ADVANCE PRAISE FOR
RESCRIPT THE STORY YOU'RE TELLING YOURSELF

Amazing knowledge, impressive experience, and a big, sincere heart; all these points just skim the surface of what Dr. Colleen Georges delivers to us every day via her classes, her publications, and her private practice. Her new book, *RESCRIPT the Story You're Telling Yourself*, is a testament to her undeniable attributes. In addition to the powerful insights found in this book, she offers us facts, strategies, and quizzes that individualizes *RESCRIPT* to the reader. Dr. Colleen systematically drives home her point that we can overcome that inner antagonist that drags us down and keeps us ruminating over our flaws and our past negative experiences. She also provides us with the keys to open our minds and to allow us to release "from the life limiting stories we tell ourselves."

~ David Mezzapelle, Bestselling Author of the
Contagious Optimism book series

You are here to shine! It's time to quiet the internal chatter that keeps you playing small, repeating the same sabotaging behaviors, and from living your best life! If you're finally ready to stop your nasty inner critic from running the show, then Dr. Colleen Georges' book, *RESCRIPT the Story You're Telling Yourself*, is a must read!

~ Linda Joy, Publisher of Aspire Magazine, Visibility Catalyst,
& Bestselling Publisher

RESCRIPT is a must-read for anyone living with a negative inner voice narrating their lives, dictating their decisions, and leaving them feeling overwhelmed, pessimistic, inadequate, or unfulfilled. The eight practices of Dr. Colleen's RESCRIPT self-authorship framework provide readers with numerous practical strategies for positively rewriting our thoughts and behaviors. Through her insights, research, stories, and exercises, she demonstrates how we can live peacefully with our past, fully in the present, and with excitement for the future.

~ Kary Oberbrunner, Author of *Your Secret Name*
& Elixir Project

In her powerful new book, *RESCRIPT the Story You're Telling Yourself*, Dr. Colleen Georges expertly guides you to heal the limiting beliefs and negative self-talk that keep you from creating the life you want. Through her own journey of recovery, Colleen shows you how to rescript your limiting story and wholeheartedly embrace the possibilities of a truly inspired life; that you have the power to transform your critical inner voice and consciously create a fulfilled life. She offers eight positive psychological practices that help you cultivate positive thoughts and actions. Colleen gives you a life-changing blueprint for creating a life of meaning, purpose, and a deep inner knowing of who you are. A must read for anyone who desires to transform their self-sabotaging beliefs into self-empowering scripts.

~ Dr. Debra L. Reble, Intuitive Psychologist,
Transformation Coach, & Bestselling Author

As a Certified Master Coach Practitioner, I can tell you that 80% of my clients struggle with the concepts of their limiting beliefs and its effects on their lives. Dr. Georges has put together a book that I would recommend to all my clients to read. The concept of RESCRIPTing the story they are telling themselves is very real and necessary for everyone if they expect to live their life in strength and confidence. She makes it very clear, your past is part of you, but you do not have to live in it every day and it doesn't define you. A must-read book for those who have experienced painful events in their past.

~ Richard J. Cavaness, Author of *The Gratitude Effect*

Dr. Colleen Georges immediately draws you in with her personal, honest account leaving readers to feel safe and validated. Practical and deep, *RESCRIPT* is full of gems, insights and exercises leading readers to unbound potential. One of the best self-help books I've encountered! You will feel like you have your life coach right in the room with you.

~ Ilana Tolpin Levitt, Career Consultant & Author of
What's Mom Still Got to Do With it?

In her thought provoking and informative book, *RESCRIPT the Story You're Telling Yourself,* Dr. Colleen Georges beautifully describes the tension between our inner antagonist and our inner advocate......the dilemma of the human journey. She shares her own personal journey as well as her professional expertise to provide a framework in guiding us to rewrite our stories and live with self-compassion and hope. A must read!

~ Dr. Catherine Hayes, International Bestselling Author of
*Everything is Going to Be Okay!: From the Projects
to Harvard to Freedom*

Life can be easier to maintain even in dire circumstances simply because you are comfortable in your current position. But you also have an option to completely change the life you're living to make it far beyond what you could imagine. In *RESCRIPT the Story You're Telling Yourself,* Dr. Colleen Georges offers readers a practical approach for silencing negative self-talk in order to change the story of your life. For anyone who has felt that limiting beliefs or self-doubt have held them back, this is a must-read. Dr. Colleen's eight practice framework helps readers control tendencies to engage in depressive rumination and regret, as well as identify their strengths, pursue their passions and purpose, and experience deeper gratitude. If you are tired of being stuck in a life you no longer want to pursue, then *RESCRIPT* is the first step in leading you in a positive direction.

~ Eric Eaton, Speaker & Author

What a powerful resource! This is wonderfully written, real-life help and compassionate guidance, solidly backed by Dr. Colleen Georges' clinical training and expertise. *RESCRIPT* is perfectly presented in playful, easy-to-access language and loaded with practical exercises for creating a positive transformation. I proudly endorse this book!

~ Michelle Lewis aka The Blessings Butterfly,
International Speaker & Bestselling Author

If you want to take charge of your story, this book is for you. Based on research, Dr. Colleen shares an impressive number of practical strategies to help you RESCRIPT your self-limiting narrative. Sharing her story, as well as others, she demonstrates how you too can change your life.

~ Dr. Vicki Kloosterhouse, Speaker, Author, & Coach

Finally, there is a step by step framework to change your debilitating inner dialogue. There is a way for us to break free of anxiety's hold on our mind. These 8 research-based steps are clever and easy to understand. Today you can create the story that was meant for you.

~ Susan A. Broussard, LMFT, Author of *It's Not Love*

If you are tired of playing the victim role and ready to take authorship of the story of your life, this is the book for you! In *RESCRIPT*, Dr. Colleen shares her personal story of transformation and an 8-step framework to help you go from powerless to limitless! You'll learn strategies to delete the pain of your past, love your present, and create the future of your dreams. Read it and transform your life!

~ Nichole Clark, Founder of More Than Moms &
Author of *The 10-Minute Refresh for Moms*

RESCRIPT is a catalyst for change and breakthrough for anyone who feels frustrated and stuck in their story. Filled with real life applications and wisdom from the author's lived experience, it promises results and freedom for anyone who will dare apply the truths and tools shared throughout this book.

~ Melanie Willard, Speaker & Author

Dr. Colleen has written an insightful and empowering book to help readers to rescript their inner stories and turn negative self-perception into something positive. Read this book - and learn from one of the best.

~ Diane Randall, M.A., Whole Living Consultant & Author

What the world needs now are truth and knowledge. Dr. Colleen Georges packs loads of this with her empowering RESCRIPT Framework on how to quiet our inner antagonist, amplify our inner advocate, and author a limitless life story. A powerful read!

~ Niccie Kliegl, CLC, RN, Author, Coach, & Talk Show Host

RESCRIPT the Story You're Telling Yourself is a fantastic read. Dr. Georges has many years of experience as a counselor, speaker, and coach. She speaks candidly about her negative story and how she RESCRIPTed it. This book will help the reader turn their negative story into a RESCRIPTed story that will allow one to live a hopeful existence. A must read for anyone who is ready to rescript and live a life filled with hope.

~ Dr. Cornelia Wenze, Author

An empowering and timely message. We can all relate to the Inner Antagonist and Inner Advocate scenarios Colleen brings with precision and humour, that will make you say, "that sounds like me!" Now as a Positive Psychology Coach, Colleen shares case studies that provide insights on how we battle with toxic thoughts and rumination. Don't suffer in silence. You can RESCRIPT your story!

~ Hyacinth Wheeler-Fraser, Author of *Journey to Wholeness: 10 Steps to Turn Setbacks into Setups*

Dr. Colleen Georges has written a smart, sensitive, and timely guide to support simple, effective implementation of the most important work there is. Fantastic.

~ Dr. Jeanine M. Staples,
Founder of the Supreme Love Project

Do you want to rewrite negatives to positives? In her book, *RESCRIPT the Story You're Telling Yourself*, Dr. Colleen helps you to quiet the antagonizing inner voice. Right from the introduction I was captured. As an author, speaker and life coach myself, I find great value in learning from Colleen's book to add more empowerment to my life and business. If you're not happy with your current life story, you can begin to RESCRIPT it with Dr. Colleen's new book *RESCRIPT the Story You're Telling Yourself: The Eight Practices to Quiet Your Inner Antagonist, Amplify Your Inner Advocate, & Author a Limitless Life.*

~ Dr. Hopelyn Mullings Brown,
Best Selling Author & Financial Coach

Colleen has hit the nail on the head in her straightforward teaching and strategy on how to change how we see ourselves by what we say to ourselves. Every person with self-limiting beliefs should take her prescription to RESCRIPT their story by attending to their inner thoughts. A brilliant, bold and blessed work that will change the lives of those who read it.

~ Donna Reiners, Speaker, Coach, & Author of
40 Days to the BRAVE New You

I believe this book will help people to unlock their fullest potential and achieve their goals. Dr. Georges provides a recipe to finding your personal and professional success! This thought-provoking and inspiring book will help millions to become their best self!

~ Dr. Yetunde A. Odugbesan-Omede, Professor & Author

RESCRIPT

THE STORY YOU'RE TELLING YOURSELF

The **Eight Practices** to
Quiet Your Inner Antagonist,
Amplify Your Inner Advocate,
& Author a Limitless Life

Keith thori!
May you script
your story filled
with love, joy,
self-compassion
+ wonderful
adventures!
Colleen

DR. COLLEEN GEORGES

AUTHOR ACADEMY elite

Printed in the United States of America
Published by Author Academy Elite
P.O. Box 43, Powell, OH 43035
www.AuthorAcademyElite.com

Cover design by Debbie O'Byrne at https://JetLaunch.net

Visit the author's website at www.ColleenGeorges.com

Paperback ISBN-13: 978-1-64085-557-1
Hardcover ISBN-13: 978-1-64085-558-8
Ebook ISBN: 978-1-64085-559-5

Library of Congress Control Number: 2019931055

DEDICATION

To my grandparents, Katherine, Steven, Ellen, and James,
for sharing your stories, your wisdom, and your love, and
for being my advocates on earth and angels in heaven.

To my parents, Lori and Peter,
for being my lifelong external advocates and
role models, and for always encouraging me
to engage my growth goals and dreams.

To my husband, José,
for being the calm, collected, and ride-or-die
partner I need and for making our story together
better than anything I could have scripted.

To my son, Joshua,
for being the light that brightens my path,
the purpose that fuels my journey, and
the infinite joy that makes this life story of ours magical.

And to my clients and students,
for teaching me so much about the
human need to recognize that we are enough
and deserve self-love and love from others just as we are.

TABLE OF CONTENTS

PART 3: THE NEW LIMITLESS LIFE STORY

FOREWORD

As a recording artist for over 30 years with many hits under my belt and a radio personality for New York's 103.5 WKTU for 20 years, visually, on paper, and on the surface, many would say that I'm quite successful. While I've never taken any of it for granted, I had an unfulfilled desire, a lifelong dream: to write and perform a one-woman show on a New York City stage. For years I talked about it with my friends, but for years I told myself, "It's just too expensive to produce, and with my career as busy as it is, and a husband and stepdaughter at home, I simply don't have the time…" Deep down, I was thinking, "Besides, who the hell do I think I am anyway?" I NEVER EVER wrote anything in that realm. But I could feel it. My soul's desire had been quieted. As a result, I was left feeling sad, unhappy, and painfully unfulfilled. At 49, I was quietly suffering. And I was acutely aware that I lived half my life already, and time was running out for me, especially in this ageist business. That's it. I'm sick of feeling like this. Time to do different. I had heard about life coaches and decided to give it a go. Desperate for my life to change, after surfing the web, I stumbled upon Dr. Colleen Georges' website: Positive Psychology Life and Career Coach. Her credentials, experience, and resume were VERY impressive. Wait. And she gave a TEDx Talk too?! OMG! I decided to give her a call.

Immediately, I felt her positivity penetrate through the phone. Hopeful at our first meeting, Colleen asked me, "So, how can I help you?" I told her about my lifelong dream of writing and performing a one-woman show. She asked, "Why do you think you haven't written it yet?" Sigh. Upon giving her my endless *reasons,* she helped me realize that it was my fear. When I told her that I simply don't have the time, she showed me that it was my Inner Antagonist ruling over me. Our Inner Antagonist tells us we can't, we won't, and we're not supposed to (fill in the blank). She helped me see that by saying I don't have the time, I had become passive. I had to learn to give a louder voice to my Inner Advocate.

Colleen helped me RESCRIPT those excuses, and my Inner Advocate said, "Of course you can do it! When you were trying to get into the music business, you knew NOTHING about it, but with hard work and putting yourself out there, you did it! And that means you can do it again. You don't have enough time? Sure, you do!" Colleen worked with me extensively, and I completed every single assignment she gave me! It took hard work, research, dedication, persistence, and sacrifice. Colleen was right. I had to stop Ruminating. I had to actively Engage in this endeavor. I began to Seek out my Strengths, instead of focusing on my weaknesses. I had to Challenge my thoughts about the show being a Catastrophic failure. I had to Restrict Regret because regret only keeps me stuck. I had to Invite Imperfection – whatever mistakes I may make will be lessons in the long run. I HAD to Pursue this Passion to write it. My soul had been whispering, "You know you want this!" And, I had to Think Thankfully – every step of this was something to be grateful for. I finally put the proverbial pen in my hand and began to RESCRIPT my story.

I worked at writing this show like I never worked on anything else in my life. And, guess what? I FOUND the time, because when it comes to your dreams, you have to make them a priority. With fingers hurting, I wrote and re-wrote the show at least seven times. I learned that I DESERVED alone-time to focus on my goal. And every time I had a doubt or a fear, and my Inner Antagonist showed its ugly face, Colleen was right there with the right words to remind me that RESCRIPTing my story is a process. I had to release my negative and fearful thinking. I had to be kinder to myself so my Inner Advocate could come through.

Because of Colleen's RESCRIPTing method, doors of unexpected greatness opened up for me. I found the time, I found producers and investors, and...I had everything I needed the whole time!

A year after my first session with Colleen, as I turned 50 years old, I got the GREATEST birthday present of my life: *No Reason to Cry*, the One Woman Show by Judy Torres was born! AND it had a Playbill too! What was intended for one weekend, turned into 28 SOLD OUT performances in a 186-seat theater in New York City! To add to the joy, I am now working on *No Reason to Cry*, the book, and a movie is in the works as well! After RESCRIPTing my story, and working my butt off, I now have nothing to fear!

There is no such thing as coincidence. Dr. Colleen Georges is an angel on earth! If you picked up this book, it's because it's time for a change. NOW! This isn't just a self-help book, it's a self-change book! It gives you the tools you need to improve every facet of your entire life! In life we all have an inner bully, our Inner Antagonist. And thank God, we also have an inner cheerleader, our Inner Advocate. I urge you to read this book, use all the wonderful resourceful worksheets that are given as well. You can do this. You can achieve all you ever dreamed of, and it starts with RESCRIPTing your life. Suffer no more. Don't hold yourself back anymore. You are the author of your story. You have been your own worst enemy, now be your own best hero! Here's to changing what you believe will be a tragedy into your absolute GREATEST story!

Judy Torres
Singer, Radio Personality, & Star and Creator of the One-Woman Off-Broadway Show, *No Reason to Cry*

A NOTE TO THE READER

You are not broken.
You are whole.
You are not inadequate.
You are enough.
You are not limited.
You are limitless.
Your story is not predestined.
You script and RESCRIPT your story.
Your story is not done yet.
You have many chapters yet to live.
Your Inner Antagonist's voice will not narrate your story.
Your Inner Advocate's volume is ready to be amplified.

Take great care with the words and tone you use when talking to yourself, you are listening intently, and you will script your story according to your own internal narrations.

Grab your pen and let's RESCRIPT!

~ Dr. Colleen

INTRODUCTION

Forrest Gump said, "Life is like a box of chocolates, you never know what you're gonna get." I still love that quote all these years later, hearing it for the first time in the summer of 1994 when the movie, *Forrest Gump*, was released. Like many viewers, I was moved by the message. The story's protagonist, Forrest, came into life with adversities. However, despite the challenges he faced, he learned to quiet the volume of internal and external antagonistic voices, become his own advocate, and author a life narrated by his belief in his capabilities. Forrest's story could have been scripted passively. He could have allowed adversities and naysayers to script his story for him with a narrative of misfortune. However, Forrest empowered himself and persevered to achieve his dreams and be a force of good in the world. In sum, he savored the chocolates that he liked from the box, but didn't believe the whole box was trash when he bit into an unpleasant flavor.

As I watched this fiction story during that summer, my life's box of chocolates had just delivered me some surprise flavors. However, unlike Forrest, I was certain I had just bitten into a box full of putrid chocolates that had poisoned me and my story forever.

I had just turned 19 in early June of 1994, after completing my first year of college with a less than stellar C- GPA. I felt defeated and inadequate. Then, in the short span of one month at the start of the summer, my first cat who I loved beyond measure had died, I learned that my boyfriend (subsequently ex) was actually married, I got arrested and charged with a DWI involving losing my driver's license for six months, and just prior to the official loss of my license, then I got into a car accident on my way home from a summer class.

It was a rough month. And, I was no Forrest Gump about it. I felt sorry for myself. And, I hated myself even more.

Without realizing it, I had been scripting a negative story for myself and about myself for quite some time. I was scripting a tragedy and this particular month was the climax. But, it wouldn't be the end of that tragic storyline. I believed I was a problem and so I continued to script my story full of problems.

It would take me several years before I channeled Forrest Gump's style of self-authorship. However, eventually, I did. I believe that, "Life is like a story, and we have more authorship over the script than we often tell ourselves."

My story has included some painful and frightening chapters—the triple rollover car crash in graduate school that struck me (literally) while sitting in traffic that should've killed me but didn't, the divorce from my first husband, the untimely and shocking deaths of two lifelong friends within a span of ten years, the illnesses and subsequent losses of close family members, the ex who crushed my young and naïve heart when he divulged he was married, the bad decision that led to my arrest and loss of my driver's license while in college, the emotionally abusive relationship I remained in for too many years, my self-destructive years, my panic attacked years, and all the years I spent listening to and believing the antagonistic voice in my head telling me I wasn't enough.

However, my story has also included many amazingly awesome chapters—meeting and marrying my husband and best friend, the birth and daily gift of our son who is the center of our world, the process and completion of my doctorate, doing a TEDx Talk, my diverse 20 plus year career working with students in higher education, the purchase of my first home, the publication of articles and book chapters, the launching and leadership of my business for over 10 years, becoming my own amplified advocate in setting and achieving my goals, life's consistent and simple joyful moments, and the unceasing blessing of my relationship with God, my parents, other human family, cat family members, and good friends throughout the years.

Maybe your chapters have involved tragedies and triumphs too. Life's box of chocolates is diversified, some taste amazing, others taste awful. We can subsequently determine that the box has positive potential and or we can conclude it's trash. We can feel excited about the surprises that await or feel dread about the ambiguity of an unknown future. We decide. While we may not know what we're gonna get, we often get more of what we tell ourselves we will get. What story do you want to tell yourself about the flavors your box of chocolates holds?

WHAT THIS BOOK WILL OFFER TO YOU

I wrote this book leveraging over 20 years of experience working with 1000+ clients and students. This book will provide you with tangible strategies to stop limiting your life by changing the way you talk to yourself (and others), shifting your focus, reframing your experiences, and taking action with positive and effective behaviors. We quiet our Inner Antagonists and RESCRIPT our stories by changing both the things we say *and* the things we do. You will learn how to live with self-love, self-compassion, hope, determination, peace with the past, and excitement for the present and the future.

I wrote this book because I want you to have the tools to free yourself from a story that is zapping you of hope and motivation, re-traumatizing and incapacitating you through analysis paralysis, keeping you replaying old and ineffective patterns, and holding you back from the people, experiences, and things you truly want in your life. I don't want you feeling trapped, stuck, unhappy, or overwhelmed when the truth is that we have so much power in our minds and through our actions to release ourselves from these life limiting stories we tell ourselves. You deserve so much better, and you too can RESCRIPT your story.

This book is for you if:

- You find yourself ruminating over what people are thinking about you, analyzing why crappy things are happening to you, or mentally reliving negative experiences from your recent or distant past...

- You are evading your dreams, goals, and things you want in life because you tell yourself you will somehow fail, believe you have no time, think it's too late for you, or you're just plain scared...

- You find yourself focusing on your shortcomings rather than your strengths, comparing yourself to others whose skills you wish you had, or struggling to identify what you are great at...

- You are catastrophizing about things that could go wrong in the near or distant future, mentally making small issues into major problems, or worrying incessantly to the point of panic...

- You find yourself regretting choices you've made in the past, wondering what could've been if you had just done things differently, or beating yourself up over mistakes you have made...

- You have been believing you aren't good enough because you aren't absolutely perfect, telling yourself you can never let anyone down or make a mistake, or telling yourself you must hide parts of who you are for fear of rejection...

- You find yourself believing that life just becomes the same old same old day in and day out, wondering how you can feel more passion and purpose, or wishing you could feel more alive and motivated... *or*

- You have been thinking that life has deprived you of many of the things others seem to have, focusing on everything you don't have while struggling to feel thankful for what you do have, or trying to fill perceived voids in unhealthy ways.

This book is not suggesting that human beings must be happy ALL of the time. Life presents us with challenging encounters and we must experience negative emotions at times in order to process and make sense out of those experiences. No one is happy all of the time—that would not be human. Negative experiences and emotions also help us to better appreciate positive experiences and emotions.

This book is about being able to face life's challenges, experience negative thoughts and emotions, process them, and move through them effectively with resilience and hope for the future, as well as peace with the past. We do not need to listen to the narrations of an Inner Antagonist who tries to make us relive pain over and over. We can quiet this Inner Antagonist and empower ourselves to move forward with strength and optimism by amplifying the voice of the Inner Advocate each of us has.

How This Book is Organized

In Part 1 of this book, we have the opportunity to examine our old limiting life stories. In order to inspect these limiting scripts, we begin with gaining an understanding of how we develop our narratives and who our narrators are. I share chapters of my own limiting life story, as well as how the process of rescripting my story led to the birth of the Eight Practices of the RESCRIPT Framework. To examine your old limiting life stories, there is a RESCRIPT Your Life Story Quiz, Life Story Satisfaction Scale, and an Old Limiting Life Story Review exercise for you to complete.

In Part 2, we cover in detail the Eight Practices of the RESCRIPT Framework. For each practice, there is a chapter dedicated to helping you understand how life limiting scripts function in our lives and how we can RESCRIPT to remove the limits we place on our stories. Each chapter is organized as follows:

- **The Limiting Scripts**: These sections describe how various life limiting scripts function in our lives.

- **Highlights from Research Studies:** These are research study results that address each focus area of the RESCRIPT framework.

- **Limiting Narrations RESCRIPTed**: These are examples of limiting thoughts/narrations, as well as these narrations RESCRIPTed to remove limits.

- **Limitless Living Library**: The Limitless Living Library has numerous practical strategies to implement and master the limitless living practices in your life. These practices engage both our thoughts and our actions, so they are in positive alignment. You do not need to implement all of the strategies in your life to live limitlessly. You can try out different strategies and see which ones work best for you. Several chapter strategies can be used to address multiple limiting thought patterns. For example, numerous strategies in the Release Rumination Chapter can be used to address limiting thinking habits discussed in the other chapters, such as Evading Growth Goals, Scrutinizing Shortcomings, Catastrophizing, Regret, Inviting Infallibility/Perfectionism, Putting Up with Passivity, and Thinking Thanklessly/Deprived. This works reciprocally for each of the chapter strategies. So, you can make minor modifications to specific limitless living strategies to address other limiting thought patterns.

- **Client/Student Stories**: These are stories of Dr. Colleen's clients and students who RESCRIPTed limiting narrations and subsequently removed limits from their life stories. Unless provided express written permission, all names and identifying information have been changed to protect confidentiality, without compromising the authenticity of clients' and students' positive RESCRIPTing.

Part 3 of this book is dedicated to your new limitless life story. Here, you will learn strategies to make RESCRIPTing a lifestyle. There is an additional section of the Limitless Living Library with numerous strategies you can utilize in various life situations where you find yourself with limiting narrations. There is also a RESCRIPT Manifesto you can recite any time you need it to keep you on your limitless life path. Finally, you will have the opportunity to script your own limitless life manifesto and new limitless life story to provide direction for your story's evolution.

PART 1

THE OLD LIMITING LIFE STORY

"Make sure your worst enemy doesn't live between your own two ears."

~ Laird Hamilton

RELIVING PLOTS WE DON'T EVEN LIKE

"You can't start the next chapter of your life
if you keep re-reading the last one."

~ Unknown

THE NARRATIVE & THE NARRATORS

Every day we are living out a story script. Our narratives unfold with comedies and tragedies, dramas and mysteries, adventures and transformations, as well as some occasional fantasies and fairytales. But, how much control do we really have over these plotlines in our narratives? Too often we feel as if the story we are living is one that has been scripted for us, one that is predestined somehow, one where we have limited control to script a different plot. Too often, we relive plots we don't even like because we believe our stories are destined to repeat patterns, even when we are sick of those particular patterns. While we don't script our entire story from introduction to conclusion—we don't get to choose all the settings, circumstances, and characters—we do get to script how we perceive, interact with, and respond to them. Just as critically, we script how we perceive, interact with, and respond to ourselves.

It's no revelation that we live in a world where there are injustices. Some face more systemic obstacles, personal challenges, and traumas in their lives than others do. We are often made

3

aware that the game of life isn't playing fair. In a world that isn't always advocating for us or the greater good, we must galvanize our own internal advocacy to rescript disempowering narratives.

Fortunately, we were created to be resilient beings. We don't control all aspects of the script, but we cannot allow our spirit to be broken. We have so much to offer the world with the diversity of our experiences, perspectives, and strengths. The negative voice in our head might try to keep us stuck in mentally reliving pain when life gets hard. We must keep on rescripting to be our own best advocate and a positive, empowered force in the world. When life is tough, we can use negative emotions like anger, frustration, and despair as fuel to be transformed into empowerment, action, and hope. We can acknowledge and feel the sting of life's challenges without giving them the power to script our entire story. It might be a journey with some bumps and bruises, but each one adds to the depth of our own character and plotline.

Each day, every moment, we are scripting our own self-stories. Our self-story is scripted from all the things we tell ourselves through our internal dialogue about who we are, why we are or aren't good enough, what we are or aren't capable of, and what possibilities the future can hold for us. Our self-story is our self-perception, and it influences our perceptions of others and the world around us. It also impacts the actions we take regarding ourselves, others, and life overall.

So, if our self-story is so important, how is it being scripted?

We have two very different, but equally influential voices, or Narrators, who talk to us in our minds—the Inner Antagonist and the Inner Advocate. As narrators, their common role is to do what narrators do—they *tell* you a story. It's either the Inner Antagonist's or Inner Advocate's point of view from which you perceive the settings, circumstances, and characters in your story. And, remember, you are the Protagonist in your story—the main character. Thus, the narrator perspective you choose to listen to also influences how you perceive yourself.

How do these two narrators differ? Let's first get to know your Inner Antagonist.

Your Inner Antagonist functions similarly to any character who is the antagonist in a story. Your Inner Antagonist is your story's opposing force. It tells you that you have disorder, conflict, weaknesses, and deficits within and around you, and that you do not have what it takes to resolve any of it. Your Inner Antagonist can also lead you to act in ways that are not aligned with your values and ultimate desires. This creates a state of cognitive dissonance—a feeling of discomfort facilitated when our values are in conflict with our actions. The stories we believe about ourselves are created both by what we say *and* by what we do.

You might be wondering—"Where does the Inner Antagonist come from?" "How did it get in my head in the first place?" "Where does it learn its language?" "Where does it derive its fuel?"

Mental Rubbernecking (AKA Negativity Bias)

Picture the scene: It's a Friday morning around 10:30am and you've taken the day off from work. You are driving down the highway to spend the day at the beach. Suddenly, traffic slows down to a crawl. What's going on? It's well after rush hour, there shouldn't be traffic like this. Could there be construction and a lane is shut down? But, there were no signs indicating road work. You try to look ahead and all you see are cars stopped for what looks like a mile ahead. You continue the slow crawl down the highway and notice traffic is starting to move again. Thank goodness. But, what was going on? Then you see it. There has been an accident on the other side of the highway. But, why on earth did an accident on the opposite side of the highway create traffic on your side? Because drivers on your side of the highway averted their attention away from their intended driving destinations, and over to the negative situation occurring across the highway. Yep, we will halt or slow ourselves down on our literal and metaphorical life journeys to fixate on something awful.

5

This specific example of focusing on the negative is so common that it warranted creating a distinct word for it—rubbernecking!

The act of rubbernecking is influenced by what researchers refer to as a negativity bias—our brain's tendency to focus more readily on negative stimuli than neutral or positive stimuli. According to Rick Hansen, best-selling author, psychologist, and Senior Fellow of the Greater Good Science Center at UC Berkeley, "your brain is like Velcro for negative experiences but Teflon for positive ones."[1] He explains that as our brains evolved, it was critical for our survival to learn from negative experiences. Thus, our brains developed circuits that record negative experiences immediately in our emotional memory. However, positive experiences, unless they are totally new or really intense, just have standard memory systems. So, for positive experiences to have a major impact on our lives, we must savor them for several seconds to move them from short-term to long-term memory. Since we rarely savor positive experiences in this way, they generally leave our memory as quickly as they came, while negative experiences are logged each time for the long-haul. The consequence of this brain wiring is that our attention is often locked on trauma, suffering, pessimism, regret, resentment, and anxiety.

In short, our brains have special circuits for mental rubbernecking! Our Inner Antagonists grow long necks to make sure they can look far and wide to spot the negative within and around us.

Bad impressions are quicker to form and more resistant to change than good ones. It typically takes numerous positive interactions with a person to make up for one negative interaction. Negative feedback has a more powerful impact on us than positive feedback. Negative experiences are more memorable and more emotionally impactful for us than pleasurable ones.

Here's a few scenarios to test the mental rubbernecking theory:

- You just had your annual performance review with your boss. She commends your dedication and shares that you have exceeded standards in nine of ten areas of your responsibility. She also shares that you didn't meet standards on the one remaining task area. You finish your meeting and go back to your desk. What do you think or do next?

- You are just taking a look at your son's quarterly report card. You scroll your eyes through five A+s, one C+, and one D. What conversation do you have next with your son?

- You went on a week-long family vacation with your partner and kids. You had a fantastic flight and the kids were so well-behaved. You got to see so many sites you'd been dreaming of seeing your whole life. You ate some incredible meals and loved all of the time you had to really connect with your family. You really needed this rest and the trip couldn't have gone more perfectly. You have a great flight back home and travel down the airport escalator to baggage claim. Suitcases come and go, but not yours. After an hour, you decide to talk with an airport staff member. You learn that no one can seem to figure out where your suitcase has gone. You had both monetary and sentimental valuables in there. How are you feeling about your trip and how might you describe it to your friends when they ask?

If after imagining yourself in these scenarios, you found yourself: 1) ruminating over why you didn't meet standards on that one task and feeling angry at yourself or your boss about it, 2) interrogating your son about why he got that C+ and D, or 3) telling your friends that your dream vacation was completely ruined, well, you wouldn't be alone!

The Media Feeds Our Mental Rubbernecking, So it Grows

Not only are we neurologically wired for mental rubbernecking, the media both counts on it and feeds on it, hence helping our Inner Antagonists get louder and louder.

Tragedies and threats are largely all we see on the news—natural disasters, terrorism, shootings, missing persons, thefts, attacks, car crashes, governmental failings, and economic downturns. Even television shows capitalize on our negativity bias, with two of the most common and popular show genres being crime and medical dramas. And countless product commercials and advertisements remind us how we must lose weight, die our gray hair, and hide our blemished skin to fix our unattractiveness.

And if you are going through a rough time and searching for supportive information on the internet, you can expect the titles of advice articles to leverage negativity bias. After a layoff, an already vulnerable job seeker searching for guidance can be assured to find countless articles online with titles like, "Why Your Resume is Getting Thrown in the Trash," "5 Mistakes You Are Making in Your Job Search Strategy," and "10 Reasons You Bombed Your Job Interview." Wow, how wildly encouraging! This doesn't motivate you to change your strategies, it makes you feel like crawling under a rock because nothing you'll ever do will be good enough! We are told in so many ways, every single day, that the world is broken and so are we.

An Over-Achieving Superego

It can be helpful to think of your Inner Antagonist as your Superego gone haywire and in beast mode. If you are familiar with Freud and psychology, you are likely familiar with the Id, Ego, and Superego. The Id is the part of our mind that desires to run buck wild, have fun, and hedonistically engage in plea-surable experiences without any thought of consequences. The Superego is the part of our mind that wants us to be moral, ethical, responsible, and good. It wants to keep us in check, do right, avoid doing wrong, and keep us out of trouble. According to Freud, the Superego dictates to us how we should and should not be, "You *ought to be* like this...You *may not be* like this..."[2] Our Ego is the part of our minds that attempts to maintain balance between the two aforementioned mind forces.

Our Superego gains its first ideas of right and wrong from its earliest influences—our parents or guardians. Once we go to school and are interacting outside of home more often, the ideas of our teachers, principals, and other authority figures are integrated. Media messages about what is good and what is bad also become synthesized into our Superego. Friends and others we admire play a role as well. Throughout our lives, our Superego has many, many teachers.

The Inner Antagonist comes into play when your Superego begins to over-achieve on the job. The Superego gets fanatical about what's right, wrong, good, bad, and begins to become painfully perfectionistic, intolerant, and punishing. This can happen for a number of reasons. In some cases, some of the voices that helped to create our Superego may be particularly critical voices. In other words, some of the people who influenced our internal ideas of good and bad may have had very rigid or even cruel ways of expressing their sentiments. An example would be a parent who repeatedly tells a child they are no good, stupid, or will never amount to anything. Physical violence from early authority figures also takes a toll. These voices and actions can fuel the Inner Antagonist.

Furthermore, the voices that form our Superego can also filter into our minds kind of like the old telephone game. In the telephone game, a message is conveyed to one person who conveys it to another, so forth and so on until the message received by the final person sounds quite different from the original message. When talking about our Superego, an original message from a teacher may have been, "You have to work harder on your writing," whereas it gets filtered in our mind as, "You are no good at school." When we do enough of this harsh filtering, the Inner Antagonist is fueled.

Individual Biological Temperament

Biologically, we are born with different temperaments—how we emotionally and behaviorally respond to stimuli in our lives. Some of us may be more easy-going, others might be more restless, some are more prone to analyze things, others are less analytical. Our temperament helps to form our overall personality, in conjunction with what we learn from our environment. However, our biological temperament can influence how critical our Inner Antagonist can be. This does not mean we can't quiet our Inner Antagonist, it simply means that doing so might be a bit easier for some than others.

Once the Inner Antagonist's voice is formed, it takes on a personality of its own. It interprets and misinterprets things in ways that harshly critique our character and behavior. With time and practice, it gets bolder, harsher, more persistent, and louder. And while it may once have been driven by others, it is now internal and a part of us.

No matter how our Inner Antagonist developed and grew in strength, it's important to understand that having an Inner Antagonist does NOT determine our story's plot or ending. And though it might sound crazy, all good stories need antagonists and a little adversity. It's the work you engage in as the Protagonist of your story, to triumph over your Inner Antagonist's voice and perception, that helps you grow and transform. This is where your Inner Advocate comes in.

Yes, You Have an Inner Advocate Too!

Your Inner Advocate has your back. It's just like any advocate character in a story. It's your ally, your supporter, your encourager, your collaborative problem solver. It rallies with you in the face of antagonism and advocates for you exactly how a good friend would. It tells you that you're strong and capable. It reminds you of all the resources you have within and around you. It reminds you of the wisdom you've gained from life experience. It tells you that you can overcome anything.

Your Inner Advocate is fueled by the positive voices, experiences, and influences throughout your life. It developed out of the one elementary school classmate who stood up for you against a bully when others didn't. It developed out of the faith your ninth-grade teacher voiced to you that she knew you could understand geometry if you stayed after school for tutoring and didn't give up. It developed out of the encouraging words your best friend gave you after your boyfriend broke up with you. It developed out of the pride your mom expressed when you graduated from college after some struggles along the way. It developed out of your job supervisor who said she saw managerial potential in you and wanted to promote you. It developed out of the server at the restaurant who complimented your haircut. It developed out of the stranger in the supermarket who thanked you for your kindness for reaching for the item she wasn't tall enough to grab.

Just as there are many voices who teach our Inner Antagonist, there are also many voices who teach our Inner Advocate. However, it is common that if we hear five compliments and one criticism, it will be the one criticism that we remember and concentrate on most. In order to amplify the voice of our Inner Advocate, we must retrain our minds to seek out and pay closer attention to the good within and around us.

Your Inner Antagonist limits you. Your Inner Advocate liberates you. Their voices are competing to narrate your script, moment by moment. While they have a major influence on your story, ultimately, they don't make the decisions. It's your actions that write your story. Whose narration will you listen to as you choose your story's plot direction and narrative?

The problem for so many of us lies in that while we all have an Inner Advocate, our Inner Antagonist is often so loud, persistent, and convincing, that we forget about our more rational and supportive story script narrator. And, like any friend you neglect, your Inner Advocate will just stop coming around. To author a limitless life story, we must learn the essential practices for quieting our Inner Antagonist and amplifying our Inner Advocate. A limitless life is a life authored by our authentic aspirations with self-compassion, kindness, resilience, bravery, zest, optimism, and faith.

I begin this book by sharing some excerpts from my old limiting life script. I introduce you to my Inner Antagonist and share how amplifying my Inner Advocate helped me to script a new story plot that ultimately gave birth to the eight practices for RESCRIPTing, which are based in Positive Psychology. You will then have the opportunity to review your own old limiting life script, learn how to integrate the eight practices into your own life, and author the limitless life story you want to be living.

DR. COLLEEN'S OLD LIMITING STORY

I was sitting on my couch and suddenly I felt like something was pressing down hard on my chest and I couldn't get any air. I could feel my heart racing and I felt terrified. It probably only lasted a few minutes, but it seemed to go on forever. I felt like I was suffocating.

This same type of experience began happening more and more. Sometimes it lasted a few minutes, other times a half hour or more. I started wondering if I could be developing asthma in my early twenties. I questioned a few people with asthma about their symptoms, but what they described to me sounded different than what I felt. I was a counseling psychology doctoral student and I had no idea I was having panic attacks.

This was about 18 years ago.

I had lived with negative self-talk and anxiety for many years before it escalated to that level. Around my early teens, my Inner Antagonist became a louder and more persistent presence in my mind. Ruminating over past decisions I'd made, replaying scenarios, and imagining what I could've done or said to change outcomes became a habit of mine. I'd mentally run through the details of things I wished I hadn't done over and over, as if thinking about them could change the past. I beat myself up over ways I believed I'd failed in relationships, school, and work. And, I felt sorry for myself over all of the things I perceived had gone wrong for me.

Like so many others who deal with issues of self-worth and self-love, I kept pretty quiet about the things going on in my own mind. Many people in my life were largely unaware of the ways I was torturing myself internally. I didn't want to bother or burden people with my thoughts and feelings, and honesty, I was ashamed of how I felt about myself and didn't want people to know. I believed it was better to pretend I was just fine. This was a function of my perfectionism. While I was blessed to have my parents, family, and friends as my external advocates, all I could hear was my Inner Antagonist.

My increasingly louder Inner Antagonist was steadily fostering a sub-conscious belief that I didn't deserve to be treated very well. Thus, I often found myself in romantic relationships with people who either disregarded my feelings or downright attempted to assert control over me. One of those relationships was severely emotionally abusive, but I remained in it for years because I believed it was the best I could do. His abusive words simply gave new language to my Inner Antagonist and fueled a growing self-punishment while any self-love I had slowly withered away.

Since I believed I'd done so much wrong in the past, I often had a pretty pessimistic outlook on the future. I worried about what could go wrong in my relationships, school, and career. I worried about everything. I played out in my mind all the potential negative scenarios that could arise in the future in hopes that by contemplating them, I could somehow control them, be emotionally ready for them, or stop them from happening.

I made a regular practice of creating catastrophes in my mind that never ended up happening. Regardless, I believed they would and thus mentally and emotionally experienced them beforehand as if they were real. As a result of my catastrophizing, I often avoided great opportunities in my life out of fear and frequently played it safe and simple. I didn't believe I was capable. I didn't think I was enough.

I not only believed I wasn't good enough, but also thought I didn't *have* enough. I thought about how I didn't yet have the relationship, job, money, house, and things I *needed* to be happy. In the interim, I felt envious of what I perceived others had. I often attempted to fill my perceived voids and deficits through buying things. But, shopping didn't fix how I felt. It just created new problems, like debt and guilt.

It was years of allowing my Inner Antagonist to narrate my story script that ultimately led me to chronic panic attacks. I suffered with progressively more frequent panic attacks for nearly two years, alongside severe lower back pain, jaw pain and dislocation, and neck pain. My body was trying to tell me something my mind refused to acknowledge.

I had been believing nearly everything my Inner Antagonist was telling me for a long time, and I scripted my story accordingly. I limited myself in many areas of my life, and felt the resultant dissatisfaction. I wanted to live a different story. But, it took time before I realized I could rescript it.

BIRTH OF THE EIGHT PRACTICES OF THE RESCRIPT FRAMEWORK

Rescripting my Own Story

Through some counseling and lots of reading, I came to realize that I lived my life with a deficit mentality—I focused on what was missing in me and my life instead of what was already there. I began putting all my effort into making real changes to the self-story I was allowing my Inner Antagonist to create for me. After reading Louise Hay's *Gratitude: A Way of Life*, I began a daily gratitude practice. I also began tracking and reframing my negative thoughts, and changing my actions accordingly. These changes were hard and I often wanted to give up. I fell off track along the way, but I kept getting back up and trying again.

14

A new story script narrator—my Inner Advocate—began to emerge. This narrator was not a stranger to me, she was familiar, she had been a part of me, but she had been the quieter one. I began to amplify her voice because I liked what she had to say. With time and the practice of truly listening to and allowing my Inner Advocate to narrate, my self-story began to brighten and the limits that my Inner Antagonist had long placed on my life story were slowly and progressively removed.

I began to love my story, including my flaws and struggles. I began to engage in things I was afraid of, but that I knew were good for me. I re-discovered that I was capable. I could hear positive external voices again, like encouragement from my parents, grandparents, and others who were my advocates. But, most importantly, I became my own advocate. I learned my life story could be limitless if I allowed it to be.

Though I was actively rescripting my own life story, the official birth of The Eight Practices of the RESCRIPT Framework would be nearly 20 years in the making.

Discovering Positive Psychology

One of the great ironies of my story is that my gift as a person and professional has always been my innate ability to see all the good in others and inspire them to see it too. This strength is what led me to fall in love with Positive Psychology.

The field of Positive Psychology was launched in 1998 by Martin Seligman during his American Psychological Association's (APA) Presidential address at the annual APA conference. He stated, "Psychology is not just the study of weakness and damage, it is also the study of strength and virtue. Treatment is not just fixing what is broken, it is nurturing what is best within ourselves."[3] I was in graduate school during this time, but I didn't dive deeply into Positive Psychology until after I completed my doctorate and was working in higher education counseling students. It was like fireworks went off for me. I discovered a perspective in psychology that fit me like a glove.

Unlike traditional psychology, which aims to take us from dysfunctioning to functioning, Positive Psychology strives to advance us steps beyond to flourishing and happiness. It focuses primarily on what is good within and around us, and helps us to use these internal and external resources to thrive and experience joy and zest for life.

In addition to developing new and unique therapeutic tools, Positive Psychology adapts and integrates tools from other theoretical perspectives, including cognitive behavioral/REBT, humanistic, solutions-focused, and narrative-based concepts and strategies, to name a few. Essentially, Positive Psychology incorporates exercises addressing how our thoughts influence our feelings and behaviors, and our behaviors influence our thoughts and feelings.

Some of the key tools of Positive Psychology had been tools I used in rescripting my own story—gratitude, strengths, positive thought reframing, forgiveness, kindness, self-compassion, optimism, meaning, and flow. They were also tools I used in counseling my students. As I read and learned more about Positive Psychology, I became more and more intentional in my use of these tools in my life, relationships, and work.

Launching a Coaching & Writing Business

After several years of work in higher education as a student counselor and department director, I had my first, and only, child. Following my passion and purpose as it evolved, I left my director role to teach college and graduate courses, and run my own small business doing career coaching and résumé writing. I had been doing both for students for years and was excited to do this work with a larger community. One of the things I loved most about the résumé writing process, was helping my students and clients see their accomplishments, capabilities, and value simply by changing the words they used to talk about themselves. I never cease to be amazed how the language we use scripts our stories. Clients who once believed a new position or even a new career trajectory was not within their reach were now able to achieve their dreams. Their stories on their résumés and language during interviews removed the limits and opened up new and exciting career chapters. Through this work, I became further invested in seeing our lives as stories, and believing our language played a crucial role in the stories we lived out.

My career coaching and résumé writing business quickly expanded to include life coaching, speaking and training engagements, facilitating community wellness groups, and authoring articles and chapters in books on self-growth. All of my work had developed some common threads—Positive Psychology concepts and tools, the importance of positively reframing our internal and external language and dialogue, and viewing our lives as stories to be continuously RESCRIPTed for greater satisfaction and joy.

Writing a Self-Growth Book & Doing a TEDx Talk

In 2015 I decided I was ready to start writing a self-growth book, a long-standing dream of mine that originated some time in high school. I had started writing one in 2003 after I finished writing my doctoral dissertation. At that time, I wrote 17 pages. Then I stopped. I meant to start it up again, but I didn't. My Inner Antagonist kept telling me it was too late. And, I let myself believe it.

So, over a decade later in 2015, I was going strong writing during the first few months of the year. I got about 40 pages in, and all of a sudden, the Inner Antagonist's voice resurfaced, it whispered at first, but eventually it got louder. It said writing a book was too much and I couldn't handle it. It said I didn't have time. It said working to make money was the more important priority. Eventually, I let myself believe it, again. And I stopped, again.

Queue 2016. A different big dream of mine came to fruition. I got accepted to do a TEDx Talk. When I learned the TEDx theme I had to frame my talk around, I thought it had to be complete serendipity—the theme was Stories. My topic came to my mind in full title within seconds—Re-scripting the Stories We Tell Ourselves. It was meant to be. I began writing and rehearsing my talk script. I incorporated some of the key Positive Psychology themes that had been leading my life and work for years, including thinking thankfully, seeking strengths, engaging growth goals, and inviting imperfection. And though my Inner Antagonist showed up to terrorize me into wanting to quit the talk in the weeks leading up to it, I amplified the voice of my Inner Advocate, walked through my fears, and did the talk anyway—as the event's opening speaker.

After I got off stage, I was met with countless audience members who came up to me and hugged me, cried, and told me it felt like my talk was meant just for them to hear. It was the most emotionally rewarding experience to know the message reached people. And, it told me that I had to hone it and spread it even wider.

So, when I decided to pick up writing that book I had begun a year earlier, something didn't feel right. It was a similar message and approach, but not quite where I wanted to go anymore. I needed first to rework my direction. I knew it had to do with rescripting, but I wasn't sure how. Then it hit me. *Rescript was both a metaphor and an acronym for a framework of practices in a life story authoring process.* I sat down at my computer to work it out. It flowed easily because the practices were all of the ones I used in my own life and in my work with my clients.

1. **R**- Release Rumination
2. **E**- Engage Growth Goals vs. Evading Them
3. **S**- Seek Strengths vs. Scrutinizing Shortcomings
4. **C**- Challenge Catastrophizing
5. **R**- Restrict Regrets
6. **I**- Invite Imperfection vs. Infallibility/Perfectionism
7. **P**- Pursue Passion & Purpose vs. Putting Up with Passivity
8. **T**- Think Thankfully vs. Thanklessly/Deprived

The Eight Practices of the RESCRIPT Framework were born.

I began writing a RESCRIPT Workbook for my clients with the practices and their strategies, created with a foundation in Positive Psychology concepts. I had started writing this book, but I didn't even know it yet. Then, I got serious. And, the real writing began. This book has been two years in the making. But, the dream of writing a self-growth book to empower others has been with me for nearly three decades. I finally quieted my Inner Antagonist's chatter about writing this book, amplified my Inner Advocate, and wrote this book. It has helped me to author an important part of my story and will help YOU author YOUR limitless life story.

RESCRIPT YOUR LIFE STORY QUIZ

Every person's limiting thought patterns vary, with certain areas of negative thinking being more salient for some than for others. This quiz is meant to help you determine what your unique life limiting thought patterns sound like. All of the chapters and tools will benefit you, even if they address areas you struggle with a bit less. This quiz simply helps to guide you in utilizing the RESCRIPT strategies that will best address what you want to change in order to author your limitless life.

Instructions: For each of the following statements, circle the level of agreement response that best fits you.

1. I frequently analyze things that I've said or done recently.
(5) Very much like me (4) Mostly like me (3) Somewhat like me
(2) Not much like me (1) Not like me at all

2. I avoid pursuing goals if there is potential for failure.
(5) Very much like me (4) Mostly like me (3) Somewhat like me
(2) Not much like me (1) Not like me at all

3. I can identify my top personal and professional strengths.

(1) Very much like me (2) Mostly like me (3) Somewhat like me
(4) Not much like me (5) Not like me at all

4. I often imagine the worst possible situations so I can be prepared if they occur in the future.
(5) Very much like me (4) Mostly like me (3) Somewhat like me
(2) Not much like me (1) Not like me at all

5. I often think about what could've been if I had made different decisions in my life.
(5) Very much like me (4) Mostly like me (3) Somewhat like me
(2) Not much like me (1) Not like me at all

6. I frequently criticize myself for the ways in which I don't meet my standard of perfection.
(5) Very much like me (4) Mostly like me (3) Somewhat like me
(2) Not much like me (1) Not like me at all

7. I frequently get so wrapped up in doing what I love that I lose track of time.
(1) Very much like me (2) Mostly like me (3) Somewhat like me
(4) Not much like me (5) Not like me at all

8. I often think about all the good people, experiences, and things I am grateful for in my life.
(1) Very much like me (2) Mostly like me (3) Somewhat like me
(4) Not much like me (5) Not like me at all

9. I don't waste my time rehashing negative things in my mind that are over and done with.
(1) Very much like me (2) Mostly like me (3) Somewhat like me
(4) Not much like me (5) Not like me at all

10. Fear and anxiety stop me from pursuing challenging goals.
(5) Very much like me (4) Mostly like me (3) Somewhat like me
(2) Not much like me (1) Not like me at all

11. I often think more about my shortcomings than I do my strengths.

(5) Very much like me (4) Mostly like me (3) Somewhat like me
(2) Not much like me (1) Not like me at all

12. I know that I can manage life's challenges and they won't cause major damage in my life.
(1) Very much like me (2) Mostly like me (3) Somewhat like me
(4) Not much like me (5) Not like me at all

13. I frequently look back on my life and think about things I wish I hadn't said or done.
(5) Very much like me (4) Mostly like me (3) Somewhat like me
(2) Not much like me (1) Not like me at all

14. Despite my imperfections, I see myself as enough the way that I am.
(1) Very much like me (2) Mostly like me (3) Somewhat like me
(4) Not much like me (5) Not like me at all

15. I often feel like my life is the same thing day in and day out, with very little excitement or deeper meaning.
(5) Very much like me (4) Mostly like me (3) Somewhat like me
(2) Not much like me (1) Not like me at all

16. I feel like good things happen for other people way more than they do for me.
(5) Very much like me (4) Mostly like me (3) Somewhat like me
(2) Not much like me (1) Not like me at all

17. I often spend time replaying unfortunate events or disappointing moments in my life.
(5) Very much like me (4) Mostly like me (3) Somewhat like me
(2) Not much like me (1) Not like me at all

18. When working towards an important goal, I don't quit even if things get difficult.
(1) Very much like me (2) Mostly like me (3) Somewhat like me
(4) Not much like me (5) Not like me at all

19. I am not usually intentional in using my strengths in my personal and professional life.
(5) Very much like me (4) Mostly like me (3) Somewhat like me (2) Not much like me (1) Not like me at all

20. When looking to my future, I think more about the negative things than the positive things that could happen to me.
(5) Very much like me (4) Mostly like me (3) Somewhat like me (2) Not much like me (1) Not like me at all

21. When I make a choice with a negative outcome, I just see it as an opportunity for learning rather than something I should regret.
(1) Very much like me (2) Mostly like me (3) Somewhat like me (4) Not much like me (5) Not like me at all

22. I try to hide my imperfections from others.
(5) Very much like me (4) Mostly like me (3) Somewhat like me (2) Not much like me (1) Not like me at all

23. I direct my energy toward engaging in opportunities that make me feel passionate and purposeful.
(1) Very much like me (2) Mostly like me (3) Somewhat like me (4) Not much like me (5) Not like me at all

24. I don't feel like I have all the things I need to be happy in life yet.
(5) Very much like me (4) Mostly like me (3) Somewhat like me (2) Not much like me (1) Not like me at all

Scoring:

For questions 1, 2, 4, 5, 6, 10, 11, 13, 15, 16, 17, 19, 20, 22, and 24 assign the following points:

5=Very much like me, 4=Mostly like me, 3=Somewhat like me, 2=Not much like me, 1=Not like me at all

For questions 3, 7, 8, 9, 12, 14, 18, 21, and 23 assign the following points:

1=Very much like me, 2=Mostly like me, 3=Somewhat like me, 4=Not much like me, 5=Not like me at all

What Does Your Story Need?
Your Score: _____

1) **24 points – Living a Limitless Life Story:** You are living a story with infinite possibilities! Your Inner Advocate is amplified, empowered, and narrating your story. You've quieted your Inner Antagonist so you release ruminations, engage growth goals, seek strengths, challenge catastrophizing, restrict regrets, invite imperfections, pursue passions and purpose, and think thankfully. Your story is an exciting adventure that gracefully flows through obstacles and plot twists, and you always come out as your own hero!

2) **25 to 48 points – Proofread Life Story RESCRIPT:** Your story is authentic with very few constraints. Your Inner Advocate is usually amplified. You're generally able to quiet your Inner Antagonist so most of the time you release ruminations, engage growth goals, seek strengths, challenge catastrophizing, restrict regrets, invite imperfections, pursue passions and purpose, and think thankfully. Occasionally, you feel you could use some help in order to live an even more adventurous story.

3) **49 to 72 points – Copyedit Life Story RESCRIPT:** Your story teeters between limits and liberations. Your Inner Advocate is sometimes amplified. You're sporadically able to quiet your Inner Antagonist, so occasionally you release ruminations, engage growth goals, seek strengths, challenge catastrophizing, restrict regrets, invite imperfections, pursue passions and purpose, and/or think thankfully. Other times you struggle to. You are ready to start a new, more exciting chapter!

4) **73 to 96 points – Stylistic Life Story RESCRIPT:** Your story feels restrained from expansion too often. Your Inner Advocate's voice is usually too low for you to hear. You're usually unable to quiet your Inner Antagonist, so much of the time you struggle to release ruminations, engage growth goals, seek strengths, challenge catastrophizing, restrict regrets, invite imperfections, pursue passions and purpose, and/or think thankfully. You are ready to RESCRIPT your story, expand your plot, and author a story that's true to you!

5) **97 to 120 points – Big-Picture Life Story RESCRIPT:** Your story feels bound by endless walls and ceilings. Your Inner Advocate is virtually silent. You have not yet learned how to quiet your Inner Antagonist, so it's a daily battle to release ruminations, engage growth goals, seek strengths, challenge catastrophizing, restrict regrets, invite imperfections, pursue passions and purpose, and/or think thankfully. You are ready to RESCRIPT your story, live authentically, and be the author of your future!

Subscale Scores:

(1) Release Rumination Subscale (Questions 1, 9, & 17): Your Score: _____
- 3 points = Low on Rumination
- 4 to 6 points = Moderately Low on Rumination
- 7 to 9 points = Average on Rumination
- 10 to 12 points = High on Rumination
- 13 to 15 points = Very High on Rumination

(2) Engage Growth Goals vs. Evading Them Subscale (Questions 2, 10, & 18): Your Score: _____
- 3 points = Low on Evading Growth Goals
- 4 to 6 points = Moderately Low on Evading Growth Goals
- 7 to 9 points = Average on Evading Growth Goals
- 10 to 12 points = High on Evading Growth Goals
- 13 to 15 points = Very High on Evading Growth Goals

(3) Seek Strengths vs. Scrutinizing Shortcomings Subscale (Questions 3, 11, & 19):
Your Score: _____

- 3 points = Low on Scrutinizing Shortcomings
- 4 to 6 points = Moderately Low on Scrutinizing Shortcomings
- 7 to 9 points = Average on Scrutinizing Shortcomings
- 10 to 12 points = High on Scrutinizing Shortcomings
- 13 to 15 points = Very High on Scrutinizing Shortcomings

(4) Challenge Catastrophizing Subscale (Questions 4, 12, & 20):
Your Score: _____

- 3 points = Low on Catastrophizing
- 4 to 6 points = Moderately Low on Catastrophizing
- 7 to 9 points = Average on Catastrophizing
- 10 to 12 points = High on Catastrophizing
- 13 to 15 points = Very High on Catastrophizing

(5) Restrict Regrets Subscale (Questions 5, 13, & 21):
Your Score: _____

- 3 points = Low on Regret
- 4 to 6 points = Moderately Low on Regret
- 7 to 9 points = Average on Regret
- 10 to 12 points = High on Regret
- 13 to 15 points = Very High on Regret

(6) Invite Imperfection vs. Infallibility/Perfectionism Subscale (Questions 6, 14, & 22):
Your Score: _____

- 3 points = Low on Perfectionism
- 4 to 6 points = Moderately Low on Perfectionism
- 7 to 9 points = Average on Perfectionism
- 10 to 12 points = High on Perfectionism
- 13 to 15 points = Very High on Perfectionism

(7) Pursue Passion & Purpose vs. Putting Up with Passivity Subscale (Questions 7, 15, & 23):
Your Score: _____

- 3 points = Low on Putting Up with Passivity

- 4 to 6 points = Moderately Low on Putting Up with Passivity
- 7 to 9 points = Average on Putting Up with Passivity
- 10 to 12 points = High on Putting Up with Passivity
- 13 to 15 points = Very High on Putting Up with Passivity

(8) Think Thankfully vs. Thanklessly/Deprived Subscale (Questions 8, 16, & 24):
Your Score: _____

- 3 points = Low on Thinking Deprived
- 4 to 6 points = Moderately Low on Thinking Deprived
- 7 to 9 points = Average on Thinking Deprived
- 10 to 12 points = High on Thinking Deprived
- 13 to 15 points = Very High on Thinking Deprived

LIFE STORY SATISFACTION SCALE

Our lives are comprised of about 10 key areas—your story's Table of Contents—and the stories we script in each of these areas can have an intense positive or negative impact on the lives we live.

1. **Relationships:** Unhealthy patterns learned from past relationships can challenge current and future relationships. Uncovering and shifting these patterns helps us achieve the meaningful connections we crave with family, friends, and others.

2. **Career:** We can sometimes find ourselves working in jobs/careers that don't bring us a sense of fulfillment or holding ourselves back from our career goals out of fear. When we illuminate our strengths, passions, and purpose, we can align our career actions with them and create greater satisfaction.

3. **Financial:** While money does not equal happiness, financial security helps ensure our basic needs are met and that we can live a lifestyle that supports our joy. Creating healthy money thoughts and habits can enhance our happiness.

4. **Living Environment:** When our living spaces and environments are in chaos, our minds can feel chaotic. Understanding what environments bring us solace helps us plan ways to organize and create these spaces.

5. **Community Engagement:** We can sometimes find ourselves feeling disconnected from our local and larger communities. Finding ways to volunteer/give back helps us express gratitude for all we have and find meaning in caring for our communities.

6. **Physical Health:** Amidst busy lives we can put our physical wellness on the back-burner and develop unhealthy habits. Creating realistic, achievable physical wellness goals and habits helps us live a happy life.

7. **Mental & Emotional Health**: Past disappointments and mistakes, daily stressors, and current challenges can take a mental and emotional toll. Learning new ways of thinking and being can help rid us of anxiety, low self-esteem, and other negative emotions and mental states, and help us reach our other life and career goals.

8. **Intellectual Growth:** Sometimes in our lives and careers, we can feel stuck in a rut of intellectual stagnation. Exploring and embarking on new intellectual growth adventures helps us to lead more enriched lives.

9. **Recreation & Relaxation:** It's easy to do only what we must on our increasingly busy to do lists, and it's often our recreation and relaxation that gets put aside. Rediscovering and reintegrating our passions and self-care practices is critical for our wellness.

10. **Spirituality:** There are times when we realize we want a connection with something larger than us. Exploring and using our greater purpose to do good in the world and express gratitude to our higher power for all we have been given helps us live more meaningfully.

On a scale from 1 to 10, with 10 being "Extremely Satisfied" and 1 being "Extremely Dissatisfied" how would you rank your satisfaction with each of these 10 areas of your life story right now?

1. Relationships: ____
2. Career: ____
3. Financial: ____
4. Living Environment: ____
5. Community Engagement: ____
6. Physical Health: ____
7. Mental & Emotional Health: ____
8. Intellectual Growth: ____
9. Recreation & Relaxation: ____
10. Spiritualty: ____

TOTAL LIFE STORY SATISFACTION: ____ out of a possible 100

Old Limiting Life Story Review

What Limiting Life Stories Have You Been Telling Yourself...

- Regarding your relationships?
- Regarding your career?
- Regarding your financial life?
- Regarding your living environment?
- Regarding your engagement within your community?
- Regarding your physical health?
- Regarding your mental and emotional health?
- Regarding your intellectual growth?
- Regarding your recreation and relaxation?
- Regarding your spirituality practices?

So, without further ado, let's begin learning how to RESCRIPT!

PART 2

THE EIGHT PRACTICES OF THE RESCRIPT FRAMEWORK

"If you ever find yourself in the wrong story, leave."

~ Mo Willems

PRACTICE #1
R- RELEASE RUMINATION

"Sometimes I wish I could tell my brain to just shut up."

~ Kristy Lee Cook

THE LIMITING SCRIPTS OF RUMINATION

You know that moment when something frustrating happens and you let yourself really think about it. All of a sudden, it feels like you've entered a dark tunnel you can't find your way out of. Your mind begins to bombard you with a litany of questions, analyses, and assessments. "How did this happen? Did I do or say something that caused this? I wonder what they are thinking about me? How will I deal with this? What can I do to fix it? Why do things like this always happen to me? Why can't I stop feeling this way? Will I ever get over this? Will things ever be good again?" Your mind is in a downward spiral going round and round and by the time you catch yourself, you've been sitting there in this state for 30 minutes, maybe even longer.

This is rumination. It's a repetitive thought pattern focused on negative feelings and experiences, as well as their causes and consequences. When you ruminate, your Inner Antagonist has grabbed the pen and is narrating your story.

When I created the RESCRIPT method, I began with rumination for a reason. It's a common challenge for many people and it feeds, facilitates, and exacerbates the issues associated with every other focus of the RESCRIPT method—in essence, we can ruminate about evading our goals, how many shortcomings we think we have, imagined catastrophes, our regrets, how we wish we could be perfect, how life is ultimately meant to feel mundane, and how we are deprived of what we need in life to be happy. Think of ruminating as spreading fertilizer on the weeds overtaking your garden. It seems like a senseless thing to do, but when we ruminate, we are basically fertilizing our mental and emotional weeds.

I also began with rumination because I know a little something about it—I'm a highly gifted ruminator. Well, I used to be at least. I utilize RESCRIPTing to release ruminations whenever they try to sneak into my brain. For too many years, I could lose hours (okay—days, weeks, months) ruminating over both the small and big things that were happening in my life. I lost hours and days ruminating over what people must be thinking after various confusing or conflictual interactions. I effectively ruminated over the experience and aftermath of a car accident for months and months. Heck, my skillful rumination helped me to make the pain of a relationship breakup last for an entire year! My point is I was a remarkable ruminator—but it wasn't a skill that served me well. I was really good at it, but I didn't want to be.

Why do we ruminate?

Why is it that despite knowing the harm rumination can cause us, it is still so difficult to contemplate stopping it? In part, we continue ruminating because on some level we believe that in doing so, we will find the answers we seek. We are very invested in our mental efforts to problem solve. Rumination gives us a false sense of control over the problem. Unfortunately, rumination is a very passive and typically distressing method for solving problems.

Rumination can also be an avoidance behavior. It keeps you stuck going around in circles in your head, instead of taking real action out in the world on the perceived problem. In ruminating, we get to avoid the potential failure or humiliation that could result from taking action.

Rumination doesn't usually *feel* like a choice. Sometimes, it can feel almost automatic, like the episode came on so quickly that we don't know how it even began. In those moments, it can feel like we lost time. For example, you are working on a report for your job and all of a sudden you realize you have been staring blankly at your computer screen for ten minutes and haven't typed a word of your report because you've been ruminating over some negative experience you recently had.

Sometimes however, we foster our rumination. By this, I mean that there are times that we send ourselves into depressive rumination episodes by selecting to isolate ourselves from others with the intent of brooding over a situation that has bothered us, repetitively playing sad songs, looking at old photos of a time or person that now spurs sad feelings, and similar types of behaviors that facilitate rumination.

Rumination tends to involve more thinking about the past rather than the future. When we ruminate, we simply recycle negative thoughts that serve no purpose or goal. Rumination is a process of focusing our mental energy on our distress, symptoms of that distress, and analyzing the causes and consequences of those symptoms. While ruminating can sometimes feel purposeful in its analysis, it is not frequently associated with genuine effort to resolve the challenges we are ruminating about. The rumination becomes almost like a state of paralysis where we are so stuck in recycling our negative analyses that we feel paralyzed to do anything concrete to address the things we are ruminating about.

There are common circumstances that facilitate rumination. If we know when we typically ruminate, we can make changes to our environment and triggering behaviors to cease the rumination before it begins or in its early stages. States and situations conducive to rumination include:

We ruminate when we are idle. If rumination were Bonnie, idleness would be her Clyde. They are partners in crime, coconspirators, ride or die. The less we are doing, the more our minds are likely to try to replay actual problems or create fake issues. When our minds or bodies aren't busy with something productive, pleasurable, or particularly intensive, our minds are more likely to wander down dark alleys. When you are alone driving in the car, or on the train or bus to work. When you are sitting in the nail salon. When you are in the shower. When you are sitting on the couch. When you are lying down in your bed to go to sleep at night. These are just a few examples of idle times ripe and ready for rumination.

We ruminate when we are overwhelmed. When our plates get too full with task upon task upon task, it can facilitate chaos in our minds. When this happens, our thoughts can begin to swirl trying to keep on top of everything. The resulting feeling of being overwhelmed can lead to ruminative thoughts.

We ruminate when we are nervous. When we get nervous about something that has happened, our brains sometimes try to make us ruminate over it. Think about how you feel after a job interview, for example. After a job interview, we might repeatedly go over our answers in our minds, pick apart every word, and wonder if there was something else we could have said or done to stand out as the strongest candidate. We might also ruminate by analyzing the interviewer's actions and words, and what they must have meant. "What did she mean when she said my level of experience was good? Did she mean good like okay, or good like excellent?" Relationships are another example. After we finish a first date, we might analyze the conversation and question if we sounded smart enough, interesting enough, or if we should have done anything differently. "When I said I love watching TV all day Saturday in my pajamas, I hope he didn't think I'm boring or lazy or totally unambitious." We might evaluate certain phrases uttered by our date and sift through them for hidden meanings. "When he said he wants to move to California one day, did he say that because he's not interested or because he wants to see if I would be interested in moving one day too?"

We also ruminate when we are upset. When something happens in our lives that ignites sadness, anger, frustration, disappointment, or other negative types of emotions, it can lead down a path to rumination. We are tempted to analyze why the situation happened, what others are thinking about us, why things like this happen to us, and so on. Once we go down this path, we can get stuck there for a while in a state of wallowing.

Being idle, feeling overwhelmed, experiencing nervousness over something that has happened, and feeling upset by a situation can be common pre-cursers to ruminating. However, it is important to understand that while our brains may ask us to ruminate, even beg and try to lure us in, we don't have to oblige. We have much more control over ruminating than we often believe we do.

What do we ruminate about?

There are a number of common things we ruminate about and ways we go about doing so. Some examples include:

- *Why-ning:* **Mulling over *why* you feel the way you are feeling** – "Why am I so sad?" "Why am I so anxious?" "Why can't I get over this?" "Why can't I get motivated?" "Why am I always so tired?"

- *Woe is Me-ing:* **Focusing on a belief that recent challenges signify that life is and will always be bad for you** – "Life is always throwing crap at me." "This is so unfair! Life is always so unfair for me." "No one is ever there for me." "I can never catch a break with anything!"

- *Gloom & Doom-ing:* **Concentrating on thoughts of the world being doomed following news of a tragedy** – "So many awful things are happening in the world; so many people are suffering." "This world is just hopeless, there's a new tragedy every day." "What's the purpose of all this suffering in the world. How could a higher power allow this?"

- *Inactive Actioning*: **Assessing how you'll deal with a problem, but in a passive way that remains in thought not behavior** – "What am I gonna do now?" "How will I ever cope with this?" "How am I supposed to fix this now?"

- *Telepathizing*: **Concluding what someone else is thinking or feeling about you** – "I bet she thinks I'm stupid now." "He probably hates me now." "She's probably thinking my idea sucks."

- *It Must be Me-ing*: **Analyzing how someone else's actions are about you somehow *or* how you are the one responsible for saving/fixing someone else** – "She hasn't texted me back. What did I do that made her mad at me?" "He was so quiet last time we talked. What did I say that made him not want to talk to me anymore?" "She had a strange look on her face in the meeting. What did I say that made her have that look?" "I have to be the one to fix this problem for him." "It's gonna have to be me that saves her from this mess she's gotten into." "It's my fault he's in this terrible situation because I didn't save him from himself."

- *I'm a Screw-Up-izing*: **Determining you are a complete and utter screw-up because of something you said, did, didn't say, or didn't do** – "I'm so utterly stupid for getting those questions wrong on the exam." "I'm the clumsiest person on earth for falling during the dance routine." "I'm so pathetic for not speaking up for myself and what I believe in during that conversation." "I'm such a failure for putting my foot in my mouth and saying that during the job interview."

In summation, when we ruminate, we are simply rehashing perceived mistakes, agonizing over opportunities we think we may have missed out on, brooding over unfair treatment from others or life overall, reminding ourselves of our perceived limitations and disastrous mess ups, holding ourselves and others to unrealistic and unhealthy standards, and perseverating on why bad things happen to us, how we'll survive, and why we can't get over it. In these mental states, our Inner Antagonist is narrating a painful tragedy.

How does ruminating harm us?

Experiencing negative thoughts is part of being human, however ruminating extensively on those thoughts can have a pretty detrimental impact on us, including intensifying to severe anxiety and depression. Rumination increases pessimistic thinking, fuels self-criticism, drains us of the energy and motivation to take positive action, and thus hinders our ability to effectively problem solve. Rumination also hinders our overall ability to focus and concentrate on more productive or enjoyable activities. Once we begin an episode of rumination, we often find ourselves pulled away mentally from the tasks we had been working on, disengaging from those we are with, and not being mentally present enough to enjoy any pleasurable activities we had been engaging in. Furthermore, ruminating can hamper our ability to fall asleep and stay asleep. As we lay our heads on our pillow at night, ruminating thoughts can create serious challenges to shutting down. These thoughts can steal several minutes and even hours of time away from our sleep time as we recycle negative thoughts, and may even contribute to waking up in the middle of the night.

The more we ruminate, the more likely we are to develop negative interpretations of events in our lives, minimizing our successes and magnifying our failures, even assuming failure will occur in situations that have not yet taken place. Continuous rumination fosters feelings of having less control over our lives and a belief that we are unable to effectively solve our problems. It ultimately leads us to become pessimistic, self-critical, self-blaming, and less confident overall.

How does Releasing Rumination RESCRIPT our story?

When we allow ourselves to release our harmful ruminations, we remove many limits from our lives. We allow ourselves to focus our thoughts on joys and aspirations, rather than sorrows and burdens. We enable ourselves to acknowledge that we don't need to be all-knowing to live in peace. We give ourselves permission to exist with hope in an imperfect world. We empower ourselves to get out of our heads and move into positive action to address what is within our control on both the small and larger scale.

HIGHLIGHTS FROM RESEARCH STUDIES ON RUMINATION

- Research by Nolen-Hoeksema, Wisco, and Lyubomirsky found that rumination weakens people's ability to problem solve and take action toward their goals, impairs interpersonal relationships, and is correlated with depression, anxiety, substance abuse, eating disorders, and self-harm behaviors.[4]

- Ward, Lyubomirsky, Sousa, and Nolen-Hoeksema discovered that non-ruminators demonstrate greater confidence and commitment to their goal plans than those who engage in excessive rumination.[5]

- Jerabek and Muoio of PsychTests uncovered that those who don't ruminate experience greater contentment with their lives, stronger abilities to effectively manage their emotions, higher self-esteem, superior self-motivation, better positive mindset, more assertiveness, deeper resilience, and less need for approval from others.[6]

- Rude, Mazzetti, Pal, and Stauble found that contemplating the causes and consequences of a recent social rejection and their role in it led to greater subsequent rumination and depression symptoms. Conversely, contemplating the larger context of the recent social rejection, including how they imagine they'll perceive the event a couple years in the future, and how an impartial observer might view the situation, resulted in less subsequent rumination and depression symptoms.[7]

- Hilt and Pollak conducted a study with children and adolescents and discovered that both distraction and mindfulness exercises are effective in getting youth out of an episode of negative rumination.[8]

LIMITING NARRATIONS OF RUMINATION RESCRIPTED

Let's examine how we can RESCRIPT the stories we tell ourselves when we ruminate:

1. "I can't believe he broke up with me. What did I do wrong? Did I say something that upset him? Was it when I asked him about his ex-girlfriend? He probably thought I was pathetic. I wonder if he regrets dumping me. I wonder if he'll call me..."

   RESCRIPTed...
   "I can't believe he broke up with me. I'm going to miss being with him. It's gonna be hard to get used to not having him around. I may never know exactly what went wrong since I can't read his mind. But, it doesn't matter because I can't control his thoughts, feelings, or behaviors. I know in the long run I will be okay. I've been here before and survived better than I originally thought I would. For now, I'm going to allow my sadness until I fully heal."

2. "My boss looked pissed this morning in the meeting. I wonder if she is angry with me. I wonder if I said something wrong in my email response to her at the end of the day yesterday. Was it when I made that joke? Did she take it wrong? I hope I didn't mess up our working relationship..."

   RESCRIPTed...
   "My boss looked pissed this morning in the meeting. I wonder if she is angry with me. Ya know, in the past when

39

I was sure I was the reason someone else looked upset, it turned out they were just stressed about other things in their life. No point in worrying about it. I'll just think maybe she is having a bad day. And if she is upset with me, she'll eventually let me know and we'll address it when she's ready."

3. "Damn, I definitely got that question wrong on the exam. I gotta look up some of the other questions. Oh man, I got those three wrong too! I wonder what else I got wrong. Did I do okay on the essay? I think I bombed this test…"

RESCRIPTed…

"Damn, I definitely got that question wrong on the exam. But, there's nothing I can do about it now, so looking up the other questions I remember won't help either. It will just make me feel worse. I can't accurately guess my performance at this point. I'm just going to have to wait to get the exam back as much as I hate waiting. If I didn't do great, I'll have to change the way I prepare for the next exam."

4. "I've had a pain in my knee for a week. Let me look up knee pain on WebMD. Rheumatoid Arthritis. Crap, I have that symptom too, and that one. I have RA. I'm gonna be completely debilitated. What am I gonna do now? Bad things always happen to me. And now my health is gone too…"

RESCRIPTed…

"I've had a pain in my knee for a week. Let me look up knee pain on WebMD. Rheumatoid Arthritis. Sprain. Overuse. Well, I was working out a lot the last few days. I really can't be certain what it is since I'm not a doctor. If it persists another week, I'll go to the doctor and get it checked out. For now, I'll take it a little easier so I don't make it worse."

5. "It's completely unfair that I was one of the people laid off! I've been there the longest and my reviews have been

great. I deserved that promotion last year, not Sharon. They just had it in for me for some reason because I never saw this coming. I always have the worst luck..."

RESCRIPTed...

"It isn't fair that I was one of the people laid off. I have been there the longest and my reviews have been great. But, I'm not the only great team member who was let go. While it feels very personal, it wasn't about any of us not being worth keeping. It was a fiscal decision, and while it sucks, life doesn't always have to be fair for me to be okay. I will be proactive and get career coaching and resume writing help. I will be okay. I've weathered other tough storms, I can weather this one too."

LIMITLESS LIVING LIBRARY – STRATEGIES TO RELEASE RUMINATION SECTION

In this section of the Limitless Living Library, you have access to a variety of strategies you can use to release rumination. As you mentally walk through this library section, you can take any of these strategies off the shelves, read about them, see which ones you like best, and "check out" the ones you want to try. Don't worry, the Limitless Living Library has no restrictions, so you are already a card-carrying library member!

If you "check out" a strategy and aren't sure what you think of it, give it a few more reads and tries. You can always return it if it doesn't feel like it's helping you to script the story you want for yourself. And, it's always there if you'd like to check it out again. Sometimes after a few reads, we find new aspects of a story we didn't notice before.

If you "check out" a strategy and find it's helping you release your ruminations, you can keep it! You don't need to return it, it's yours now. So, it becomes a part of you and your RESCRIPTed story.

In addition to these strategies, you can modify and use strategies from other chapters to release your ruminations. The Limitless

Living Library provides resources for you to move into positive thought and action, so you can quiet your Inner Antagonist and amplify your Inner Advocate!

Release Rumination Strategy #1:
Helping or Harming Review

It's always a good practice in life to review the reasoning behind why we do the things we do and determine if our current strategy is the most effective path to our end goal. Reviewing why we ruminate and examining if it's achieving its intent is no different.

During or following your next episode of rumination, ask yourself the following:

1. What is/was my purpose/intent in this episode of rumination?

2. How does/did this rumination harm me?

3. How does/did this rumination help me?

4. What is/was avoided through this rumination?

5. What is/was addressed through this rumination?

6. What would I say to a friend who was ruminating over this?

7. What more effective things could I say to myself right now?

8. What more effective strategies exist to achieve my original purpose/intent?

9. What did I learn about my rumination from this review?

Release Rumination Strategy #2:
Alter Analysis into Action

One of the most common underlying intentions of rumination is to foster a feeling of control over a situation where we have limited control. The process of analyzing all the factors of a situation can make us *feel like* we are taking control of it and doing something about it. Earlier in the chapter, we talked about the concept as "Inactive Action-ing" – ruminating over how we'll deal with a problem, while not actually doing something to address it. However, in essence, all forms of rumination are inactive attempts at resolving an issue.

Furthermore, episodes of rumination frequently occur when we were in the middle of trying to do something else. Thus, our rumination analyses often take us away from more productive or pleasurable actions we were engaged in just before we began ruminating.

One of the most effective ways to squash rumination, as well as genuinely deal with the issue we are ruminating about, is to alter our analysis into actions by determining what part of the situation we control.

Sometimes, we may find there are several aspects we control. For others, our control may be quite limited. The actions below are examples of things that can be done with various levels of control in a situation:

- "Instead of ruminating that the director must think my report is terrible, I can call her to ask if she's reviewed my report, and if so, what she thinks about it."

- "Instead of ruminating that the reason my friend was so quiet last night is because she's angry with me, I can call my friend to ask if she is angry with me about something."

- "Instead of ruminating that my injury is going to take forever to heal and that it will mess up my life, I can do all the things the doctor suggested to care for my injury and heal steadily."

- "Instead of ruminating over whether the company made a hiring decision yet, I can send a follow-up email to reiterate my interest and check on my candidacy for the job."

- "Instead of ruminating over my house foreclosure, I can start doing some research and making phone calls to find a new home."

- "Instead of ruminating in the pain of losing my best friend since she passed away, I can honor her and savor the blessing of knowing her by making a picture collage of our times together."

No matter how much or how little control we have, action empowers us, while analysis keeps us stuck. Taking action teaches us that although we may feel pain, anger, sadness, disappointment, frustration, and other difficult emotions, we can still simultaneously keep our lives moving forward. It's not the difficult emotions that are bad, they are part of life, it's when we wallow in them for too long and allow them to debilitate us that they become severely problematic.

The next time you find yourself in an episode of rumination, immediately ask and answer these questions (in your head, out loud, or on paper):

1. What control do I have over what I am ruminating about?

2. What action within my control will I take now to address what I am ruminating over?

3. What more productive or pleasurable pursuits did this rumination take me away from?

4. What steps will I take right now to move forward and do something more productive or pleasurable?

Once you have the answers, take action as quickly as your situation permits. And, once you have taken the action(s) that are within your level of control, commit yourself to letting your ruminations go by telling yourself, "I've taken action on what is within my control. Analyzing this further doesn't serve or move me forward. It's time to go back to doing what I was doing before I began ruminating." You can repeat this, or abbreviated versions of it, as many times as you need to until the ruminating thoughts stop.

Release Rumination Strategy #3:
Remove Your Rumination Routines

Becoming more aware of the context surrounding our periods of rumination can help us to remove rumination routines we may have. Sometimes we are inadvertently doing things that are facilitating rumination.

It is helpful to ask yourself:

1. Are there particular times of the day that I ruminate? When?

2. Are there particular locations where I ruminate? Where specifically?

3. Am I typically alone, with others, with a particular person just before/during episodes of rumination?

4. Are there particular events that typically trigger my ruminations? Which ones?

5. How long do my periods of rumination last?

6. Are there things that tend to stop my ruminations? What are they?

Furthermore, contemplate if there are contexts in which your rumination *does not* typically occur:

7. When, where, who, and what *does not* seem to facilitate rumination?

Consider how you can utilize this information to remove rumination routines by doing something different than you usually do for contexts that facilitate rumination. Perhaps non-facilitating contexts hold some solutions. Or, maybe you can engage more quickly in things that have stopped your ruminations in the past. Here are some examples:

If you ruminate in bed after waking up, try keeping some affirmations on your nightstand and reading/reciting them just after you wake up. Or, try getting yourself out of bed more quickly and jumping into action to start your day. If you ruminate in bed at night as you are trying to sleep, empower your Inner Advocate to recount the things you are grateful for from your day instead. If you ruminate while exercising or driving, try singing to music you love or listening to an audio book that you have wanted to read. If you ruminate while sitting alone and idle on your couch, try reading a book, or researching something online you have been interested in. Try meditating, or doing another fulfilling activity that relaxes and engages you. If you ruminate when you are in a rush to go somewhere, consider building in extra time by getting up earlier or taking care of some things at night before you go to bed so you have enough time and don't need to feel rushed.

These are just a few examples to generate ideas, but you can do anything that feels like it might change up routines that have been facilitating your ruminating. Give it a try!

Release Rumination Strategy #4:
Shorten or Schedule Your Stress for Later

Episodes of negative mental analysis rarely wait for a convenient time to strike. They come on when you are trying to study for an exam, work on a project at the office, read a good book, get a massage, or spend quality time with your family or friends. Got something more important to do right now than stress? Shorten your stress episode or schedule it for later!

When you start to notice the distracting negative contemplations, say to yourself, "I've got other more important things I need to do right now, so I'm gonna make this quick." Then, take a look at your watch and give yourself 10 to 20 minutes of stress time. Once your time is up, tell yourself, "Okay, I've done my stressing, now back to what I was doing before!"

Or, you can tell yourself, "This will need to wait until later." Then, take a look at your daily calendar and pencil in your stress in a 10 to 20-minute open space on your schedule later on. You can label it Stress Time, Drive Myself Crazy Time, Over-Analyze Time, Deal With It Later Time, or anything you like. If your brain tries to trick you into thinking about it earlier, calmly remind it, "I'm not doing this now, I've scheduled this for later" and then go back to the more productive or enjoyable things you were doing. Once your scheduled stress time arrives, stress away, but only for 10 to 20 minutes. If you decide you no longer feel like stressing now, don't! But if you want to, go ahead, but keep an eye on the clock. When your allotted stress time ends – STOP! Tell your stress that its time is up. Then, resume other more pleasurable or important activities. You control your mind and your time!

Release Rumination Strategy #5: Alternate Your Analyzing

Still struggling to stop your mind from analyzing something unproductive, unpleasant, and/or unhealthy? Alternate your analyzing! Hey, if your mind *really* wants to analyze something *right now*, give it something more purposeful and pleasant to focus on!

Were you in the middle of a work project when your ruminating began? Consider some aspects of your work project that could use a little analytical thinking. Were you in your car driving and listening to music when the rumination began? Try analyzing the lyrics of the songs you are listening to? Were you with a friend at dinner just trying to enjoy her company when you started ruminating? Alternate your analysis to helping her resolve a problem she was sharing or assess the best places in the area to go for ice cream after dinner. Even if you were just sitting on your couch idle when you began ruminating, start assessing the steps needed to get started on a passion project you have been wanting to begin.

To facilitate your alternate analysis, talk back to that Inner Antagonist that's trying to make you ruminate. You can speak to it out loud or in your mind, whichever makes the most sense based on your situation and location. Tell it, "Nope, I'm not going to analyze that right now, it has no positive purpose. But, if my brain really wants to analyze something right now, I'll analyze _____ instead."

Sometimes, if you can't beat the analysis, you can just join it by alternating it to something more positive!

Release Rumination Strategy #6:
Put Your Distractors in Detention

So, here's the deal: Your distractors, those pesky ruminating thoughts about things that don't serve you, are kind of like kids trying to distract you while you are doing work in a classroom. Remember being a kid in school trying to take a test, and there was that one kid who was whispering to you, "Psst, psst, psst, hey…" Sometimes they took it up a notch and tossed a little crumpled piece of paper at your back to get your attention. But, it was just enough to throw you off track from remembering your answers and focusing on your test! When the teacher noticed what they were doing, sometimes these kids got detention during recess. Well, what if you could put your distractors in detention!

When you notice a pesky, distracting, ruminating thought trying to throw you off your task at hand, imagine the thought as that kid in class saying "psst, psst," and throwing paper at you during a test. But this time, you are both student and teacher, and you can assign detention. Tell your thought distractor, "You know you aren't supposed to be doing that right now. I'm sorry, but I'm going to put you in detention." Imagine yourself removing that thought from the front of your mind, and putting it in a quiet, locked room way in the back of your mind, away from you and everything else. It can't bother you anymore, it's in detention until further notice.

Release Rumination Strategy #7:
Cap the Complaining

Productively addressing a problematic situation is positive. Rehashing it over and over is less helpful. If we want to stay stuck in a story that's limiting our life, one of the very best things we can do is complain—when something goes wrong, when something annoys us, we can tell as many people as possible, or even better, we can post about it on social media!

However, we *don't* want to remain stuck in a life limiting story, yet, we still might find ourselves complaining. Hmm, what's up with that? In part, we often don't realize we are complaining, especially if it has become kind of a habit. Furthermore, we generally don't realize how negatively impactful complaining can be in our lives.

Let me first define what I mean by complaining. For the purposes of this practice, complaining refers to expressing discontent, verbally and/or in writing, to multiple people, with a greater desire to tell it than to gain insight into resolving it. We ALL do this sometimes. It is when it becomes a habitual practice that we hamper our mental and emotional wellbeing.

Think of it this way, what we talk about, we give energy to—energy through our thoughts, words, emotions, actions, and time. When we spend that much energy on something, like complaining about any particular situation, we think it must be pretty important. If it wasn't important, why would we put so much effort into maintaining it? Ironically, it may not even be all that important, but we've been telling others, and in turn, ourselves, that it is important, so we believe it is. Hence, we continue fueling it.

Thus, it slowly drains energy from us in the process. It wears us down talking and thinking about negative things over and over. We get further dragged into perpetuating the negativity when all those we complained to check in to ask how we are doing. Even if we were ready to move on, we've been pulled back into talking about it again. So, the cycle of telling ourselves a negative story just drags on.

Am I suggesting we bottle up our feelings tightly about unpleasant experiences? Of course not, I'm a therapist and coach, that would be unhealthy! Particularly with serious issues we face in our lives, sharing with others for support and guidance can be quite helpful for devising solutions. Discussing an issue in order to raise awareness so action can be taken is both important and productive. Understanding our intent in talking about our challenges is key. Are we seeking to foster awareness, gain support, get ideas, or produce positive action? Or, are we simply rehashing problems and annoyances in our lives?

Learning to cap complaining is like building any new habit, it takes time and consistent practice. There are some simple guidelines you can follow to help you build this habit.

After a situation occurs that you feel discontented with, pay closer attention to your thoughts during and following. In particular, pay attention to thoughts that sound similar to, "Oh, I gotta tell people about this!" "Nobody would ever believe this crap just happened to me." "See, nobody believes me when I say I have bad luck!" "Alright, I need to vent."

If you find yourself having thoughts in line with these, the next thing you want to do is say to yourself, "Okay, I know complaining to a bunch of people about this is just going to perpetuate my negative feelings." Then ask yourself, "In talking about this situation, what type of emotional support am I looking for and who in my life is most likely to give that to me?"

Once you have determined who will best provide the support you seek, contact that individual and share away. You can rant or cry if it helps you release. However, once you have let out your feelings for 15-30 minutes—stop. At this point, if there are ideas and solutions the person can help with, talk about them (and put them into practice if useful). However, cease complaining simply to complain.

Afterwards, you may still desire to tell others about your discontent. Resist this urge, especially if the issue was more of a frustration or annoyance, like a fender bender, a person who was rude to you at a store, or a cranky colleague. If the issue is more serious, like losing a job, chronic health problems, a relationship breakup, or the death of a loved one, still remain selective in who you share with. When we are going through tough times, we benefit from support from those who have a deep caring for us and who can help us devise solutions and coping strategies. However, we still must not be indiscriminate in our sharing, as it can hamper our resilience if we focus solely on our challenges rather than on our amazing human capability to triumph over our challenges.

Consistently capping complaining helps it become a new habit. Over time, we feel much less of a desire to complain. In fact, we actually desire not to complain because we see how much more content we feel and how much less ruminating we do when complaining is not using up excessive energy in our lives.

Release Rumination Strategy #8:
Turn Off the Telepathy Switch

"What are they thinking about me?" "What is he thinking about this situation?" "What does she think that I'm thinking about her?"

Well, let me just turn on my telepathy switch so I can know their thoughts.

So, let's just be real – WE CAN'T READ MINDS. Nope. Sorry. You can keep trying to mind-read someone else's thoughts if you want to, but it's not going to work. That switch you're using—can you picture it in your mind? It's like the switch on a child's old, beat up, battery-less toy. It's fake, not hooked up to anything, not real. It's not doing *anything* in the on position. So, just turn it off.

Yea, it sounds rather silly when you think of it like that doesn't it? But, that is in essence what we so often do when:

- We just finished an interview or a first date.

- We had an awkward interaction with a friend.

- We are in the middle of doing a presentation.

These are just a few examples of times when nerves and insecurities might try to turn on our telepathy switches. We think that if we could just replay every aspect of the interaction or situation, we might figure out what others are thinking, and then we can *finally* feel calm and secure.

But, that's not how life works. We are not telepathic and we don't get to know what other people are thinking. They don't get to know what we are thinking either. All of this is a good thing. We do not need to know what anyone else is thinking about us or any situation in order to feel calm and secure. We must generate our calm and secure feelings from within.

The next time you find yourself ruminating about what someone else must be thinking, picture that nonsensical telepathy switch in your mind and say to yourself, "That telepathy switch isn't real, it's not wired to anything or anyone else's mind, it doesn't work, and I don't need it anyway!"

Release Rumination Strategy #9:
Take Off the Control Cape

No one is the center of the universe. No one is all-knowing. No one is all-powerful. No one holds mystical powers to control the minds, emotions, and actions of other human beings. And, usually, we know this.

Yet, when a person we know—is too quiet today, is cranky today, looked at us with a strange facial expression, doesn't respond quickly enough to our call/text/email—we can do something amazing. We can magically transform into a character out of a comic book—THE central, all-knowing, all-powerful being who is in sole control of this person. With our Control Cape draped over our shoulders, we know for certain—"It was surely I who said, or did, or didn't say, or didn't do something (I don't know what) to make you think/feel/act this way. Let me sift through my mind with my superpowers, review every interaction we've recently had, to uncover how I am responsible." Or, perhaps, "There is surely something I *must* do to fix your problems, as I, with my superpowers, am the one who can save you."

But, you see, your story is not a fiction story. And you know what that means? It means you don't control anybody else, only yourself!

Sometimes we dislike ambiguity so much, and desire more control in life so much, that we mentally conjure controls that we don't actually have. And, our other insecurities feed into this when it comes to "It Must Be Me-ing" focused ruminations, like desires not to let people down or to not be disliked.

But, when you really break it down, each of us has MANY influences and factors in our lives that impact the things we think, feel, and do. And when we are "It Must Be Me-ing" we totally ignore these numerous factors, assuming we are the most central and powerful influence of all over another person's thoughts, feelings, or actions.

How many times have you done this kind of ruminating and ultimately learned a person's actions had absolutely nothing to do with you? Seriously, how many? Or, how often have you found that all your save-someone tactics have been futile, because it turned out they needed to take responsibility for themselves. Remind yourself of this the next time you go putting on your Control Cape. Then, imagine yourself in that comic book inspired control cape. Recite to yourself, "I am not the central, all-knowing, all-powerful being in control of this person's actions. They have lots of other things happening in their lives that could be impacting their behaviors. I cannot make anyone else do anything. Analyzing this is a waste of my time." Next, picture yourself taking the control cape off.

Now, go spend your valuable time using your real, non-fictional strengths to script the story you want to be living.

Release Rumination Strategy #10:
Let It Go Letter

Sometimes life gets tough. People let us down or betray our trust. Adversities and traumas occur in our lives. Tragedies occur in the world. We find ourselves wondering why life can be so unfair, replaying all the hurts. We find ourselves digging deeper and deeper into a tunnel of ruminative despair. We don't know where to begin to pull ourselves out. And, ruminating just keeps us in the hole. It keeps us thinking there's no way out. It keeps our energy focused on the darkness, and slowly works to shut out all the light.

When our shoulders are heavy with the weight of life's disappointments and challenges, we can double a ten-pound weight to twenty simply by keeping our thoughts focused on our troubles.

We want to let it go because on some level we know—the despair won't let go of us if we won't let go of it. But, where do we even begin?

We start by getting it out of us. Get out a piece of paper, a pad, or start a Word document on your computer. Think about the focus of your anger, sadness, or frustration. Is it a particular individual? Or, is it just life overall?

Address your letter accordingly, "Dear Jim," or Dear Life,"

Now, write about how the person or life has treated you unfairly and how this has made you feel. Then, commit to letting go of harmful thoughts, emotions, and behaviors that have resulted from this unfair treatment. Share what beneficial thoughts, emotions, and behaviors you commit to experiencing now that you have let go of the harm.

Do not share the letter with your transgressor (if an individual) or anyone. This letter is just for you. Each time you find your mind trying to dwell again on the negative thoughts and emotions surrounding this experience, read this letter to yourself, quietly or out loud.

Letting go is not the same as forgetting or condoning the transgression. It is an act of self-compassion to allow you to release ruminations of toxic experiences and feelings that are harming you. In holding onto these toxicities, we simply allow them to victimize us over and over and over again.

Here are some very brief examples of things a Let It Go Letter might say:

Dear Life,

When I found out that I was getting laid off from my job after 15 years, I felt angry, disillusioned, and ashamed. I felt like my career would never get back on track and no one would ever want to hire me again. And then, to have my car completely break down and find out I needed knee surgery within the next two months, I've been trying to figure out why life is out to get me. I've spent the last few months being really pissed at life and ruminating over how unfair all this has been, feeling resentful, and basically hopeless. But what I am realizing is that I'm the only person who can pull me out of this rut, and all my ruminating is doing is just digging me deeper into it. So, I'm choosing to let it go—the anger, resentment, shame, hopelessness—I'm letting go of all of it. I'm replacing the rumination and crappy feelings with pride for 15 strong years at the company and for saving enough money to buy a new car, and resilience for how I healed after my surgery. I'm choosing to feel secure in my skills and experience, and hopeful about future career opportunities. Life is not my enemy and I'm strong enough to thrive no matter what.

Sincerely,
Alex

Dear Jim,

When you suddenly told me our marriage wasn't working, that you had fallen in love with someone else, and that you wanted a divorce, I felt blindsided, betrayed, angry, and broken-hearted. I felt like all my dreams for our life together had been stolen from me and I could never have happiness again. Ruminating on what you did, why something like this happened to me, and the devastation I felt has been really weighing on me these last six months. I know I don't deserve to be burdened with this anger and pain, so I'm committing myself to letting the toxic feelings go. I'm giving them up. I don't want them and I am choosing to stop carrying them around with me everywhere I go. I'm choosing to replace the toxic feelings with new positive feelings of gratitude for what I've learned from our relationship—the good and the bad, hope for a more authentic relationship in my future, empowerment that I am strong and will achieve all of my dreams, and conviction that my happiness comes from within me, not from anyone or anything else outside of me.

Sincerely,
Janet

Writing and reading your letter whenever you need to helps you to truly let it go. And, it helps you to replace the pain and anguish with hope.

Release Rumination Strategy #11: Calm & Compassionate Cognitions

Ruminating thoughts aren't often calm, compassionate thoughts (except the aspect that feels sorry for ourselves or the world, that I suppose is a type of compassion, though not a particularly healthy one). When we ruminate, we are often focused on feeling upset with ourselves, others, and/or life overall. Increasing compassion can be a helpful strategy for releasing ruminations.

Compassionate thinking removes judgements and absolutes. Here are some examples you can use to create more calm and compassionate cognitions during an episode of rumination.

Agitated & Uncompassionate Thought: "I'm never going to be able to get a good job again after being let go from my company."

Calm & Compassionate Thought: "I am skilled and experienced and will find a great job again after experiencing this layoff."

Agitated & Uncompassionate Thought: "This restaurant server is horrible. She's so slow and messed up my order. She's totally ruined my dinner out tonight."

Calm & Compassionate Thought: "This restaurant server seems to be having an off night. Maybe it's because it's busy tonight or maybe she has some other stresses happening in her life. That's okay, it's not really a problem, her slower pace gives me more time to talk with my friend over dinner."

Agitated & Uncompassionate Thought: "Life seriously sucks all the time now. I can never catch a break."

Calm & Compassionate Thought: "Life may be tougher for me right now, but it isn't all bad. I have things in my life to be grateful for."

The next time you are stuck in an episode of rumination, try listening to the agitated and uncompassionate aspects of what you are thinking, and intentionally infuse some calm and compassion into your cognitions.

Release Rumination Strategy #12: Mindfulness Over Madness

Rumination episodes can sometimes *feel* like madness—like an irrational virus that takes control of your mind and makes you lose track of everything else happening in the moment. Practicing mindfulness meditation and breathing can help bring us back to awareness of the present moment. It involves intentionally and non-judgmentally paying attention to the present moment. As founder of the UMass Mindfulness-Based Stress Reduction Program, Jon Kabat-Zinn states, "You can't stop the waves, but you can learn to surf."[9]

If you are noticing yourself feeling distress in a ruminative episode, you can try the following:

- Focus your attention on the sensations arising in your body.

- Now, sit still with your back straight and close your eyes.

- Concentrate your mind on the present moment.

- Slowly take a deep breath in through your nose, feeling your lungs fill with air.

- Hold your breath and count to three in your mind.

- Now, slowly exhale your breath while relaxing the muscles in your face, jaw, neck, shoulders, back, chest, arms, hands, fingers, stomach, buttocks, legs, feet, and down through your toes.

- You may notice sounds, physical sensations, thoughts, and emotions. It's okay. Just bring your attention back to your breathing.

- Ruminative thoughts may still be floating through your mind. You don't need to criticize them, analyze them, or fear them. You are human and these thoughts are simply part of the human experience.

- Whenever you notice your attention has drifted off to ruminative thoughts, simply acknowledge the drift, and bring your attention back to your breathing.

- Continue to focus on your breathing and repeat the steps as needed.

This exercise helps us to recognize that ruminative thoughts are not to be feared. They are fleeting. They are part of being human. And, they eventually drift away. You can practice aspects of mindfulness meditation wherever and whenever, whether active or inactive, with others or alone. It's about becoming present, aware, and calm.

Release Rumination Strategy #13:
Dwell on the Positive

The opposite of ruminating is savoring, or in other words, dwelling on the positive. When you find yourself dwelling on the negative, refocus your lenses to see all the good. Even when we make an error in judgment, we learn something, and that error does not erase all the great decisions we've made. When we experience the loss of a relationship, job, home, or other losses, the good experiences we had don't cease to exist, we get to keep them in our memories. Simply because something ends, doesn't mean we must begin thinking of it as completely bad and forever tainted.

When we hear about something tragic that has happened to someone we know or don't know, receive shocking bad news, or when we experience a challenge or even a trauma, we don't have to keep revisiting the disillusionment or pain. We can feel and process our feelings, but we don't have to keep swimming around in them. We can subsequently re-focus our lenses on the good experiences in our lives.

Here are some questions you can ask yourself to start dwelling on the positive:

1. What positive new ways will I choose to perceive the situation I've been ruminating about?

2. What positive wisdom did I gain from the situation I've been ruminating about?

3. What positive actions will I take in life as a result of the wisdom I've gained?

4. If there's a loss involved, what positive memories will I continue to cherish?

5. If an error in judgment was involved, what great decisions have I made in the past and what positive outcomes have arisen from them?

6. What positive experiences have I had in my life and what successes have I achieved that I'll ponder and savor right now?

7. What positive people, characteristics, and other resources do I currently have in my life that I'll ponder and savor right now?

8. What positive events have I witnessed or kind actions have I seen people take that I will focus on instead?

Release Rumination Strategy #14: Ruminating Thought RESCRIPTing

Consider some common, recent, and/or long-standing ruminations you have experienced in various areas of your life that have kept you stuck in a life limiting story. Using the ruminating thought RESCRIPTing examples and other illustrations from this chapter as a guide, RESCRIPT some of your ruminating thoughts into statements that are more realistic, encouraging, and empowering.

What ruminations will you release through RESCRIPTing...

1. Regarding your relationships?
   • Ruminating Thought:
   • RESCRIPTed:

2. Regarding your career?
   • Ruminating Thought:
   • RESCRIPTed:

3. Regarding your financial life?
   - Ruminating Thought:
   - RESCRIPTed:

4. Regarding your living environment?
   - Ruminating Thought:
   - RESCRIPTed:

5. Regarding your engagement within your community?
   - Ruminating Thought:
   - RESCRIPTed:

6. Regarding your physical health?
   - Ruminating Thought:
   - RESCRIPTed:

7. Regarding your mental and emotional health?
   - Ruminating Thought:
   - RESCRIPTed:

8. Regarding your intellectual growth?
   - Ruminating Thought:
   - RESCRIPTed:

9. Regarding your recreation and relaxation?
   - Ruminating Thought:
   - RESCRIPTed:

10. Regarding your spirituality practices?
    - Ruminating Thought:
    - RESCRIPTed:

Commit yourself to releasing these ruminations, knowing they do not serve you.

Release Rumination Strategy #15:
Acknowledgements & Affirmations

To retrain our brains to make a habit of releasing rumination takes regular practice. Daily, weekly, monthly, or whenever you need them most, recite these rumination releasing acknowledgements and affirmations. These help us to acknowledge the realities of what we do and do not control, and what we do and do not need to live our lives fully, happily, and healthily. They also help us to affirm the ways we will choose to think and act positively and empoweringly throughout our days.

I acknowledge and affirm that...

- Mentally analyzing what others are thinking will never make me a mind reader.

- Unfair things sometimes happen in all people's lives and ruminating about them will not change that.

- I cannot make another person think, feel, or do anything if they do not want to, thus ruminating about how I will go about trying to do so is a waste of my time.

- I do not need to know what others think of me in order for me to think confidently about myself.

- I do not need to know why others do the things they do in order for me to feel confident in my interactions with others.

- I do not need to know why things happen in life for me to live hopefully.

- I do not need to control others' thoughts, feelings, or actions in order to be in control of my own thoughts, feelings, or actions.

- Other people's negative moods or attitudes often have absolutely nothing to do with me, and overanalyzing what I did to create them does not serve me.

- Simply analyzing how I will manage a problem does not help solve the problem, only taking some type of positive action can help resolve the issue.

- Telling myself how much of a screw up I am doesn't erase mistakes or missteps, it just keeps me reliving them and makes me feel worse about myself.

- Diving deeply into thoughts of sad times in my life doesn't change the sad things that happened, it just gives the sadness power to envelop and overtake me.

- I am allowed to feel sadness, anger, frustration, disappointment, and other negative feelings sometimes and I am fully capable of processing them and then letting them go.

ABBIE'S STORY

Abbie was in a rut when she first reached out to me to work together. She had been let go from her position as a marketing associate with a fortune 500 company just a few months earlier and was struggling to find another job. It had been her first full-time job out of college and initially, she was thrilled to be working for a big name company. However, she quickly began to feel overwhelmed. Her supervisor piled on the work, and she struggled to keep up. When there were mistakes or something was not completed as quickly as requested, her supervisor became extremely critical.

She began to feel daily anxiety at the office and started doubting her capabilities. The one thing she felt kept her positive during this stressful period was a new relationship with a guy she had strong feelings for. However, after a few months, he broke off their relationship and she felt crushed. Then after months of stressful work days, she was told she was being laid off. While on some level she felt relieved to be done with the toxic work environment, she mostly felt demoralized, insecure, and resentful.

And with lots of time suddenly on her hands, she found herself spending most of it ruminating. She incessantly ran through memories of her negative moments at work and analyzed why she couldn't keep up with the work, why her supervisor was so unfair to her, why she was out of work and living with her parents when her friends were working and living in their own places, and what her former colleagues must be thinking and saying about her now. Then, she'd ruminate over her relationship breakup— why didn't he feel as strongly for her as she did for him, did he ever think about her now, and why she couldn't catch a break in relationships when all her friends were dating.

The constant ruminating did no service to her job searching and interviewing. It simply made her feel worse and worse about herself and less and less hopeful that anyone would ever hire her. And, she swore off relationships altogether because she never wanted to go through something like that again. After months of analysis paralysis, she reached out to me for help getting unstuck.

Abbie and I did a lot of great work together. But, one of the key areas we worked on was releasing ruminations. With faithful practice using RESCRIPTing techniques, Abbie began releasing her ruminations. She became more aware of their triggers and patterns, and how to stop them in their tracks before they consumed her. She began seeing her past experiences and future possibilities differently. But, most importantly, she began to see herself differently. She rebuilt her self-esteem and her hopefulness.

Abbie began applying for positions in industries she felt more passionate about, and was offered a marketing specialist position in the healthcare industry. After a few months on the new job, Abbie moved into her own apartment. She also began dating again. The first date she went on ended up being a great one and a keeper. Abbie has since gotten married and in within the first six months in her new position, she was promoted. She's now been with the company for three years.

Abbie learned how to keep ruminations in check and how to positively RESCRIPT her story.

PRACTICE #2

E- ENGAGE GROWTH GOALS VS. EVADING THEM

"The sooner you step away from your comfort zone; the sooner you'll realize that it really wasn't all that comfortable."

~ Eddie Harris Jr.

THE LIMITING SCRIPTS OF EVADING GROWTH GOALS

Growth is change. And, you've probably heard or uttered the phrase, "Change is scary." Well, at least that's what we often tell ourselves. Change is really just doing and managing something different from before. We make it scary by repeating this phrase to ourselves whenever a change presents itself in our lives.

So, why is it that we keep ourselves stuck in situations and stories we don't want simply because we fear the change that comes with engaging our growth goals?

In part, we fear change because we don't know exactly what it will look or feel like. Change is ambiguous. Even when aspects of our current story are dull, uncomfortable, unpleasant, disappointing, or painful, we know what our current discontent looks and feels like. And sometimes that knowledge is enough for us to hang on to that discontent and evade the ambiguity of change. Our Inner Antagonist often tricks us into believing that the change we are contemplating might be worse than how things are right now.

Before we examine the reasons why we evade our growth goals, we must first understand a bit about how goal setting operates in our lives.

When we want to reach a goal, we are generally hoping to do one of four things:

1) Engage Growth by seeking to perform to a self-set standard or out-perform our own personal best in a particular area. This type of goal tends to be *most intrinsically motivating* and often has the *most positive outcomes*. Example Goal: Erin strives to memorize and confidently deliver a 20-minute speech for her class because she wants to sharpen her public speaking skills.

2) Engage Growth by seeking to out-perform or reach the level of others'/another's best in a particular area. This type of goal tends to have the *second most positive outcomes*. Example Goal: Chris strives to deliver a longer, more informative, and more interesting speech than his classmate Jim.

3) Evade Failure by trying not to perform poorly according to a self-set standard or trying not to under-perform our previous achievement in a particular area. This type of goal tends to have the *second least positive outcomes*. Example Goal: Kara wants to avoid saying words like "um," "uh," "ya know," and "anyway" during her speech.

4) Evade Failure by trying not to under-perform others'/another's achievement in a particular area. This type of goal tends to be *least intrinsically motivating* and often has the *least positive outcomes*. Example Goal: Shawn wants to get through his speech without sweating or having his voice shake so he avoids looking silly in front of his classmates Joe and Kevin who are great presenters.

Goals that strive to engage growth rather than evade failure typically lead to greater satisfaction during the pursuit of the goal, as well as have a stronger likelihood of achieving desired outcomes. Why is this? In part, it is easier to measure our progress toward a goal that engages growth, whereas goals that seek to evade failure are more ambiguous and thus it is harder to determine if we are making progress on achieving them.

However, a really important factor is in the language of the goal itself and the tone it sets. When our goals include evasive language, it sets a fearful, insecure, and incapable tone. Furthermore, when our goal involves language focused on what we don't want, then what we don't want is what we are putting out into the universe. In effect, we sometimes inadvertently create more of what we don't want in our lives. It also keeps our attention focused on something negative during the goal pursuit, which is neither satisfying nor motivating.

On the other hand, when we rescript our goals to engage growth, we are using action words that move towards something positive, rather than away from something negative. This kind of language is empowering. It makes us feel stronger, braver, and more capable. Plus, we are using language that focuses on what we do want, thus we put a positive outcome into the universe. Hence, we create energies and actions that script the stories we want to be living. While pursuing this type of goal, our attention is focused on positive language and outcomes which is both satisfying and motivating during the pursuit of our goal.

What does evading vs. engaging language sound like when contemplating goals?

Below are examples of goals one could potentially have in each area of life. You can see the simple differences it makes to RESCRIPT the language of a goal that evades failure and instead make it one that engages growth. As you read, imagine the energy and outcome you would be focused on, depending upon whether the goal engages or evades. What feelings does each evoke in you?

1. **Relationships:**
   1. Evade: "To not be alone on Friday nights." vs. Engage: "To spend time with friends on Friday nights."
   2. Evade: "To stop being so quiet and closed off on first dates." vs. Engage: "To talk more readily and openly on first dates."
2. **Career:**
   1. Evade: "To not bomb this job interview." vs. Engage: "To demonstrate confidence during this job interview."
   2. Evade: "To stop doing the same old job at my company." vs. Engage: "To get a promotion at my company."
3. **Financial:**
   1. Evade: "To stop incurring so much debt." vs. Engage: "To start paying more than the minimum payments on my credits cards."
   2. Evade: "To not waste so much of my paycheck." vs. Engage: "To start putting away money from my paycheck into my savings account."
4. **Living Environment:**
   1. Evade: "To stop renting an apartment." vs. Engage: "To buy a house by the end of the year."
   2. Evade: "To stop letting messes pile up in the living room." vs. Engage: "To start cleaning up the living room at the end of each day."
5. **Community Engagement:**
   1. Evade: "To stop being so disconnected from my community." vs. Engage: "To join a community board or volunteer initiative."
   2. Evade: "To stop being complacent about community issues I care about." vs. Engage: "To contribute to community issues I care about by volunteering at the food pantry."
6. **Physical Health:**
   1. Evade: "To not be overweight for my height." vs. Engage: "To be a healthy weight for my height."

2. Evade: "To stop being so lazy in the morning." vs. Engage: "To start going on my treadmill for 15 minutes each morning."

7. **Mental & Emotional Health:**
   1. Evade: "To stop being so pessimistic." vs. Engage: "To start being more optimistic."
   2. Evade: "To stop beating myself up over perceived mistakes." vs. Engage: "To be more self-compassionate, saying encouraging things to myself when I make a mistake."

8. **Intellectual Growth:**
   1. Evade: "To not fail the exam." vs. Engage: "To get an A or B on the exam."
   2. Evade: "To stop putting off getting this certification." vs. Engage: "To enroll in the certification course today."

9. **Recreation & Relaxation:**
   1. Evade: "To stop making no time for fun." vs. Engage: "To start making time to do things I enjoy, like painting."
   2. Evade: "To stop working to the brink of exhaustion." vs. Engage: "To begin making time for daily meditation.'

10. **Spirituality:**
    1. Evade: "To stop feeling so disconnected from my higher power." vs. Engage: "To start thanking my higher power for all the days' blessings before I go to sleep."
    2. Evade: "To stop feeling negative about life and humanity." vs. Engage: "To intentionally perform kind deeds for others to conjure more positive feelings about life and humanity."

Consider some goals you may have for yourself. How might you RESCRIPT them? There will be exercises at the end of the chapter that will help you script positive growth engaging goals for yourself!

Why do we evade growth goals?

Fear of failure clearly plays a big role in why we evade our growth goals. Fears may stem from childhood goal pursuit and achievement experiences and the feelings connected to those experiences. Fear of failure can be developed when we have pursued a goal and did not achieve it according to our own or another's (parent, teacher, coach, classmates) expectations. It can derive from experiencing some form of negative consequence (parental punishment, a poor grade from a teacher, reprimanding from a coach/mentor, social out-casting from friends) and subsequently feeling shame or embarrassment. These memories remain with us along with the resulting feelings that can get reignited in later years when we once again contemplate engaging our goals, especially if these negative experiences were numerous.

Things we tell ourselves to avoid failure include:

- "I have no time right now."
- "It's just too hard to do this."
- "I won't be able to do it well enough."
- "I'll just end up disappointing people."
- "Maybe this goal isn't all that important anyway."
- "I should just put this off for now until I have the time, skills, and fearlessness required to achieve it."

Basically, our Inner Antagonist psyches us out. It tells us we can't, and if we do try, we will only look stupid and feel ashamed. So, why bother at all? Thus, we avoid the impending shame we fear could be awaiting us if we try and fail.

We also sometimes fear success. I'm sure you've heard of fear of success. Maybe you've wondered why on earth someone would fear success. Success is a good thing, right? Success is indeed a good thing, however, sometimes we fear the change that will come along with that success. Perhaps it will require more work, more pressure, major lifestyle changes, or a greater public spotlight we don't feel ready for. In essence, fear of success is really just fear of failing to effectively manage and maintain the changes associated with the success.

Many clients have said to me, "I can't wait to stop being afraid so I can finally _____." But, most of the time, this isn't how goal pursuit works. We don't engage our goals *after* we finally stop being afraid. We typically begin to feel less fear once we've experienced success. But, we can't experience success unless we initially feel the fear and move towards our goals anyway.

Another important factor related to evading or engaging our goals is the degree to which we feel we have control over the events in our lives. Some individuals are more likely to attribute their success or failure to their own internal capabilities or actions. However, other individuals may be more likely to attribute their successes or failures to factors outside of themselves, like other people or life circumstances not within their control. The reality, of course, is that both can be true—we control some things and don't control other things. However, learning to focus on our own internal impact on goal achievement is more motivating. What we believe we control, we are more likely to take action upon. And, learning to see failure as a common, acceptable, and sometimes necessary part of the goal pursuit process is important. Then, perceiving internal control over aspects of our failures does not equate with inadequacy or eternal defeat. It simply means we have gained information to aid us on subsequent attempts at goal pursuit. It helps us edit our efforts based on what we learned. Furthermore, we can simultaneously learn to make peace with and work around the aspects of our goal pursuits that we do not control.

How does evading growth goals harm us?

The way we look at goal achievement can be the difference between doing things that facilitate our success or doing things that facilitate failure. In essence, our thoughts influence our

71

actions and thus we create exactly what we tell ourselves is going to happen. When we operate out of fear of failure, our Inner Antagonist takes the reigns, and without even realizing it, we start getting in our own way. Getting in our own way can include things like, procrastination, setting unrealistic expectations, overcommitting, and lack of genuine effort or practice. In a way, these can be attempts to protect ourselves from the pain of the expected and feared poor performance. We can just tell ourselves, "Well, I really never put my whole heart into it. Who knows what could've happened if I had." "It was just way too hard with everything I've got going on right now. It's just not a good time. I'll just try again when I have less going on." Despite the attempts to self-protect with excuses, the end result is sabotaging our success, which can facilitate anxiety, depression, and poor self-esteem.

How does Engaging Growth Goals RESCRIPT our story?

Ultimately, engaging our growth goals versus evading them (and the fear of change, failure, or success associated with them) is the difference between a life filled with courage, accomplishment, progress, and confidence rather than one comprised of trepidation, resignation, stagnancy, and insecurity. In order to achieve our dreams, we must amplify our Inner Advocate by walking through fear into the unknown, trusting that we have the resources within us to conquer obstacles, be resilient through failures, and manage the changes ahead. When you finally open yourself up fully and completely to your dreams, the universe opens itself up fully and completely to you.

This has most certainly been my experience in moving through my fears to engage my own growth goals. Specifically, engaging one of my most feared goals completely changed my life. Like many people, I spent my teens and young adult life terrified of any form of public speaking. I was more confident in elementary school, but once I hit junior high and my hormones kicked in, things took a nose dive.

I can remember one of the first presentations I had to do alone in junior high. I worked myself up as I sat waiting to present, telling myself I'd forget everything and look stupid. Once I stood up behind the podium and looked out at my classmates, my heart began to race and I felt like I couldn't breathe. I could feel my palms sweating and my hands start to go numb. I felt heat rising up into my chest and up along my neck and cheeks. I tried to speak and no words would come out. It was as if I had a mute button and accidentally pressed it. Then I heard ringing in my ears, my vision zeroed in, and I fell backwards into a chair that was, by the grace of God, right behind me. Somehow, I didn't lose consciousness. I remember my teacher and a few of my friends rushing over to me and asking if I was okay. Everyone else was just staring at me. All I knew was that I was so painfully embarrassed that I wished I could disappear and never have to see any of them again. Mentally and emotionally taking that failure experience to a whole other level, from that moment forward, speaking in front of groups made me believe I could die. I don't know that I fully deciphered between that death being real or metaphorical.

Most of my subsequent (forced) class presentation experiences were not as terrible, but they were not good either. My heart palpitated, my palms sweat, I turned red from my chest up to my cheeks, I felt like I was running out of breath as I gasped out my words, and afterwards felt embarrassed and defeated. I told myself I was terrible at public speaking and should try to avoid it at all costs.

And in college, I strategically worked to do just that—avoid public speaking. If I learned a course or instructor required it, I wouldn't take that class or instructor. I think I had one or two group presentations where my part was really quick and I survived them. I didn't even raise my hand to speak in class as I began to feel as if I couldn't do that right either. But overall, I was getting good at avoiding public speaking. Unfortunately, this skill did not fill me with any kind of pride and certainly diminished my confidence.

Once I got to graduate school, it became evident that public speaking would be unavoidable. I had to speak in my much smaller classes and had to do presentations in most of my graduate courses. I started wanting to get better at it. I began hating how much I feared it and how that fear impacted me. But despite the desire to improve, I continued to avoid any non-required public speaking. While many of my classmates started teaching, presenting at conferences, and leading therapy groups, I stuck to my one-on-one counseling and did no presenting that I did not have to do. Soon came the moment that would shift things.

One thing I was doing in grad school was a lot of research. I had served as a Research Assistant for a professor for three years when she asked me if I could substitute teach a class for her while she was at a conference. Although my brain was screaming "NO!," my mouth said, "Yes." But over the weeks leading up to that class, my Inner Antagonist's voice got super loud and persistent. At the last minute I made up some excuse and bailed on her. Our once very close relationship was negatively impacted. And, I felt like garbage—both for what I did to her and for what I kept doing to myself because of my fear.

Not long afterward, I completed my doctoral program and started my first full-time job in higher education. And, a mentor of mine presented me with a proposition, "Would I co-teach a college course with her?" Clearly, due to my public speaking fears, I didn't have any actual interest in teaching. But, I did have a desire to get more comfortable with public speaking. I said, "Yes," and this time I kept my word. I was terrified, but I read, organized, planned, and prepared...a lot. And, every time my Inner Antagonist began narrating critiques of my abilities, I talked back to it with confident phrases. I was crazy nervous that first day in front of the classroom, but having my mentor by my side helped a lot. I reminded myself that it had been helpful presenting with a group when in college.

After my first class, I was on a natural adrenalin high. I was never prouder of myself. And I LOVED how it felt to feel that pride—a pride that only comes when you push through fear to do something you want to do, but thought you couldn't. I wanted more of that feeling.

I have been teaching in classrooms, leading workshops, and doing keynote speeches for 14 years now. It's one of the environments where I feel my happiest and most authentically me. I love the feeling of synergistic, reciprocal learning and passion that transpires between me and my students/participants.

Who would've known I'd love presenting so much?! I sure didn't. I'm so grateful I gave myself the opportunity to find out.

Changing the way I was narrating my story played a crucial role in RESCRIPTing my story with completely new and exciting plotlines. We all have the power to RESCRIPT limiting narrations that stop us from engaging our growth goals.

SOME HIGHLIGHTS FROM RESEARCH STUDIES ON ENGAGING GROWTH GOALS

- A study by Shahar, Kalnitzki, Shulman, and Blatt discovered that those who are high in self-criticism are less internally motivated toward their goals, make less progress toward their goals, and experience poorer future goal expectations.[10]

- Powers, Koestner, and Zuroff found that self-criticism is correlated with rumination, procrastinating on goals, and diminished goal progress.[11]

- Wang, Shim, and Wolters discovered that motivational self-talk is connected with diminished avoidance of challenges and higher goal engagement.[12]

- Locke uncovered that goal commitment and achievement are facilitated by believing in your task-specific capabilities, setting goals that are specific and challenging, and believing the goal is both important as well as attainable.[13]

- Jerabek and Muoio of PsychTests discovered that goal achievers are significantly more likely than non-achievers to visualize themselves successfully accomplishing their goal, plan out how they'll accomplish their goals and overcome obstacles, break down large goals into smaller steps, start goals immediately instead of procrastinating, and keep themselves motivated with small rewards for accomplishing benchmarks on their way to success.[14]

LIMITING NARRATIONS OF EVADING GROWTH GOALS RESCRIPTed

Let's examine how we can RESCRIPT the stories we tell ourselves when we evade growth goals:

1. "I wish I could go back to school, but I can't since I'll have to take math again and I suck at math."

   RESCRIPTed...

   "I want I go back to school, but it might be tough taking math again because it was never my greatest subject. Let me check out the college's website to see if they offer math tutoring. They do! This is important to me and although the math may challenge me, it's worth it for me to get my degree."

2. "I really want to take this job, but I can't since I'll have to do public speaking and it terrifies me."

   RESCRIPTed...

   "I really want to take this job, but I'm really nervous about the public speaking. I get so scared talking in front of groups. But this job is such a great opportunity. And, I won't be talking in front of groups more than once a week. I'm going to see if I can join my local Toastmasters, take a class, and maybe get a mentor so I can build my skills. I don't have to be the best speaker, just good enough to do that part of my job."

3. "I really wish I could go to that conference across the country, but I can't because of my fear of flying."

   RESCRIPTed...

   "I really want to go to that conference across the country, but I'm so scared of flying. It's such an amazing opportunity to meet the leading researchers in my field. Maybe I can get a colleague to go with me. It would help to have the moral support. Or, I could try to go to the regional conference since it's a much quicker flight to help ease me into flying. I can practice some strategies to manage my nerves. The learning and networking are worth it."

4. "I want to make more friends now that I'm retired, but I can't because I get so nervous about meeting new people."

   RESCRIPTed...

   "I want to make more friends now that I'm retired, but I get so nervous meeting new people. Maybe it would be easier if I try meeting people at a place I feel comfortable, like the library. I'm there all the time for books. I could start going to their learning programs and workshops. Maybe I could meet people who are interested in similar things who may also be looking to meet new friends."

5. "I truly want to get healthier, but I'm just too busy with everything I have going on to exercise."

   RESCRIPTed...

   "I truly want to get healthier, but it's so hard to find time in my schedule to exercise. Maybe if I spend a little less time on social media and use that time for exercise. I can start slowly—20 minutes on Mondays and Wednesdays after I pick the kids up from aftercare. I could try a dance DVD and the kids can do it with me. That will make it feel more like play for all of us."

LIMITLESS LIVING LIBRARY – STRATEGIES TO ENGAGE GROWTH GOALS SECTION

In addition to these strategies, you can modify and use strategies from other chapters to engage your growth goals!

Engage Growth Goals Strategy #1:
Helping or Harming Review

Contemplate your experiences evading growth goals in your life and ask yourself the following:

1. What are some goals I have evaded because of fear?

2. What specific fears have stopped me from pursuing my goals?

3. How has evading my goals harmed me?

4. How has evading my goals helped me?

5. What do I gain by continuing to evade my goals?

6. What do I miss out on, put up with, or lose by not engaging my goals?

7. What do I say to myself when I'm trying to convince myself to evade my goals?

8. What would I say to a friend who was evading goals because of fear?

9. What more effective things could I say to myself regarding engaging my goals?

10. What did I learn about evading my goals from this review?

Engage Growth Goals Strategy #2:
Pledge to Pass Up Permission

These are YOUR goals and dreams. This is YOUR story. So, why would you put the pen in someone else's hand by seeking validation (hence permission) to script the story you want for yourself? But sometimes, that is just what we do. We want to go after a goal, and we run it by a bunch of people waiting to see if the consensus is that we should indeed pursue this particular dream. Then if too many people seem unsure, unsupportive, unconvinced, unenthused—we bail on the goal. But, who said you needed a permission slip in the first place? The next time you catch yourself seeking validation to determine whether you should pursue your dreams or not, ask yourself:

1. What am I hoping to achieve by seeking permission to pursue my goals?

2. What are the reasons I believe I should let someone else decide if my dreams are important enough?

3. In what ways would I be empowered if I gave myself the permission I am seeking?

Now, take the following pledge:

I, _____, pledge to pass up permission to pursue my dreams and goals. I am not a child, I am a strong and capable adult who is responsible for my own future.

I know better than anyone else what I want for my life story and no one else can better determine what I am capable of achieving. I will galvanize my internal and external resources to realize my dreams.

You run you—no one else runs you. If you want it, that's enough. Now go get it!

Engage Growth Goals Strategy #3: "Will" it into the World

When we decide to set goals, it's generally because these goals are things that really matter to us. So why do we so often use passive words and phrases when talking about these goals? "I *want to* register for a Spring semester graphic design class." "I'm *thinking about* putting away an extra $200 at the end of each month to increase my savings." "I'm *planning to* register for Match.com tonight so I can start dating again." "I'm *gonna try to* look at job search sites today so I can find a new job I love." When we speak passively, we are likely to be passive. Passive words often equate with inaction. However, when we make a very simple change and use the word "will" we often will ourselves into action. "I *will* register for a Spring semester graphic design class!" "I *will* put away an extra $200 at the end of each month to increase my savings!" "I *will* register for Match.com so I can start dating again!" "I *will* look at job search sites today so I can find a new job I love!" Each time you hear yourself say to yourself or someone else that you *want to, are thinking about, are planning to, are gonna try* to work on a goal, stop yourself, amplify your Inner Advocate, and restate passionately – "I WILL!" WILL your dreams into the world!

Engage Growth Goals Strategy #4:
Lead with the Least Labor

Say what? Yup, when you have a huge list of tasks on your list, one of the ways to start tackling your tasks is to lead with the task requiring the least amount of labor. This is the equivalent of taking small steps down a ladder into cold pool water. It gets you to the destination by doing the easier thing—walking in slowly and steadily instead of diving into the deep end.

What tasks on your list require the least amount of time or effort? Work on these first. Then you get to cross these off your list and feel a quicker sense of accomplishment. This can be a big motivation booster. Another way to use this strategy is to start the goal achievement process with committing to working on your goal for just 30 minutes a day. We can all find 30 minutes in our daily schedules (yes, I know sometimes even that *seems* impossible). This is not too much labor to ask, its achievable, and it still provides a sense of accomplishment in the end. We can always increase the labor as we progress towards our goal.

Engage Growth Goals Strategy #5:
Tackle the Toughest Task

Yes, this is an opposite approach, and also effective. Sometimes slow and steady is the answer, while other times fast and furious is what feels right. What is the hardest task on your list, the one you dread and try to evade the most? This is the equivalent of diving quickly right into the deep end of the cold pool water. It's harsher, but it deals with the tough part right away. Try tackling the toughest task first! Once you complete that more effortful task, you will feel an immense sense of accomplishment for getting it over and done with. Then all the other tasks will seem like nothing in comparison!

Engage Growth Goals Strategy #6:
One Task at a Time

Multitasking is the magic word these days, as in "I really need to multitask better!" However, multitasking isn't the only way to goal achievement, and it isn't always the most effective way. When we are working toward goals, we often overwhelm ourselves into quitting because we are trying to take on too many changes all at once. Be careful and observant with yourself. You are overdoing it and headed for burnout and/or Quitsville if you notice that your new goal commitment calendar for Saturday reads something like, "7-8am treadmill, 8-10am study for certification exam, 10am-12pm work on business proposal, 12pm-1pm lunch, 1-3pm volunteer at animal shelter, 3-4pm set up dating profile online…." It doesn't all have to happen in one day, one week, or even one month. Pace yourself. Be realistic. Consider your mental, emotional, and physical health—all will suffer if you try to do it all at once! Spread out your goal-related tasks to make them more manageable, reasonable, achievable, and healthy. One task at a time!

Engage Growth Goals Strategy #7:
Salvage Success Strategies

You've achieved goals before. How did you do it? How did you push past your fears, create the time, and move through challenges along the way? Sometimes the answers to what we can do to reach a new goal are in strategies we've used to successfully achieve previous goals. So, take inventory! Sit down and answer the following questions:

1. What are at least five goals I have achieved that challenged or scared me and that I feel proud of?

2. What success strategies did I use to achieve these goals?

3. What motivated me in the past to move past my fears and dive into the discomfort of an important goal?

4. How can I salvage these success strategies to achieve some of my current goals?

Engage Growth Goals Strategy #8:
Seek a Success Sidekick

Having a little trouble reaching your goal solo? Maybe you could Seek a Success Sidekick (accountability partner) to be in on it with you! Do you know anyone who has also expressed reaching the same type of goal as you or even a different goal? Ask them if they would like to partner up! You could text one another at the start and end of each day to motivate one another and check on each other's progress! This is another great way to achieve a goal—you keep one another accountable, give each other guidance, cheer each other on, and celebrate success together!

Engage Growth Goals Strategy #9:
Brief Brain Breaks

Whereas there are times we may evade our goals, there are other times we get so immersed in working on goal related tasks that we can burn ourselves out. There is a difference between being in the zone or in a flow state (a feeling of productivity and enjoyment while immersed in goal pursuit activities) and being burnt out (a feeling of non-productivity and exhaustion while immersed in goal pursuit activities). Sometimes we treat the latter like it's the former and keep pushing ourselves. The thing is, once we are feeling that burnout, the ideas and excitement are tough to recharge simply by pushing through (or pushing against, really). I know, I know, deadlines. Yes, deadlines are real and are often associated with the pushing against that we do. This is what Brief Brain Breaks are for. They are convenient because they can be quick, and useful because they recharge us. What is a brain break? It is something as simple as laying down with your eyes closed, or sitting back in your work chair with your eyes closed for 15 minutes. It could be sitting outside or taking a quick nature walk for 15 minutes. If you can and would like to make it longer, go for it! But, 15 short minutes will do. During that period of time, you keep your mind thinking peacefully and calmly and take a brain break from your tasks/work. This might be facilitated by breathing slowly, envisioning a beautiful and peaceful place you love, or savoring the beauty of nature. The most effective brain breaks involve lying down, closing your eyes, and/or being in nature. The next time you are feeling that burn out and tell yourself, "I gotta push through," give a Brief Brain Break a try instead!

Engage Growth Goals Strategy #10: Daydream Your Desired Destinations

This exercise is designed to help you begin daydreaming the destinations you desire in each area of your life story. When we visualize what our desired life story looks like, we can begin thinking, feeling, and behaving in ways that move us closer to those destinations, as well as begin limiting the thoughts, feelings, and actions that move us farther from those destinations. When we daydream our desired destinations, put them into words, and envision them in our minds, we can make more informed decisions that are aligned authentically with who we are and what we ultimately want. Daydreaming our desired life story helps us identify the "whys" that create the foundation of our visions—the underlying themes of what brings us feelings of joy, passion, meaning, security, success, and ultimately happiness.

Read the questions for each area of your life story and use them as a GUIDE to jot down thoughts about your desired destinations. You DO NOT have to address EVERY question. Write your daydreams in the present tense as if they are already happening right now. For instance, instead of writing "I want to do _____," write "I am doing _____." For example, "I am living in a small town in Maine, in a colonial home with woods for a backyard." For some life areas you may have many daydreams, for others just one or two—not every area will be as salient for you, but each help create a balanced life story. If you have a partner/spouse, you can (but do not have to) also engage them in daydreaming individual desired destinations, discussing them together afterwards, and determining strategies for merging your daydreams together.

1. **Relationships**:
   - What is your relationship like with your spouse/partner? Kids? Family? Friends? Pets?
   - How much time do you spend with your spouse/partner daily? Kids? Family? Friends? Pets?
   - How do you spend your time with your spouse/partner? Kids? Family? Friends? Pets?
   - How do you and those you are living with manage home-related responsibilities? Who handles what and how?
   - What are you giving to others? What are you not giving to others?
   - How are you asking for and receiving support when you need it?
   - How are you maintaining your relational boundaries?
   - How are you achieving your relationships goals?
   - Who have you decided to let go from your life?
   - What negative habits have you eliminated from your relationship practices?

- What other ways are you nurturing your relationships?
- How are you feeling now that you have reached your desired relationship destinations?

Desired Relationship Destination Daydreams:

2. **Career:**

- What industry are you working in?
- What kind of work are you doing?
- What projects are you most frequently working on?
- Do you have your own business or work for someone else?
- Do you work alone or with others?
- Do you work in an office, from home, outdoors, or in another setting?
- Are you managing others?
- How are you interacting with your supervisor? Colleagues? Supervisees?
- Does your work involve travel? How much?
- Do you have a regular, structured schedule or a varied schedule?
- How many hours a week do you work? Is it the same each week, or does it change depending on what you do?
- How are you remaining engaged at work?
- How are you crafting your job around your strengths, passions, and larger life purpose?
- How are you achieving your career goals?
- What negative habits have you eliminated from your career practices?
- What other ways are you nurturing your career?
- How are you feeling now that you have reached your desired career destinations?

Desired Career Destination Daydreams:

3. **Financial:**

- How much money do you make per month?
- What kinds of benefits and insurance do you have?

- What is the pattern of your income stream? Do you have regular, predictable income, or does it vacillate depending on what you are doing?
- How much money do you have in savings?
- How are you paying down debts?
- How much disposable income do you have available each month? How much of it do you save? What are you saving it for? How much do you spend? What do you spend it on?
- How are you achieving your financial goals?
- What negative habits have you eliminated from your financial practices?
- What other ways are you nurturing your finances?
- How are you feeling now that you have reached your desired financial destinations?

Desired Financial Destination Daydreams:

4. **Living Environment:**

- Where do you live?
- What is your home like?
- How are you keeping your home clean, decluttered, and organized?
- What surrounds your home?
- What is the neighborhood like?
- What are the characteristics of your community?
- How are you achieving your goals related to the environment you live in?
- What negative habits have you eliminated from your living environment practices?
- What other ways are you nurturing your living environment?
- How are you feeling now that you have reached your desired living environment destinations?

Desired Living Environment Destination Daydreams:

5. Community Engagement:

- How are you contributing to your local community? The larger community? Global community?
- What volunteer opportunities are you engaging in?
- How much time do you give yourself daily/weekly for community engagement pursuits?
- How are you achieving your community engagement goals?
- What negative habits have you eliminated from your community engagement practices?
- What other ways are you nurturing your community engagement?
- How are you feeling now that you have reached your desired community engagement destinations?

Desired Community Engagement Destination Daydreams:

6. Physical Health:

- How much sleep do you get each night?
- What exercise do you do? Where do you do it? How frequently?
- What do you eat and drink more of? Less of?
- How does your body feel most days?
- How are you achieving your physical health goals?
- What negative habits have you eliminated from your physical health practices?
- What other ways are you nurturing your physical health?
- How are you feeling now that you have reached your desired physical health destinations?

Desired Physical Health Destination Daydreams:

7. Mental & Emotional Health:

- How are you managing stress and life challenges?

- How are you managing your time, prioritizing tasks, eliminating time wasters, and balancing? To-Do Lists? Calendars?
- What are you doing for regular self-care?
- How much time are you dedicating daily/weekly to self-care?
- How are you treating yourself? Speaking to yourself?
- How are you savoring and being fully present in positive experiences or beautiful surroundings?
- How are you achieving your mental and emotional health goals?
- What thoughts and emotions are you experiencing more of?
- What thoughts and emotions are you experiencing less of?
- What negative habits have you eliminated from your mental and emotional health practices?
- What other ways are you nurturing your mental and emotional health?
- How are you feeling now that you have reached your desired mental and emotional health destinations?

Desired Mental & Emotional Health Destination Daydreams:

8. **Intellectual Growth:**

- How are you expanding your knowledge?
- What topics/subjects are you learning about?
- What are you reading?
- What documentaries are you watching?
- What courses are you taking? Are you taking them online, in a classroom?
- How much time do you give yourself daily/weekly for intellectual growth pursuits?
- How are you achieving your intellectual growth goals?
- What negative habits have you eliminated from your intellectual growth practices?

- What other ways are you nurturing your intellectual growth?
- How are you feeling now that you have reached your desired intellectual growth destinations?

Desired Intellectual Growth Destination Daydreams:

9. **Recreation & Relaxation:**

- What rest and relaxation practices are you engaging in?
- How much time do you give yourself daily/weekly to rest and relax?
- What fun/recreational activities are you engaging in?
- How much time do you give yourself daily/weekly to engage in fun/recreation?
- What are you doing to express creativity?
- How do you spend your evenings? Weekends?
- How often do you take day trips, weekend trips, vacations? Where are you traveling to?
- How are you achieving your recreation and relaxation goals?
- What negative habits have you eliminated from your recreation and relaxation practices?
- What other ways are you nurturing your recreation and relaxation?
- How are you feeling now that you have reached your desired recreation and relaxation destinations?

Desired Recreation & Relaxation Destination Daydreams:

10. **Spirituality:**

- What role does spirituality play in your life?
- How are you integrating spiritual practices into your daily life?
- How are you engaged in connecting with a higher power on a personal level? On a group/community level?
- How does spirituality help you make meaning of your life and experiences?

- How does your spirituality guide your daily actions?
- How are you living your greater purpose in life?
- How are you achieving your spiritual goals?
- What negative habits have you eliminated from your spiritual practices?
- What other ways are you nurturing your spirituality?
- How are you feeling now that you have reached your desired spirituality destinations?

Desired Spirituality Destination Daydreams:

Engage Growth Goals Strategy #11: Define Your Desired Destinations' Design

Once we have daydreamed our desired destinations, we can define our desired destinations' design—hence, we can **set positive, precise, and pragmatic goals** that are connected to our daydreams!

What makes a goal positive? A positive goal is written to engage versus evade. It is also written in "I will" not "I want." An evading goal would address what you "don't want" and what you "won't do," whereas an engaging goal addresses what you "do want" and what you "will do."

What makes a goal precise? A precise goal is very specific about what you will accomplish, how you will accomplish it, and by when. Being precise helps you to focus your efforts, make your goals a priority in your schedule, determine milestones, track your progress, meet deadlines, and feel excitement about getting closer to your goal.

What makes a goal pragmatic? A pragmatic goal is realistic. It considers your current state of affairs, the internal and external resources you have available to you, and strategies you have used previously to achieve your goals. A pragmatic goal should stretch your current skills and comfort zone, while remaining achievable.

Here are some examples of positive, precise, and pragmatic goals connected to desired destination daydreams:

- If one of your desired destination daydreams is to write an e-book, a positive, precise, and pragmatic goal might be, "I will complete writing an e-book by six months from today about a topic I have previously written articles and blog posts on, utilizing my previously written material for chapter ideas and content. I will give up one hour per day of social media and television time and write my book one hour each day during that time."

- If you are currently a Marketing Associate and one of your desired destination daydreams is to become a Marketing Director, a positive, precise, and pragmatic goal might be, "I will complete my MBA in Marketing online within the next two years to gain the knowledge and credentials necessary to become the Marketing Director within my organization, so that I can build my career, increase my salary, advance my organization, and cultivate the talents of my team."

- If one of your desired destination daydreams is to make an extra several thousand dollars each year in income, a positive, precise, and pragmatic goal might be, "I will make an extra $15K each year, which I will assess monthly by focusing on earning an extra $1300 per month by adding a new service to my business, which will total just over $15K in a year."

- If one of your desired destination daydreams is to spend more one-on-one time with your spouse, a positive, precise, and pragmatic goal might be, "I will schedule a weekly lunch date with my husband during our lunch hours, so we can spend more individual time together talking and connecting."

- If one of your desired destination daydreams is to lose some weight to improve your health, a positive, precise, and pragmatic goal might be, "I will lose 20 pounds by four months from today by eating 1200 calories daily and exercising 15 minutes per day."

For each area of your life story, convert your daydreams into designs!

** Worksheet available in Appendix A and in my free "RESCRIPT Your Story Workbook" available at www.ColleenGeorges.com **

Engage Growth Goals Strategy #12: Realization Roadmap

Now that you've daydreamed your destinations and defined their designs for each area of your life, it's time to convert your destination designs/goals into a Realization Roadmap! A realization roadmap is comprised of "If/Then" or "When/Then" statements that support your goals by determining in advance when, where, and how you will achieve them. They are often attached to a specific day/time and actions you already take as part of your regular routine.

For the Destination Design/Goal, "I will lose 20 pounds by four months from today by eating 1200 calories daily and exercising 15 minutes per day," some Realization Roadmap actions could be:

- "When I finish brushing my teeth each morning, then I will get on my treadmill for 15 minutes."

- "If I feel the urge to eat junk food, then I will grab some raw veggies to snack on instead."

- "When I finish changing into my pajamas at night, then I will sit down at the kitchen table and plan out my meals/calories for the next day."

In essence, you are chunking down each of your goals into specific steps/actions to achieve them. Contemplate any research you need to conduct, people/places you need to contact, things you have to write up, or other specific actions you need to take to work towards your goal. Brainstorm the steps involved in achieving your goals and then you can use your brainstorming list to create your Realization Roadmap actions.

Give it a try!

** Worksheet available in Appendix B and in my free "RESCRIPT Your Story Workbook" available at www.ColleenGeorges.com **

Engage Growth Goals Strategy #13: Dream Depiction

Many of us are very visual people, meaning we learn through visual depictions of informational material and are inspired by visual depictions of ideas and dreams. Creating a Dream Depiction (vision board) that covers each area of our lives (Relationships, Career, Financial, Living Environment, Community Engagement, Physical Health, Mental & Emotional Health, Intellectual Growth, Recreation & Relaxation, Spirituality) can be a motivating and fun way to represent our goals and dreams. Your first step is to review your Desired Destination Daydreams, Destination Designs/ Goals, and Realization Roadmap to get ideas. Then, get yourself a big poster board, some magazines and newspapers, and some assorted art supplies from the craft store. Peruse the magazines, newspapers, and internet for words, quotes, pictures, and other visuals that are connected to your daydreams, designs, and road-map. Cut out/print out your dream depictions and paste them on your poster board using your own unique creativity, style, and organization. Post your Dream Depiction somewhere in your home where you will see it every day. Take time each day to really look at it and imagine yourself achieving your goals and dreams. Savor what you see, visualize yourself living it. Use your Dream Depiction daily for inspiration to attain your aspirations.

Engage Growth Goals Strategy #14:
Weekly Commitment Calendar

Create a Weekly Commitment Calendar by plotting out your realization roadmap actions that will repeat each week – placing them in their intended day/time slots. Also input your typical daily tasks (work, school, picking kids up from school, cooking, etc.). Build in some buffer time for the unexpected. Post your Weekly Commitment Calendar in a place or places where you can see them and be kept reminded. At the end of each week, check off the actions you completed to track your progress!

Another great way to create a Commitment Calendar is to use Google Calendar. Here are some directions if you've never used it before: https://support.google.com/calendar/answer/37095?hl=en.

One of the features allows you to input repeat activities (things you do each day, each week, or each month at specific times – basically, a Commitment Calendar). You can install the Google Calendar app on your phone and carry your Commitment Schedule with you: https://www.google.com/calendar/about/.

You can also share your calendar with others, for example your partner, so you don't double book evening or weekend plans!

** Worksheet available in Appendix C and in my free "RESCRIPT Your Story Workbook" available at www.ColleenGeorges.com **

Engage Growth Goals Strategy #15:
3 Ps Weekly Action Agenda

The partner to your Weekly Commitment Calendar is your 3 Ps Weekly Action Agenda (Professional, Personal, Passions). Select a day each week to sit down somewhere quiet and create your Weekly Action Agenda for that week (I suggest Sunday as it is the start of the new week). First, put in the starting date for that week—for example, Week of 1/6/2019. Then, make a column for each of your 3 Ps:

- **Professional:** Actions related to work and/or school that are "have to dos".

- **Personal:** Actions related to home, errands to run, appointments, phone calls to make, etc. that are "have to dos".

- **Passions:** Actions related to your Passion Projects/Goals in any area of your life—your "want to do" goals.

Then, designate a day of the week you will have the action completed by. Establishing a date of completion is critically important—this is going to help you prioritize what needs to get done first and what actions can wait a bit longer.

Now, make sure your actions are broken down into smaller steps that feel less overwhelming! For example, instead of writing the professional task, "1) Write 15-page marketing report" create a few actionable steps as separate Action Agenda items, such as "1) Write intro section of marketing report, 2) Write digital marketing section of marketing report, 3) Write traditional marketing section of marketing report."

If there are additional action items that pop up during the week— the unexpected undertakings—you can add them to your list as the week goes along and assign them completion dates as well.

Your list should only focus on this week, as not to overwhelm you with items that are not yet priorities. So, for projects or tasks that are longer term (two weeks away or more) that you want a running visual reminder so you don't forget, use the Longer Term Projects or Actions section at the bottom of your Action Agenda. These longer term items do not need to be chunked down into smaller tasks yet, you can keep them broad for now (until they become higher priority).

Now, take a look at your Weekly Commitment Calendar to see where you can dedicate time to your Weekly Action Agenda tasks. If you are using Google Calendar, you can also add in times to work incrementally on your actions so they are completed by your designated day of the week. It's just one more tool for accountability and commitment.

As you complete a task, CROSS IT OFF with a thick line all the way through it! This action feels good—it lets us feel successful and motivates us to keep going, knowing we CAN DO THIS! And, at the end of the week when you see all those thick, crossed off lines, you see how much you accomplished in just one week!

If you like using pen and paper, buy yourself some wide/letter ruled note pads to create your 3 Ps Weekly Action Agenda, or you can use my worksheet!

** Worksheet available in Appendix D and in my free "RESCRIPT Your Story Workbook" available at www.ColleenGeorges.com **

Engage Growth Goals Strategy #16:
Time Thief Tracker

If you have been feeling overwhelmed trying to take action on your goals, you are not alone. When we embark on new goals, we can often tell ourselves, "I just don't have time for anything else!" And while you may already be busy, you can always find time for your goals if you want to achieve them badly enough. We just need to figure out what your time thieves are. We all have them—things like social media, emails, texting, game apps, internet surfing, Netflix binging, etc. Usually, we have no idea how much time we spend on time thieves each day. So, to take back our precious time, we need to track where it's going.

For one week, track how you spend your time each day (specific morning routines, driving, work tasks, personal tasks, specific time thieves, etc). At the end of the week, tally up the time spent on your time thieves to determine the top ones. Then, set more reasonable time limits (specific times of day and time spans) for the time thieves. Determine how many hours you get back to dedicate to your goals!

** Worksheet available in Appendix E and in my free "RESCRIPT Your Story Workbook" available at www.ColleenGeorges.com **

Engage Growth Goals Strategy #17:
Unexpected Undertakings Tracker

Another reason we can get frustrated while trying to implement the actions of our goal plan is because life doesn't always seem to get the memo that we have a plan. Life often has other plans. However, in our own plan, we stack our tasks so tightly, often back-to-back, with no time available to be a buffer for unexpected undertakings. Thus, after dealing with the unexpected undertakings, we don't get to all of our planned goal tasks and we become frustrated and resentful. We have to build in time for the unexpected.

For one week, track what unexpected undertakings arise each day (doctor appointment for a sick child, mechanic appointment for a broken car, plumbing appointment for a busted pipe, craft supply shopping trip for a kid's art project we just learned of, a work project for a colleague who called in sick, etc). At the end of the week, tally up the time spent on these unexpected undertakings to determine the time each required. Then, take inventory of the time dedicated to such tasks all week and estimate how much time you want to build into your schedule each day for unexpected undertakings. You can literally label it Unexpected Undertakings on your calendar. You can put your time in one spot on your calendar or break it up and disperse it. It doesn't really matter how you do it, it's an item there as a buffer that can be moved around where and if needed, allowing you to still complete your planned tasks when unexpected things arise. And the other perk—if nothing unexpected occurs that day, you can use that time to catch up on upcoming tasks, as self-care time at the end of your day, or basically for anything you want!

** Worksheet available in Appendix F and in my free "RESCRIPT Your Story Workbook" available at www.ColleenGeorges.com **

Engage Growth Goals Strategy #18: Rise & Round-Off the Day Routines

Routines propel success. In particular, the ways we kick off and culminate our days have an important impact on what we accomplish. Those who are most productive, generally begin and end their days with a particular self-customized routine. Starting your own custom Rise & Round-Off the day Routine is a great way to reach your goals! Most morning or evening routines are approximately 30 minutes to a few hours in length, depending on what you would like to accomplish during those times. So, the first step is deciding what types of activities you want to incorporate into your routines. I am providing some possible activities below that could be incorporated into Rise and Round-Off Routines.

For Round-Off the Day Routines, tackling decision making tasks is a smart choice, such as selecting and laying out your outfit and/or kids' outfits for the following day, determining the next day's meal items, and making your lunch and/or kids' lunch for the following day. This ensures less rushing around in the morning! A different kind of decision-making task to include in your evening routine is planning out what you want to accomplish the following day—things related to your "have to do" tasks and your "want to do" goal-related actions. This helps you feel more prepared for the following day. Another thing you can include in an evening routine is tasks related to straightening up the house, like folding and putting away laundry, washing or putting away dishes, and putting away miscellaneous items that are laying around the house. If you spend 10 to 20 minutes on these tasks each evening, it stops things from piling up and feeling overwhelming. Maintaining order also means things are easier to find and feels less chaotic overall, as a mess in the home often contributes to frazzled thoughts in our brains.

Moreover, a great way to round off your day is to do something fun, such as reading a book you love, watching a show you enjoy, listening to a radio program you love, or engaging in a hobby. This is a little way to unwind and reward yourself for a day well spent. Doing something that relaxes you at the end of your night is nice as well, like drinking a cup of decaffeinated tea or sprinkling some relaxing essential oils on your pillow just before bed. Additionally, you might consider ending your day with some inspiration, such as watching a TED Talk, listening to an inspirational podcast episode, or reading some positive affirmations. This helps to keep your mind on things that are positive and motivational. Another thing that is calming and positive to do before bed is contemplate what you are grateful for that day (more on this in the Think Thankfully chapter). And, if you live with family, you will want to incorporate family time into your evening routine, as well as making sure your routine includes disconnecting from doing work for your job.

It's important to note that planning out your sleep time is also critical. Research suggests that somewhere between 6.5 and 8 hours of sleep is best for our health and productivity.

Let's say you go to sleep about 11pm. Here is a sample Round-Off the Day Routine:

- 8:00pm: Get the kids showered/bathed and in pajamas.

- 8:30pm: Do a family gratitude review of each person's day and put the kids to bed.

- 9pm: Watch a sitcom with my spouse while drinking a cup of decaf/herbal tea.

- 9:30pm: Plan out tomorrow's "have to do" and "want to do" goals.

- 9:45pm: Straighten up around the house.

- 10:00pm: Make tomorrow's lunches and select/lay out clothes.

- 10:30pm: Read positive affirmations.

- 10:45pm: Sprinkle my pillow with Lavender essentials oils and lay my head on my pillow to go to sleep.

Now, let's talk about some things you might consider for your daily Rise Routine. Much like your evening routine, your morning routine should include some inspirational activities like gratitude, affirmations, manifestos, and/or an inspiring video or audio book. Also like your evening routine, if you live with family, you will want to incorporate time talking and connecting with your family members. If you set your day's tasks and goals in advance the evening before, you can review them during your morning routine, and possibly spend some time working towards one of your goals/passion projects. This will get you feeling organized and give you an immediate sense of accomplishment as you begin your day!

Incorporating some form of exercise into your rise routine is a great way to get yourself energized and boost your endorphins. Other ways to feel energized when you rise are taking your shower in the morning, making a cup of coffee you can drink in a mug that has words or phrases that inspire you (for the coffee drinkers!), and/or drinking a big glass of cold water to cleanse your system. If you are seeking a sense of peace in the mornings, you might try a walk outside, yoga, or meditation as part of your routine. Or perhaps, you want to get a head start on your work and info for the day by tackling some work emails, reading news articles, or browsing through your social media.

Let's say you want to rise at 6am (7 hours sleep if you fell asleep about 11pm). Here is a sample Daily Rise Routine that is the companion of the sample Round-Off Routine:

- 6am: Get up (resist the snooze button) and brush my teeth.

- 6:15am: Get on the treadmill. During this time, my spouse gets the kids up and dressed.

- 6:35am: Take a shower, get dressed, and put on my makeup. During this time, my spouse gives the kids breakfast and they brush their teeth.

- 7am: Walk the kids to bus stop while talking with them about their day, and then walk back home.

- 7:20am: Make a cup of coffee in my "Wake with Gratitude" mug, eat breakfast, and spend some time working on my goal of developing an entrepreneurial business plan.

- 7:50am: Talk with my spouse about one another's plans/ goals for the day as my spouse finishes getting ready for work.

- 8:10am: During my drive to work, listen to an inspirational audio book in my car and drink an 8 oz. bottle of water.

These, of course, are simply sample Rise and Round-Off the Day Routines. Yours has to fit you and what you want. The best way to find out what works is to brainstorm some ideas with allocated times and then try them out. We learn by trying (and failing). By failing, I mean that what you plan may not work out how you anticipate. Things may take longer than you think, it may be harder to get up earlier than you anticipate, or glitches may occur. The first week is always the hardest, and it typically takes at least 21 days of doing the same thing daily to create a habit/ routine. You may want to incrementally work toward your new desired sleep and wake times initially, versus jumping right into trying your new times. You also may want to introduce some aspects of your desired new routines and get them down first before trying all aspects of your routine at once. A routine begins with trial, error, modification, and more modification until you find one that fits great for you. It could be shorter or longer than the sample plans, could include more or less activities, and certainly different activities. But, once you find routines that work, they will get you organized, save you time and energy, give you a feeling of accomplishment, enhance your belief in what you are capable of, and move you closer towards reaching your goals.

Your turn to try out your own Rise and Round-Off the day Routines!

Engage Growth Goals Strategy #19:
Triumph Tracker

How often do you write down your accomplishments? What if you amplified your Inner Advocate and jotted down every personal and professional triumph/achievement you are proud of at the end of each week? How many awesome things would you have to celebrate at the end of the month? The end of the year? Give it a try! We are fueled by our successes and triumphs. In acknowledging, tracking, and savoring them, we boost our confidence to tackle our next big goals!

** Worksheet available in Appendix G and in my free "RESCRIPT Your Story Workbook" available at www.ColleenGeorges.com **

Engage Growth Goals Strategy #20:
Compensate Completion

Too often when we achieve our tasks or goals, we don't even reward the success, instead we simply ask ourselves, "Okay, what's next?" Instead of jumping right to the next task or goal, what if we rewarded the completion? Compensating completion for tasks relevant to our goal pursuit, as well as achievement of the ultimate goal, is a great motivator! Consider some things you really enjoy doing—perhaps getting a massage, going to a concert, or taking a day trip to a place you've been wanting to visit. Or, it can be even simpler things that you already do and enjoy, that could be utilized as mini-compensations, like reading a chapter in a book you love, watching your favorite Netflix show or a movie, or spending time on social media. Brainstorm a list of big and little things you enjoy doing, or want to do, that can be used as compensations for completing the steps to your goal and the achievement of your goal. Use these rewards only after your completions. You can even take this a step further and develop a Completion Compensation Plan for yourself, using similar When/Then statements like the ones from your Realization Roadmap. For example, "When I complete the first section of my business plan, then I will compensate myself with 20 minutes browsing Facebook," "When I complete working on my book for two hours, I will compensate myself with watching an episode of Westworld," or "When I complete my certification course, I will compensate myself with a day trip to Longwood Gardens, PA." These compensations of step completion and ultimate goal completion not only feel great, but they get you into an important habit of work first, play later. We get our fun, which we all need, but we get it only by working toward our goals. It's a great way to inspire motivation and discipline!

Engage Growth Goals Strategy #21: Own Your Awesome

Sometimes when we achieve success, we want to be humble—we think and say things like, "It was nothing," "Well, I had a lot of help," "Anyone could have done it," or "I got lucky." Sure, maybe we don't want to brag, but owning and celebrating the awesomeness of our successes is an important part of the journey! It allows us to really feel and experience the exhilaration of our hard work and end results, while simultaneously building our confidence and belief in all the great things we are capable of. So, the next time you feel like downplaying your achievements, amplify your Inner Advocate and try instead telling yourself or others, "It was a lot of work, and I am so happy to see the amazing results!" "Thank you. It feels really good to see all my time and passion culminate in this kind of success!" and "After lots of effort, now I'm going to savor, celebrate, and soak up how good it feels to create something so awesome!" When you complete a task or goal, SAVOR the experience! Feel the pride and tell yourself you are awesome for putting in the time and effort to make your dreams a reality.

Engage Growth Goals Strategy #22: Destination Designing Rituals

When we create a ritual for something, we make it sacred and deem it greatly important. When you set rituals for your Destination Designing/Goal Setting—you make the process meaningful and most conducive to being creative and intentional. You might consider doing a Destination Design Ritual quarterly/seasonally, and have a particular location you go to each time, like a cabin in the woods, the beach, or something simpler like the park, a local hotel room getaway, your backyard, or even a special room in your home. If you live someplace where the weather changes quite a bit throughput the year, you could have different locations for each of your four Destination Design Ritual sessions (park in spring, beach in summer, backyard in fall, woodsy cabin in winter). The idea is to repeat that same process each year to make the process sacred, to make your goals sacred.

During your sessions you could set a similar process for goal setting. If you are indoors, perhaps you might dim your lights, burn some incense (or light a candle, diffuse some essential oils), pour a cup of tea or glass of wine, and then begin writing. If you are outdoors, you might lay down a blanket on the grass to sit on, make yourself a little picnic, spend some time taking in nature, and then begin writing.

During each session, you want to do two things—1) take inventory and savor/celebrate what you accomplished toward your goals in the last few months and 2) Reassess/reestablish your goals for the next season/cycle. Your final ritual of the year is super fun—in this session you can review and celebrate your accomplishments for the entire year and set your goals for the following year! It can be fun to do that final ritual session around New Year's Eve.

If you like, you can do one or more of these sessions with a partner/spouse or even as a family. It can be a great time to connect, get to understand one another's unique dreams, see how some of your unique goals might intertwine, and determine how you can support one another in reaching them.

Brainstorm times of year, locations, and practices you might be inspired by for your own Destination Designing Rituals!

Engage Growth Goals Strategy #23:
Evading Growth Goals Narration RESCRIPTing

Consider some recent and/or long-standing growth goals you have been evading in various areas of your life that have kept you stuck in a life limiting story. Using the narration RESCRIPTing examples and other illustrations from this chapter as a guide, RESCRIPT some of your growth goal evading thoughts into statements that are more realistic, encouraging, and empowering.

What growth goals that you've been evading will you engage through RESCRIPTing...

1. Regarding your relationships?
   - Evading Growth Goals Thought:
   - RESCRIPTed:

2. Regarding your career?
   - Evading Growth Goals Thought:
   - RESCRIPTed:

3. Regarding your financial life?
   - Evading Growth Goals Thought:
   - RESCRIPTed:

4. Regarding your living environment?
   - Evading Growth Goals Thought:
   - RESCRIPTed:

5. Regarding your engagement within your community?
   - Evading Growth Goals Thought:
   - RESCRIPTed:

6. Regarding your physical health?
   - Evading Growth Goals Thought:
   - RESCRIPTed:

7. Regarding your mental and emotional health?
   - Evading Growth Goals Thought:

- RESCRIPTed:

8. Regarding your intellectual growth?
    - Evading Growth Goals Thought:
    - RESCRIPTed:

9. Regarding your recreation and relaxation?
    - Evading Growth Goals Thought:
    - RESCRIPTed:

10. Regarding your spirituality practices?
    - Evading Growth Goals Thought:
    - RESCRIPTed:

Commit yourself to engaging your growth goals!

Engage Growth Goals Strategy #24: Acknowledgements & Affirmations

Here are some acknowledgements and affirmations you can recite any time you need a boost in your goal engagement motivation!

I acknowledge and affirm that...

- Evading my goals may feel easier in the short-term, but it can make things feel harder for me in the long-term by keeping me stagnant and scared.

- I do not need to get rid of my fears before I act on my goals. I can walk through my fears towards my dreams.

- Discomfort does not equal danger or destruction. My goal pursuit will challenge me, but it will not harm me.

- Telling myself I don't have time and now isn't a good time to work towards my goals is just an avoidance mechanism, I can and will create time because I matter.

- I am fully capable of resisting urges to invest in distractions and procrastination.

- I can and should reward and celebrate the steps I take toward achieving my goals.

- I have successfully completed tough goals before and have developed strategies I can use to achieve tough goals now.

- I can effectively manage, be resilient through, and use what I learn from any missteps along my path toward my goals.

- Neither fear nor failures will ruin me. I am much bigger and stronger than both of them.

- A life spent evading my goals is not a life well-lived. I desire and deserve a life filled with accomplishment and fulfillment.

JUDY'S STORY

When I first played back Judy's voicemail, I had to hit replay to make sure I heard her name right. It was a name I knew well, I sang and danced to her music back in middle and high school (and in the years since…still do!). I've listened to her DJing on the radio over the years since then. She is beautiful, successful, and talented. And, she wanted to hire a life coach.

I fully admit I was star-struck when I returned her phone call.

When I first spoke with Judy, she shared that while she had success in the music and radio industries, she had some other professional dreams that remained only in her mind's eye for too long. The most long-standing of those dreams was to do a one-woman show off Broadway, sharing her life's story to inspire others to persevere through life's challenges.

She pushed this dream aside for years out of fear. She feared she may not be able to break into something so different from the things she had previously done in her career. She feared she couldn't find time in her already packed personal and professional schedule to do the prep work. She feared that although she really wanted it, she had no idea where to begin to make it a reality.

Maybe it would just be too difficult. As a result of these thought patterns, Judy had effectively evaded one of the most important goals of her life and career.

However, Judy is one of the hardest working women I've ever met. She felt the fear and did the work anyway. We examined her fears, she started to acknowledge how she had achieved the seemingly impossible at other points in her life, and she began RESCRIPTing the stories she was telling herself about what she was capable of and what her future could hold. Judy created a vision board with her show taking center stage of her vision of what she would achieve. We plotted out the steps to her goal one action at a time, examined and reworked her schedule, and made the steps to her dream a priority in her calendar.

Judy took charge of her dream and fully engaged herself in achieving her goal. She worked hard. Really hard. There were many long days writing, rewriting, rehearsing, and memorizing. Some days she was absolutely exhausted.

Nevertheless, she persisted.

The first three dates for Judy's one-woman show sold out in less than one hour. She got the experience of holding her very own Playbill. And, she TOTALLY ROCKED her opening weekend (I know…I was there!). She did so much more than she imagined. She was authentic, dynamic, elegant, funny, and most importantly, so very inspiring to all who watched and listened to her story. Her show was such a success that it generated overwhelming requests for more dates. Judy has since performed 28 more shows to date!

Judy engaged her goals despite her fears, and the reward is she is living her dream. And, she brought me to happy tears when she thanked me in her Playbill, "Special thanks to my life coach, Colleen Georges, you gave me the tools to get unstuck and find the courage to write and tell my story, not just imagine it!" We all have a little Judy in us just begging to be unleashed.

PRACTICE #3

S- SEEK STRENGTHS VS. SCRUTINIZING SHORTCOMINGS

"If you judge a fish by its ability to climb a tree, it will live its whole life believing that it is stupid."

~ Albert Einstein

THE LIMITING SCRIPTS OF SCRUTINIZING SHORTCOMINGS

"What's wrong with me?"

As a helping professional, I have been asked this question by clients countless times.

The follow up question is generally something like, "How can I fix it?" This question infers the underlying assumption of brokenness—something is broken in me and requires fixing.

Through our internal narration, we ask ourselves questions like these as well. It often comes out as a loud, yelling, and reprimanding voice from our Inner Antagonist, "What's *wrong* with me!?" followed by a sad, nervous, puzzled, and desperate voice of our Inner Antagonist pondering, "How can I *fix* it?!"

Can you hear what these voices sound like in your imagination right now?

Have you heard them in your *own* head?

Most of us have at one time or another, but some of us hear these voices a whole lot. Maybe too much.

Now imagine this instead, what if the narration in your head spent as much, or better yet, *more* time asking, "What's *right* with me?" and "How can I *use* it?"

A little harder to imagine? It can be harder to imagine because many of us have fewer actual experiences asking ourselves questions like these to draw upon for our imagination. This is the voice of our Inner Advocate. And, we want to amplify it.

But first, let's try to understand this tendency toward scrutinizing our shortcomings.

What does it mean to scrutinize our shortcomings?

When we scrutinize our shortcomings, we are mentally focusing on our "*in*capabilities." Not a real word, I know. But I use it for purposes of clarity. It means we are putting our energy toward examining the things we believe we are incapable of doing or doing well. We nitpick the things we perceive we are not good at. We dissect all the ways in which we feel we don't perform well in various areas of our lives.

But there's more. We often determine that because of our perceived shortcomings, there's things in life we just won't be able to attain. There are experiences we'll just have to do without, because we've fallen short in what it would take to achieve in those areas.

Here are some examples to demonstrate what this type of mental narration might sound like in various areas of our lives.

1. **Relationships**: "I'm just not a funny, quick-witted kind of person, so I feel like people always think I'm too boring to be friends with."

2. **Career**: "I'm terrible at delegating, that's why I can never get anything done."

3. **Financial**: "I'm the worst at tracking my expenses, that's why I can never save money."

4. **Living Environment**: "I'm just not creative with decor, so my house looks so plain."

5. **Community Engagement**: "I'm so shy and reserved, I'll never be able to get more involved in my community."

6. **Physical Health**: "I'm just not an athletic person, so exercising never works for me."

7. **Mental & Emotional Health**: "I'm just naturally a high-strung, restless kind of person, so I'll never be able to have any peace and calm in my life."

8. **Intellectual Growth**: "I'm awful at math, so I'll never get my degree since math is required."

9. **Recreation & Relaxation**: "There's just no hobbies I'm any good at, so I can't find anything to do for fun."

10. **Spirituality**: "I just suck at being consistent, so I could never maintain any spiritual practices in my life."

When we scrutinize our shortcomings, we are often making extreme value judgements against ourselves. We make black and white assumptions. "I'm not good at ____. This is bad. Thus, I will never be able to _____."

Why do we scrutinize our shortcomings?

Shortcomings Bring Negative Consequences. Or, so that's what we learn. It doesn't take us long in life to learn that if you don't perform something to a particular external standard, there could be negative consequences. We can make lots of inferences and generalizations from these experiences.

For instance, let's say I get a low grade on several math tests as a kid. My teacher and mom tell me they are disappointed, and that this is a problem that needs to be fixed. As a child, this disappointment may feel more like removal of acceptance and love. And, I might translate "this is a problem that needs to be fixed" to "this is a weakness that needs to be fixed." I get it in my head that I'm no good at math, and I spend a lot of time thinking about how this shortcoming has caused me problems, it will cause me more problems, and I should fix it. But, I don't know how.

We're Kind of Wired That Way. Remember mental rubbernecking? Since we experience our shortcomings as facilitating negative consequences, those negative consequences can be processed by our brains as a threat. Our brains are wired to scan for threats and get as much information about them as we can to protect ourselves. Thus, scrutinizing our shortcomings can be perceived as self-protective.

Everybody's Doing It. Focusing on weaknesses and trying to fix them is a common narrative. The field of psychology has long studied psychological disorders with the intent of discovering the path to mental and emotional wellness. The medical field has studied physical diseases with the intent of uncovering the path to physical wellness. Companies have studied their business failings and losses to determine the path to organizational wellness.

Clearly psychology, medicine, and corporations have each made excellent strides in remediating the problems they've been studying. Numerous effective treatments, remedies, and interventions have been developed over the years.

And, so we follow suit—simply studying and attending to the shortcomings and weaknesses works…right?

Well, it's really only half the picture we are viewing when all we do is examine the shortcomings, disorders, diseases, or failures. We still don't know what makes a person or organization thrive and flourish. To get that information, it's best to study strengths—like psychological wellness, physical, and organizational wellness—what strengths are fostering this wellness and how can we leverage it.

Or in other words, "What's right and how can we use it?"

So, why do we not seek out our strengths?

We're Less Wired This Way. Since our brains are wired to scan for threats to our well-being, seeking out and focusing on our strengths is less of a mental priority. It takes instruction and lots of practice to train ourselves to seek strengths.

"Don't brag." Did a parent, a teacher, or someone else ever say that to you when you were a kid or throughout your life? Or maybe similar phrases like, "Don't be egotistical," "Don't be so full of yourself," "Don't get a big head," or "Don't be narcissistic."

The advice was in all likelihood said with well-meaning, good intentions. What it may have intended was for you not to act like you think you are better than anyone else. Seems like sound advice—we are, indeed, no better than anyone else, and probably don't want to give off such an impression. So, what's the problem?

Well, it's that strange telephone game-like filter we have in our brains that we talked about in the Engage Growth Goals chapter. We are told one thing and it filters through our brains and is transformed into something similar, but not the same—"Don't talk about what you're good at" and "Don't think about what you're good at."

When I've worked with clients on their resumes and to prepare for job interviews, I've found that one of the most common reasons they are seeking help is expressed in phrases like, "I'm just not good at talking myself up," "I have a tough time figuring out what my accomplishments and strengths are," and "I have a hard time telling people what I'm good at."

Most of us are taught to be humble from an early age, and we take on this humility like an oath. "I, _____, pledge to never acknowledge that I am good at something."

Okay, perhaps that's a little extreme, but you get the picture.

How does scrutinizing shortcomings harm us?

Spending too much time focusing on the things we believe we can't do and are not good at can be detrimental to our self-esteem. We begin to define ourselves by these limiting labels and often subscribe ourselves to the limits we believe they put on us. If you have noticed, I have used the word perceived before shortcomings a lot. There is a big reason for this. There is a decent likelihood that the shortcoming we believe we have is not real, but simply a perception we have developed and hung onto. Once we believe it, we make it so. We tell people about it, we tell ourselves about it, and it feels more and more real. We behave in ways that reinforces that the shortcoming is a real thing. We also act in ways that reinforce the limits the shortcoming places on our lives.

Let me give an example, if a child does not perform well in several sports in gym class, and is not picked repeatedly for teams by her friends as a result, she may begin to tell herself, "I'm just not an athletic person." She may take this belief with her throughout her schooling and life, avoiding all things sports and exercise related, because she has labeled herself "not athletic." She may also ignore moments that demonstrate any athleticism because they do not fit with her existing belief. As an adult, she may avoid exercising, because she still carries this label. Until one day, she catches on to her Inner Antagonist's game, removes the "not athletic" shortcoming label, and makes exercising a part of her daily routine.

Alright, alright, that girl is me. My point is, sometimes the shortcomings aren't even real. A skilled baseball, basketball, and football player I am not, but also not hopelessly unathletic.

Some shortcomings may indeed be legit. But, that doesn't mean they have to be critically limiting for you.

How can we leverage our strengths in the face of shortcomings?

So, my dad can build and install anything. I've watched him over the years because I really, really wanted to be able to do that. I think it's the most amazing capability. And, I used to spend a lot of time watching those home renovation shows dreaming of being able to do the stuff they were doing. It was a recurring shortcoming that frustrated me.

I really wanted to put a hardwood floor in my kitchen, as well as a tile backsplash. But, I recognized that measuring and using power cutting tools for wood and tile was not within my strength repertoire. This bothered me for a while. Finally, I intentionally sought to capitalize on the strengths I do have to make this happen one way or another. I am strong at doing research, coming up with alternative ideas, being resourceful, developing plans and strategies, and being perseverant.

I researched, read tons of reviews, watched videos, and ultimately found a faux wood flooring made from vinyl and a gel-based faux tile backsplash. I was able to cut with a box cutter, easily recut when I messed up the measurements, and install it all myself. Most people think it's all real...until I tell them. I always tell them...because I'm proud of what I did!

The purpose of my story is to share that if we look at shortcomings only, we miss out. We tell ourselves we can't do something because we believe a particular strength is the only way to get there. But when we seek out our strengths to solve a problem, we can achieve our goals in a different way.

How does Seeking Strengths RESCRIPT our story?

To go back to the quote at the beginning of the chapter—don't be a fish trying to climb a tree feeling weak and stupid. Be a fish swimming in the water feeling strong and smart.

When we know and use our strengths intentionally and regularly, we boost our overall satisfaction with our lives. We also become more creative goal achievers! Knowing our shortcomings is not a bad thing at all. But, we should know just as much, if not more, about our strengths. Then we can spend time using and cultivating them. With the appropriate balance and synergy, we can use our knowledge of our shortcomings and power of our strengths to propel our success and happiness in every area of our lives.

SOME HIGHLIGHTS FROM RESEARCH STUDIES ON SEEKING STRENGTHS

- Gander, Proyer, Ruch, and Wyss found that intentionally using your strengths in new ways leads to increases in happiness and reductions in depression.[15]

- Research by Wood, Linley, Matlby, Kashdan, and Hurling uncovered that strengths use facilitates well-being, diminished stress, and increases positive emotions, vitality, and self-esteem.[16]

- Lavy and Littman-Ovadia found that intentionally using your strengths in the workplace is correlated with greater productivity, organizational citizenship, job satisfaction, engagement, and positive emotions.[17]

- Linley, Nielsen, Wood, Gillett, and Biswas-Diener revealed that strengths use supports people in achieving their goals and leads to greater well-being.[18]

- Quinlan, Swain, Cameron, and Vella-Brodrick found that youth who participated in a school-based strengths program reported higher levels of positive emotions, classroom engagement, autonomy need satisfaction, strengths use, and lower levels of class friction than the control group.[19]

Limiting Narrations of Scrutinizing Shortcomings RESCRIPTed

Let's examine how we can RESCRIPT the stories we tell ourselves when we scrutinize shortcomings:

1. "I forgive people too easily."

   RESCRIPTed...

   "I forgive people easily. While some may consider that a weakness, I see it as a strength. I have a gift for letting go of anger, hurt, and the desire for revenge."

2. "I'm way too idealistic."

   RESCRIPTed...

   "I'm pretty idealistic. Some have called it a weakness, Pollyanna, and unrealistic. But, no matter what I encounter in my life and in this world, I always see the potential for hope and possibility. And because I can see it, I pave the way towards its realization. My idealism is a strength."

3. "I'm terrible at so many things."

   RESCRIPTed...

   "There are certain things I struggle with, and I definitely don't possess every skill. Nobody else does either. But, fortunately I also have many strengths and I use them daily to overcome my challenges and achieve my goals."

4. "I wish I could be great at writing like Jessica."

   RESCRIPTed...

   "My friend Jessica is a fabulous writer. I truly admire her gift. It's not my greatest strength, but I've asked Jessica for some guidance. I'm an okay writer, but I work hard at it, and am getting better and better. One of my greatest strengths is perseverance. When something is important to me, I always keep at it and won't quit even if it's really tough."

5. "I just don't have the right skills to be successful at my job."

RESCRIPTed...

"Sometimes, I feel like I have a lot to learn at my new job. But, I have been taking some online courses to develop those skills. Fortunately, I have some strengths that have been really beneficial to the team, like my technology and budgeting strengths. We all contribute something different—no one needs to have all the same strengths because the synergy of our strengths makes the team work amazingly."

LIMITLESS LIVING LIBRARY – STRATEGIES TO SEEK STRENGTHS SECTION

In addition to these strategies, you can modify and use strategies from other chapters to seek your strengths!

Seek Strengths Strategy #1: Helping or Harming Review

Contemplate your experiences scrutinizing your perceived shortcomings in your life and ask yourself the following:

1. What are some perceived shortcomings I have scrutinized about myself?

2. What is my purpose/intent for scrutinizing these perceived shortcomings?

3. How has scrutinizing my perceived shortcomings harmed me?

4. How has scrutinizing my perceived shortcomings helped me?

5. What do I gain by continuing to scrutinize my perceived shortcomings?

6. What do I lose by continuing to scrutinize my perceived shortcomings?

7. What would I say to a friend who was scrutinizing perceived shortcomings?

8. What more effective strategies exist to achieve my original purpose/intent?

9. What did I learn about scrutinizing my perceived shortcomings from this review?

Seek Strengths Strategy #2: Survey Your Strengths

How do you get to know and make friends with your strengths? One great first step is to take survey instruments that help you assess them! Utilize the two leading strengths assessments to discover your strengths, the VIA (Values in Action) Survey of Character Strengths and CliftonStrengths. The VIA Survey is FREE, assesses your highest of 24 character strengths, and can be taken online at www.viacharacter.org. CliftonStrengths is a fee-based survey that assesses your highest of 34 strengths, and can be taken at www.gallupstrengthscenter.com. After taking these surveys, you can spend some time on the survey websites reading and getting more familiar with your unique strengths.

What are your top five VIA Character strengths?

1. VIA Strength #1:
2. VIA Strength #2:
3. VIA Strength #3:
4. VIA Strength #4:
5. VIA Strength #5:

What are your top five CliftonStrengths?

1. Clifton Strength #1:
2. Clifton Strength #2:

3. Clifton Strength #3:
4. Clifton Strength #4:
5. Clifton Strength #5:

Seek Strengths Strategy #3:
Top Ten Triumphs of Your Lifetime

What do you consider to be your Top Ten Triumphs of your life thus far—your proudest personal and professional accomplishments to date? These are the moments you accomplished something that filled you with great confidence in your capabilities. Do some brainstorming. Now, make a list of your Top Ten Triumphs of Your Lifetime to date, and contemplate the strengths you utilized to achieve each particular accomplishment!

Triumph #1:
Strengths Used:

Keep it going!

Seek Strengths Strategy #4:
Easy Peasy

A task that's easy for you may not be easy for everyone. If you think it's Easy Peasy, you are probably using some strengths to do it! Ask yourself the following questions to determine Easy Peasy task strengths:

1. What academic subjects have always come easily to you?
   • Strengths Used:
2. What personal or professional tasks do you accomplish without much thought and effort?
   • Strengths Used:
3. What activities or projects have you jumped right into because you knew you would get it right away?
   • Strengths Used:
4. What tasks have you picked up or learned very quickly?
   • Strengths Used:

5. What can you do well that you can't explain how you do it when asked about it?
   - Strengths Used:

Seek Strengths Strategy #5:
The "Go To" Guru

If you have ever been referred to as the guru for something or the "go to" person for a particular task, you've definitely got some unique strengths happening in those areas! Each of us has areas where our work stands out as exceptional or where we express particular talents. Ask yourself the following questions to determine your "Go To" Guru task strengths:

1. What types of things do friends, colleagues, or family members always go to you for knowledge, input, or assistance?
   - Strengths Used:
2. What do the people who know you best say you are the guru of?
   - Strengths Used:
3. What have you done that someone knowledgeable in that field has told you that you could make a living doing?
   - Strengths Used:
4. What things have you done where your work was recognized for being exceptional?
   - Strengths Used:
5. If you were to win a talent show, what would it be for?
   - Strengths Used:

Seek Strengths Strategy #6:
Rewrite Your Résumé

Now that you have written down your top triumphs (several of them career-related), and determined your massive list of strengths/superpowers, it's a great time to Rewrite Your Résumé! Why? Well, for one, at some point you may want to use it, and two it's a great exercise in rescripting the language and stories you use to describe yourself professionally. Write yourself a nice, new introductory summary that highlights the strengths you've discovered. Showcase the stories of your proudest career accomplishments and the strengths they demonstrate. Re-word your job descriptions to incorporate more action words, ownership of what you've accomplished, strengths, and triumphs. Do the same for your education and training sections, and highlight your volunteer work. Use powerful, strength-based language throughout. When you are done, read over your rewritten résumé and relish in all you have accomplished with your unique superpowers and imagine all you still have to offer!

Seek Strengths Strategy #7: Galvanize Your Gifts to Get Your Goals

Once we know what our gifts/strengths are, we can seek them out to use whenever we need them. What's really cool is that we can be very intentional to Galvanize Our Gifts to Get Our Goals! Review your Destination Designs/Goals for each area of your life—how can you craft each part of your story around utilizing your strengths? Each day, take a look at your Commitment Calendar and/or Action Agenda for the day and contemplate which gifts you can use today to reach your "have to do" and "want to do" goals. Pencil in the strength(s) you can leverage next to your specific goals and be intentional in using them in your achievement efforts. This not only moves us toward the things we want, but further cultivates our strengths and keeps our minds and actions focused on those strengths. Give it a try!

Seek Strengths Strategy #8: Strengths for Service Week

Once we know our strengths, we can use them more intentionally to do good in the world. We can use our unique Strengths for Service. This is a little exercise to get you seeking out your strengths to help others over the course of one week/seven days! It is a great way to focus on our strengths and has the perk of doing good.

First, select the seven strengths you want to use during your Strengths for Service Week.

1. Strength #1:
2. Strength #2:
3. Strength #3:
4. Strength #4:
5. Strength #5:
6. Strength #6:
7. Strength #7:

Second, use the Random Acts of Kindness (RAK) website to help you develop a list of seven acts of service/kindness you can complete over seven consecutive days that will capitalize on seven of your top strengths (one strength a day for one week): www.randomactsofkindness.org/kindness-ideas.

Third, carry out one act of service/kindness a day for seven consecutive days using seven of your strengths. You don't have to limit yourself to the ones you selected or planned, you can allow spontaneous acts to unfold as well. What did you do each day?

1. Day #1:
2. Day #2:
3. Day #3:
4. Day #4:
5. Day #5:
6. Day #6:
7. Day #7:

Finally, reflect on how it felt to use your strengths intentionally to serve others.

Seek Strengths Strategy #9:
Stretch Your Existing Strengths

So, you have got it down to a science how you use your strengths in your personal and professional life. But, are there ways you haven't thought of? Contemplate how you could Stretch Your Strengths and use them in ways you haven't used them before that take you beyond your comfort zone, expand your growth, and help you solve problems. For example, if Love of Learning is one of your strengths, and you feel your résumé could use more training experience, perhaps you could flip that strength and use it to train someone at work on an area you have mastered in your unceasing self-education. Or, if Strategic is one of your strengths, maybe you could volunteer to offer consulting to a different department in your organization that is struggling to develop a strategy to a critical problem they are facing on an issue you want to gain more experience with. Brainstorm some ways you could Stretch Your Strengths and propel your growth!

Seek Strengths Strategy #10:
Cultivate New Capabilities

If you have taken the VIA and CliftonStrengths surveys and feel you want to Cultivate New capabilities that are lower on your strengths assessment, the VIA and Gallup websites offer specific suggestions and activities to do just that! Now, let me be clear, this is NOT about scrutinizing our shortcomings. It's about leveraging what we are great at to expand our strengths repertoire. Browse the VIA (www.viacharacter.org) and Gallup (www.gallupstrengthscenter.com) websites for ideas!

Seek Strengths Strategy #11:
Compliment Others' Capabilities

Yep, this exercise is about others…while simultaneously being about you too. When we make a practice of paying attention to and Complimenting Others' Capabilities, a few really cool things happen. First, the part about others—they feel good that we noticed and acknowledged what they are great at. That recognition also encourages them to use that capability more often. Second, we feel good about ourselves for taking the time to make someone else feel good. Third, we are less likely to experience envy regarding that person's strength because we aren't hiding from it—we acknowledged it. We allow ourselves to celebrate that strength along with them. Maybe we even learn from them. Basically, everybody wins. So, each day, make a point to notice and acknowledge the strengths of those you interact with—colleagues, supervisees, supervisors, family, friends, neighbors, and strangers alike!

Seek Strengths Strategy #12:
Scrutinizing Shortcomings Narration RESCRIPTing

Consider some recent and/or long-standing perceived shortcomings you've been scrutinizing in various areas of your life that have kept you stuck in a life limiting story. Using the narration RESCRIPTing examples and other illustrations from this chapter as a guide, RESCRIPT some of your scrutinizing shortcomings thoughts into statements that are more realistic, encouraging, and empowering.

What perceived shortcomings have you been scrutinizing that you could instead seek your strengths through RESCRIPTing...

1. Regarding your relationships?
   • Scrutinizing Shortcomings Thought:
   • RESCRIPTed:

2. Regarding your career?
   • Scrutinizing Shortcomings Thought:
   • RESCRIPTed:

3. Regarding your financial life?
   • Scrutinizing Shortcomings Thought:
   • RESCRIPTed:

4. Regarding your living environment?
   • Scrutinizing Shortcomings Thought:
   • RESCRIPTed:

5. Regarding your engagement within your community?
   - Scrutinizing Shortcomings Thought:
   - RESCRIPTed:

6. Regarding your physical health?
   - Scrutinizing Shortcomings Thought:
   - RESCRIPTed:

7. Regarding your mental and emotional health?
   - Scrutinizing Shortcomings Thought:
   - RESCRIPTed:

8. Regarding your intellectual growth?
   - Scrutinizing Shortcomings Thought:
   - RESCRIPTed:

9. Regarding your recreation and relaxation?
   - Scrutinizing Shortcomings Thought:
   - RESCRIPTed:

10. Regarding your spirituality practices?
    - Scrutinizing Shortcomings Thought:
    - RESCRIPTed:

Commit yourself to seeking your strengths in every area of your life!

Seek Strengths Strategy #13: Acknowledgements & Affirmations

Here are some acknowledgements and affirmations you can recite any time you need a boost in your strengths seeking!

I acknowledge and affirm that...

- Scrutinizing and criticizing myself for my perceived short-comings doesn't motivate me, it deflates and discourages me.

- I can know what I'm great at and still be humble and kind.

- Knowing my strengths does not make me narcissistic.

- I don't have to be great at everything to recognize I'm great at lots of things.

- My strengths are gifts I can share to positively impact the world.

- I can intentionally galvanize my strengths to achieve my goals.

- Using strengths language in how I talk and write about myself enhances my confidence.

- Complimenting others for their capabilities makes both them and me feel good.

- I can draw upon what I do exceptionally well to cultivate new capabilities.

- I can seek out my strengths to solve problems and tackle challenges I have yet to dream of.

- I've already accomplished a lot using my strengths and I am going to achieve so much more seeking my strengths out every time I need them.

MY STUDENTS' STORIES

I have had the great pleasure of teaching undergraduate and graduate students for many years now. One of my greatest teaching experiences has been creating my own Positive Psychology-based course. I incorporated a multitude of Positive Psychology exercises into the course, and had students utilize them in both their professional and personal lives.

With regard to seeking strengths, I asked my students to do the following:

- Take the free online VIA Character Strengths Assessment.

- Use each of their top five strengths to carry out one help-ful act daily for others.

- Reflect upon their experience.

Their heartfelt reflections on this exercise moved me. One of my favorite strength use stories was from a student who intention-ally used one of his top five strengths—Kindness. It was a snowy winter day, so he went outside to shovel out his car. Noticing another person struggling to dig out her car, he went over to her car and shoveled her out. Seeing what he was doing, a neighbor jumped in and started to help as well. Together, they helped two more people shovel out their cars. After they finished and stopped for a moment, they noticed something amazing. Several others who saw what they were doing jumped in and began doing the same thing for their neighbors. Within a short period of time, the entire street of cars was completely shoveled out from this snowball effect that began with his kindness.

Students cited some beautiful impacts from the exercise. They felt more connected to humanity as a whole during and afterwards. They found that seeking out ways to use their strengths to help others made them feel happier and more peaceful throughout their day. They were surprised to find that the positive effects of using their strengths to help someone else lasted longer than the effects of buying something they really wanted. Giving their strengths to others actually made them feel more appreciative of other people. And, it made my students significantly more aware of the fact that they had important strengths that they could offer to the world.

PRACTICE #4

C- CHALLENGE CATASTROPHIZING

"I've got 99 problems and 86 of them are completely made up scenarios in my head that I'm stressing about for absolutely no logical reason."

~ Unknown

THE LIMITING SCRIPTS OF CATASTROPHIZING

You want to know who knows a ton about catastrophizing?

I do! And, I don't just mean some theories and concepts. Nope. I've got years of hands on experience with this. That's right, I can catastrophize like nobody's business!

In all seriousness, of each of the eight RESCRIPT practices, this is the one that challenges me the most, even though I know I need to be challenging it. I listen closely for the signs of my Inner Antagonist attempting to throw me into catastrophe mode. Most times, I catch it and challenge it quickly, but sometimes I have to work a little harder to quiet my Inner Antagonist. Last night I looked at my book writing deadlines, and low and behold, it started yacking at me. It took a little longer than usual, but

I quieted it down. And, today my Inner Advocate is running things again.

Catastrophizing is the mental process of exaggerating the meaning and magnitude of a perceived challenge and dramatizing the perceived adverse consequences. It's when our minds transform discomfort into danger or destruction. When we catastrophize, we assign negative meaning to something neutral or uncomfortable and make it seem like it's actually an *inherently bad* situation that *will* cause major problems.

Catastrophizing is a product of anxiety and a heightened version of worry. Anxiety involves fear and apprehension of the unknown. Worry is a repetitive contemplation about unpleasant things that might occur in the future. Catastrophizing takes worry to another level by mentally conjuring progressively worse and worse outcomes to a specific worry topic. It's a horror movie with infinite terrifying sequels.

Catastrophizing typically involves asking ourselves a series of "What if...?" types of questions:

- "What if I go up to the podium and forget my speech?"
- "What if I take this new job and I hate it?"
- "What if I go on the date and she thinks I'm boring?"
- "What if I can't save enough money for retirement?"
- "What if I my daughter gets on the plane and it crashes?"
- "What if my husband's heart palpitations mean he's having a heart attack?"
- "What if my girlfriend hasn't called me because she's gonna break up with me?"
- "What if my boss didn't give me the project because she's gonna lay me off?"

Through asking ourselves these questions, we fuel underlying fears of being out of control and/or lacking the characteristics or resources to effectively problem solve. The process of asking these questions also helps to perpetuate our feelings of ambiguity, and thus continue exploring further possibilities, even those that might be considered improbable. The further down the "what if" spiral we go, the more a thing that was originally neutral or uncomfortable becomes threatening, dangerous, and destructive in our minds.

Why do we catastrophize?

Our Inner Antagonist's catastrophic thoughts can be elicited by internal or external stimuli. For instance, a series of bad headaches could lead someone to a catastrophic thought that they have a ruptured brain Aneurysm. Or, driving on a highway could lead someone to a catastrophic thought that they will get into a car accident. Often, the trigger situation elicits a memory of a previous situation, which leads us to interpret the trigger situation based on the outcome of the previous one, and we emotionally and behaviorally respond accordingly.

Using the previous examples, if a person had a cousin who recently passed away from a ruptured brain Aneurysm, that person's bad headache might elicit this memory and lead them to catastrophize about their bad headaches. Or, if someone had a car accident while driving on a highway, their memory of this experience could be evoked while driving on a highway and lead to catastrophic thoughts. The memory could be of something that has happened to us directly, to someone we know, or even something we've seen or heard about. Catastrophizing can also be evoked by situations that are more loosely connected to a memory. For example, if you were late to a work meeting once and perceived some kind of issue arising from your lateness, you might begin to catastrophize when you are running a bit behind schedule to go to a social gathering.

The catastrophizing that can occur during a panic attack is similar. I remember that when I had my first panic attack, I thought I was developing asthma. This was elicited by memories not long before of seeing someone close to me having an asthma attack. The memory evoked a belief that I could lose air, suffocate, and die. There are also many people who catastrophize that they are having a heart attack during panic attacks because of the heart palpitations and tightness in the chest they experience. This can be evoked by memories of a previous heart attack, memories of someone else having a heart attack, or hearing about this happening to someone.

When we catastrophize, our Inner Antagonist goads us into fixating on particular aspects of a situation that supports our catastrophic belief, and we often ignore other non-supportive details. This can hamper our ability to accurately assess the situation because, in that moment, we are so fixated on everything we think is bad about it.

Furthermore, when we catastrophize, there is often something happening in our brains that believes that if we just mentally run through 15 million different scenarios of all the worst things that could happen, we might be able to control or stop them from happening. It's a really ineffective attempt at taking control of that which we feel so out of control. Unfortunately, it doesn't work. The process of catastrophizing renders us feeling even more helpless and makes us feel paralyzed to take useful action.

What do we catastrophize about?

Each of us has our own unique triggers and predictions when it comes to catastrophizing as a result of our life experiences. However, there are some common themes that our Inner Antagonist might fixate upon. We might catastrophize these types of things happening to ourselves or to others:

- Prognosticating major health issues, illnesses, or diseases (chronic disease, rare mystery health issue, terminal illness, etc.).

- Envisioning major physical, mental, or emotional harm (stranger related danger, abuse, freak accident, etc.).

- Anticipating a major transportation related disaster (car, plane, bus, train, etc.).

- Foreseeing the loss or destruction of property (an iron left on causes fire, doors unlocked enables break-in, natural disaster causes major damage, etc.).

- Expecting betrayal, abandonment, rejection, or ridicule from a loved one or from social circles (cheating, leaving, emotional cut-off, social ostracizing, etc.).

- Presuming a failed task performance (public speaking, sports, job interview, work project, parenting, etc.).

- Fear of losing self-control in front of other people (inability to stop oneself from speaking or behaving inappropriately around others).

How does catastrophizing harm us?

If you've ever catastrophized, you know the harm it can cause. When you catastrophize, you mentally and emotionally (and sometimes physically, in the case of panic attacks) experience trauma before any real problem actually arises. In many ways, it feels like torture. It debilitates us from taking helpful actions on real issues and tricks us into experiencing the anguish of fake issues. Catastrophizing can even contribute to phobic disorders (social phobia, agoraphobia, glossophobia, acrophobia, etc.), which creates even greater limits in our lives.

Fortunately, there are numerous strategies to challenge catastrophic thinking. The strategies not only help to alleviate stress in the moment of a catastrophe episode, but also teach us to get faster at catching and challenging worrisome thoughts before they become catastrophic, and slowly train us to change the way we think overall.

How does Challenging Catastrophizing RESCRIPT our story?

When we challenge our catastrophizing, we begin to see the flaws in our negatively skewed logic. We start to recognize that most of the things we've worried ourselves to death over never came to the terrifying fruition we believed they would. We also see that when we have experienced challenges, we typically survived them much better than we anticipated. We are better able to understand how worrying and catastrophizing about the future does not mean we suddenly take control of future outcomes. We also begin to understand that while we may *want* to know what the future holds, we don't *need* to know. We begin to see that we can hope for and believe in a positive future. When we challenge catastrophizing, we amplify our Inner Advocate and thus regain control of our emotions and significantly alleviate feelings of anxiety and panic. We free ourselves to feel confident and have faith in ourselves and the future.

SOME HIGHLIGHTS FROM RESEARCH STUDIES ON CATASTROPHIZING

- Pisarik, Rowell, and Thompson found that college students' catastrophic thinking about their skills, decisions, performance, and future outcomes facilitated career development anxiety, which manifested in hot flashes, nervousness, tension, sleep issues, and pervasive feelings of angst, frustration, fear, and irritability.[20]

- Arnow, Blasey, Constantino, Robinson, Hunkeler, and colleagues uncovered that chronic pain sufferers who engage in higher levels of catastrophic thinking report significantly more instances of their pain interfering with their ability to carry on with daily activities, work/housework, and recreational/social activities, than those with low levels of catastrophic thinking.[21]

- When we catastrophize, we immerse ourselves in an overly pessimistic view of what the future will bring, instead of allowing ourselves to perceive our future through a lens of hope and optimism. Jerabek and Muoio of PsychTests discovered that optimists are considerably more likely than pessimists to see the good in even the most disagreeable of people, see the positive aspects of bad situations, believe they can handle whatever challenges come their way, view problems from multiple perspectives, feel satisfied with their personal relationships, and be in good physical health.[22]

- Research by Sugiura and Sugiura uncovered that when we resist engaging in catastrophic thinking, it diminishes a multitude of forms of psychological distress including reducing worry, depression, social anxiety, phobias, generalized anxiety, and obsessions and compulsions.[23]

- Sullivan, Adams, Ellis, Clark, Sully, and Thibault discovered that individuals with PTSD who received treatment such as empathic reflection, guided disclosure, thought monitoring, problem solving, and goal setting reduced catastrophic thinking tendencies and returned to work following disability leave more quickly than those with higher levels of catastrophizing.[24]

LIMITING NARRATIONS OF CATASTROPHIZING RESCRIPTED

Let's examine how we can RESCRIPT the stories we tell ourselves when we catastrophize:

1. "I know I'm gonna bomb this exam and then I'll probably fail the class and get kicked out of school!"

   RESCRIPTed...
   "I don't feel totally ready for this exam. I'm not sure how well I am going to do. But, I'm going to go in hopeful and do the best I can. If it doesn't turn out great, I will get extra help for the next one and change my study habits."

135

2. If I go on this date, it's probably gonna be as horrible as all the other ones, and I'll be alone for the rest of my life!"

   RESCRIPTed...
   I've had some cruddy dates these last few months. But, it doesn't mean that this one will be cruddy too. And, even if it is, it's not a foreshadowing of anything. All I can do is keep putting myself out there and keep believing that the right relationship is in my future. It may just require some more trial and error."

3. I know I'm gonna say something stupid during this interview and probably never get a decent job!"

   RESCRIPTed...
   I get so nervous before interviews, but so do lots of people. I think I'm going to hire an interview coach to do some mock interviewing and give me feedback and suggestions so I can get ready for this one. And even if I do struggle at some points, each interview is good practice. Eventually, I'm going to nail it."

4. If I do this presentation, I know I'm gonna forget my speech, look like an idiot, and everyone will think I'm stupid!"

   RESCRIPTed...
   I'm so anxious about this presentation. But, I've been rehearsing like crazy and really know my speech inside and out. Even if I fumble a bit, no one else will know because they don't know what my speech looks like, only I do! Plus, if they do notice my nerves at all, what difference does it really make? I won't die. It just means I'm human."

5. I've been getting these headaches for days—what if I have a brain tumor and I'm gonna die!"

   RESCRIPTed...
   I've been getting these headaches for days. I might be staring at my computer too much or possibly not getting enough sleep. Let me try to lighten up my screen time

and go to sleep earlier the next couple of days. If the headaches still persist, I'll make a doctor's appointment to get it checked out."

LIMITLESS LIVING LIBRARY – STRATEGIES TO CHALLENGE CATASTROPHIZING SECTION

In addition to these strategies, you can modify and use strategies from other chapters to challenge your catastrophizing!

Challenge Catastrophizing Strategy #1: Helping or Harming Review

During or following your next episode of catastrophizing, ask yourself the following:

1. What is/was my purpose/intent in this episode of catastrophizing?

2. How does/did this catastrophizing harm me?

3. How does/did this catastrophizing help me?

4. What is/was avoided through catastrophizing?

5. What is/was addressed through this catastrophizing?

6. What would I say to a friend who was catastrophizing over this?

7. What more effective things could I say to myself right now?

8. What more effective strategies exist to achieve my original purpose/intent?

9. What did I learn about my catastrophizing from this review?

Challenge Catastrophizing Strategy #2: Break the Catastrophe Chain

Episodes of catastrophizing are generally brought on by situations that tap into some of our deeper insecurities and fears. Something occurs, then we assign a bigger meaning to it, creating a chain of thoughts that quickly transform a discomfort into a destructor.

When visualized, catastrophizing episodes look like links in a chain. The crazy thing is they generally occur so quickly that we just see the first link and the last link. We *perceive* them as *directly* connected to one another. It can be helpful to examine the links in the middle of the chain so we recognize how many more situations and assumptions are linked in between the triggering event chain link and the catastrophe chain link we've imagined. When we do this, we can break the chain---we can see that there is *no direct connection* between the triggering chain link and the catastrophe chain link.

When catastrophizing, we see this (example):

I failed my first college Introductory Psychology exam >>> My future is completely destroyed!

Under further examination, we can see this (example):

I failed my first college Introductory Psychology exam >>> I might fail other Psychology exams >>> I might fail my Psychology classes >>> I might fail other classes too >>> I'll have a horrible GPA >>> I'll never get into a Psychology doctoral program >>> I'll never be a Psychologist >>> I'll have to work at a crappy job I hate >>> I'll be miserable >>> My future is completely destroyed!

How do we uncover these middle links in the catastrophe chain?

Start back at the first link, and ask yourself:

1. What specifically worries me about _____ (the triggering event chain link)?

2. What specifically worries me about _____ (the next chain link)?

Example:

Q: What specifically worries me about failing this Psychology exam?

A: That I might fail other Psychology exams.

Q: What specifically worries me about failing other Psychology exams?

A: That I might fail my Psychology classes.

Continue the Q&A until you arrive at the catastrophe chain link.

Now, look at how many things would need to occur and how many assumptions need to be made in order to connect the triggering event chain link with the catastrophic conclusion chain link.

Consider how many opportunities there are between the event that occurred and the catastrophic conclusion you've drawn to make a plan and take positive action.

1. What positive actions can you take to replace the negative chain link assumptions to help facilitate a more positive conclusion?

Example:

I failed my first college Introductory Psychology exam >>> I speak with my TA about the questions I got wrong to understand the material better >>> I go to the college learning center for study strategies, time management, and test anxiety coaching >>> I implement the strategies I learn >>> I improve my grades on future Psychology exams >>> I improve my grades on all of my course exams >>> I maintain a strong GPA >>> I get into a Psychology doctoral program >>> I become a Psychologist >>> I work at a job I love >>> I'm fulfilled >>> My future is fabulous!

1. What is the first action(s) I can take right now?

Much like with rumination, we want to Alter Analysis into Action. Now, go act on what is within your control in order to Break the Catastrophe Chain!

Challenge Catastrophizing Strategy #3: Evidence For & Against

When we are catastrophizing, it helps to examine the situation a bit closer to understand what we are basing this catastrophic conclusion upon in the first place. The next time you find yourself catastrophizing over something, ask yourself the following questions.

1. What evidence do I have that supports this catastrophizing thought? Basically, what has occurred that would indicate the catastrophic conclusions I've come to believe?

2. What evidence do I have that does not support this catastrophizing thought? What has occurred that would indicate that this catastrophic conclusion is unlikely?

3. After reviewing my evidence, what revisions would I like to make to my conclusions?

Challenge Catastrophizing Strategy #4: Catastrophes that Never Happened

So, pretty funny thing about those catastrophes we are expecting—most of them never actually happen. Yup. We spend hours, days, weeks, months (sometimes even longer) worrying and traumatizing ourselves over them. Time we wanted to be doing other more productive or enjoyable things. And then.....no catastrophe.

Think back to times recently or longer ago when you agonized needlessly, worried yourself sick, and anticipated the worst in a situation, and the catastrophe didn't even happen:

Situation #1:

1. What catastrophe did you think was going to happen?

2. What actually happened?

Keep it going!

What information can you take away from this exercise?

The next time you catch yourself catastrophizing, remind yourself of these situations. Consider how much time you unnecessarily spent in mental and emotional agony. Tell yourself, "Most of the catastrophes I imagine never even happen. I won't torture myself needlessly over this. I will remain calm and confident."

Challenge Catastrophizing Strategy #5: Choose an Alternative Conclusion

Do you remember those story books that would let you choose a bunch of different possibilities for how the story could end? Think of when you watch the digital release of a movie, and the bonus scenes have alternate conclusions the writers, producers, and director were considering? Or, most recently, think of Netflix's Bandersnatch (which is awesome!). You are the writer, producer, and director of your story—so, which alternative conclusions would you like to choose for your story? The possibilities are endless.

First, think of a recent or current situation in your life where you have been scripting a catastrophe.

1. What event/situation occurred that elicited catastrophic thinking?

2. What catastrophic conclusion(s) have you been choosing to accept for your story in this present situation you are facing?

Now, start brainstorming some alternative conclusions. Get creative!

3. What are some possible fabulous, fantasy-like conclusions you could choose? These are conclusions you feel are amazing, but think they're less likely.

4. What are some positive, plausible conclusions you could choose? These are conclusions you feel would be good outcomes and could be possible.

5. What are some totally anti-climactic conclusions you could choose? These are conclusions you feel would be harmless and uneventful, and could be possible.

6. Of ALL the conclusions you've chosen to contemplate, which one(s) do you think is/are most probable to actually occur?

Below is one example for each type of conclusion:

Event/Situation: My boss tells me that she wants me to do the keynote speech at the annual regional conference where hundreds of industry colleagues will be present.

- **Catastrophic Conclusion**: I'm going to bomb this speech in every way possible, all my industry colleagues will think I'm an idiot, and I'll be completely ostracized in my field.

- **Fabulous, Fantasy-Like Conclusion**: I'm going to do the most informative, engaging, poised, and confident keynote speech that the conference audience has ever seen, thus my industry colleagues will be so impressed that any door in the field I want to walk through will be open to me.

- **Positive, Plausible Conclusion**: I'm going to do a strong speech, it will have some nice highlight moments, my colleagues will enjoy it, and new opportunities in my field will be open to me.

- **Anti-Climactic Conclusion**: I'm going to do a good speech, not bad, not great, no major issues, no major highlights, thus my industry colleagues will think it's fine, and my career will go on just as it has been.

- **Most Probable**: I think something in between the Positive, Plausible Conclusion and Anti-Climactic Conclusion is most probable. I'm going to work towards preparing as much as possible to make it as strong as I can, and hey, maybe I can even achieve a little of that Fabulous, Fantasy Conclusion! No matter what, I'm going to be proud of what I do accomplish since public speaking is scary for me.

Challenge Catastrophizing Strategy #6: What's on Your "I Survived" Tee-Shirt?

Catastrophizing often is fueled by a belief that we cannot handle challenges that may come our way. When we catastrophize, we are telling ourselves we are too weak and incapable to figure out how to manage a problem. But, I bet you've managed a problem before. I bet you have coped with a tough situation you didn't know you could handle. I bet you've survived some struggles in your years on this planet. What's on Your "I Survived" Tee-Shirt? When you ride a steep, loopy roller coaster, you can get one of those tee-shirts. Imagine if you got one each time you survived a major life challenge.

1. What challenges in life have you survived?

2. What challenges have you endured that turned out to not be as awful as you catastrophized them to be?

3. How did you survive these experiences?

4. What actions did you take that helped you manage, cope, or effectively address the issues you faced?

5. What internal and external resources did you call upon to manage during and after?

6. What surprised you about how you got through these experiences?

7. What resources can you draw upon to manage future challenges?

See, you have and can survive through challenges. The next time you are facing something that elicits catastrophizing, review this exercise and let your Inner Advocate remind you of the resources that have gotten you through tough times before. Sometimes, just knowing you did it before boosts your confidence!

Challenge Catastrophizing Strategy #7: So, What If it Did Happen?

When you are at the height of being convinced that your worst-case catastrophe will happen, another option is to just go with it. Well, kind of. You can go with letting yourself believe it for the time being, but with some inquiry involved. Ask yourself the following questions:

1. If the worst did happen, would it create destruction? Or, would it create discomfort? How so?

2. If the worst did happen, what actions would I take to manage it?

Now, calmly tell yourself, "It's not happening right now. I'm okay right now. I will stop stressing right now. I will allow myself peace right now. Whatever happens in the future, I can and will handle it mentally, emotionally, and behaviorally. I have the internal and external resources I need to cope."

Challenge Catastrophizing Strategy #8: Say Your Name

When you find yourself going into a brain spin over something stressful, speak to yourself by name (in your head or out loud is even better if location permits). This reminds you that YOU are in control and you CAN reason with yourself and calm yourself. "Colleen, you are fine." "Colleen, this isn't as big as your brain wants you to believe it is." Colleen, you've got this!" Decide what phrases you need to say to yourself, but no yelling or reprimanding allowed. Use a calm, rational, and neutral tone of voice, and only affirming, positive, encouraging words, addressing you by name.

Challenge Catastrophizing Strategy #9:
Speak Calmly to Your Rambling Inner Antagonist

Your Inner Antagonist is loud. It tries to make sure it's heard. It rants, complains, freaks out, and can jump from one thought to the next really fast! When it starts rambling like this, you need to help it calm down. After all, it's a part of you and you don't need it riling you up! As soon as you hear your Inner Antagonist begin the ramble, start to speak slowly, softly, and with a neutral tone of voice back to it, "S..l..o..w d..o..w..n, let's stay c..a..l..m." "Let's think about this situation s...l..o..w..l..y, let's not race to conclusions we know nothing about." "You can remain calm, you don't need to allow yourself to escalate." "Slow down your thoughts. That helps you think clearly." Continue to speak to yourself slowly and softly until your thoughts slow down and you can think more clearly about the situation that ignited your Inner Antagonist.

Challenge Catastrophizing Strategy #10:
Call Upon Your Inner Advocate

Your Inner Advocate has your back, it's your ally, your supporter, it encourages you exactly how a good friend does. When your Inner Antagonist tries to steal the scene, call your Inner Advocate onto the stage. Call upon it – "Okay, Inner Advocate, I could really use your rational reasoning right now." "Inner Advocate, I want your advice and inspiration to manage this situation." Sometimes you just need to step back from a situation and remind yourself that your Inner Advocate is available and ready to step in as long as you call upon it.

Challenge Catastrophizing Strategy #11:
Drop A Barrier Between You & Anxiety

When you have something big coming up that has often set off your anxiety and catastrophizing, try imagining the anxiety as separate from you versus a part of you. Envision yourself standing in a big, plain, empty room. Anxiety is the only other entity in the room with you. It's on the other side of the room and your job is to keep it away from you. The good news is you have a magic power, you can drop an infinitely long and infinitely high barrier down in front of you, and anything on the other side of that barrier can't touch you. Now, drop down your barrier. All you can see now is that barrier. You can't even see anxiety anymore because it's on the other side. It can't see you and it can't touch you. You are completely safe from it.

Challenge Catastrophizing Strategy #12: Disrupt (vs. Erupt) the Volcano

When we are anxious about something in our lives, we can experience a variety of physical symptoms and sensations. Sometimes anxiety can feel like something stirring in our stomachs that heats up and churns and tries to make its way up our bodies, making our skin hot, making us sweat, racing our heartbeat, making it hard to breathe, burning up into our brains, and into a swirl of chaotic, irrational thoughts. Think of this type of anxiety – also known as a state of panic - as a volcano.

Through practice, we can learn to disrupt the volcano before it erupts into a panic state. When you feel your stomach begin to churn, imagine the anxiety as lava deep down in your stomach. Your job is to keep that lava down as it tries to rise. Speak calmly and slowly to yourself out loud and in your mind as your mind tries to race. Calmly and kindly assure yourself you are going to be just fine. You've made it through this before and you will again. Pay attention to the sensations in your body. If your face is expressing your anxieties, close your eyes, neutralize your facial expressions. Breathe slowly in through your nose, and slowly out through your mouth. Continue this breathing process. Keep your eyes closed. Imagine the lava simmering down, it has stopped bubbling and rising, its going back down. Your skin is feeling cooler, your heart is slowing down, you are breathing easily. You've disrupted the volcano.

Challenge Catastrophizing Strategy #13:
Cool it with the Crystal Ball

So, you can see the future, huh? You're psychic? An oracle? Come on now. You can't see any images of the future in that crystal ball—you're just making things up! We don't like ambiguity, so we replace it with conjecture. Unfortunately, catastrophizing conjectures are torturous to have spinning around in your brain. The next time you start catastrophizing over something, imagine yourself hovering over a purple crystal ball pretending you can see some looming doom ahead. Then cool it with that clairvoyance and tell yourself, "I don't know what's going to happen. And, that's okay. I don't like not knowing, but I can live with it. It's sure better than torturing myself with bleak assumptions about my future."

Challenge Catastrophizing Strategy #14:
Hand it Over to Your Higher Power

Faith is freedom. One of the most meaningful and powerful things you can do when you are feeling driven to catastrophize is stop, sit back, take a deep breath, and Hand it Over to Your Higher Power. Trust that your Higher Power is watching over you and will provide you with the internal and external resources to manage any challenges you may face. Our Higher Power talks to us all the time, but we must quiet our minds to listen. Be still and quiet, and allow your Higher Power to guide you. Together, you've got this!

Challenge Catastrophizing Strategy #15:
Catastrophizing Narration RESCRIPTing

Consider some recent and/or long-standing catastrophizing you have done in various areas of your life that have kept you stuck in a life limiting story. Using the narration RESCRIPTing examples and other illustrations from this chapter as a guide, RESCRIPT some of your catastrophizing thoughts into statements that are more realistic, encouraging, and empowering.

What catastrophizing will you challenge through RESCRIPTing...

1. Regarding your relationships?
   - Catastrophizing Thought:
   - RESCRIPTed:

2. Regarding your career?
   - Catastrophizing Thought:
   - RESCRIPTed:

3. Regarding your financial life?
   - Catastrophizing Thought:
   - RESCRIPTed:

4. Regarding your living environment?
   - Catastrophizing Thought:
   - RESCRIPTed:

5. Regarding your engagement within your community?
   - Catastrophizing Thought:
   - RESCRIPTed:

6. Regarding your physical health?
   - Catastrophizing Thought:
   - RESCRIPTed:

7. Regarding your mental and emotional health?
   - Catastrophizing Thought:
   - RESCRIPTed:

8. Regarding your intellectual growth?
   - Catastrophizing Thought:
   - RESCRIPTed:

9. Regarding your recreation and relaxation?
   - Catastrophizing Thought:
   - RESCRIPTed:

10. Regarding your spirituality practices?
    - Catastrophizing Thought:
    - RESCRIPTed:

Commit yourself to challenging catastrophizing!

Challenge Catastrophizing Strategy #16: Acknowledgements & Affirmations

Here are some acknowledgements and affirmations you can recite any time you need to boost your confidence in your capability to challenge catastrophizing!

I acknowledge and affirm that...

- No one can predict the future (unless you are a legit psychic!).

- I do not need to conjure negative outcomes when I don't know the outcome.

- Not knowing what the future holds does not mean the future is dangerous.

- I may not like ambiguity, but I can live with it.

- Most of the catastrophes I've created in my mind never actually happened.

- I have managed through challenges before and can call upon strategies I used in the past to handle future challenges that may arise.

- I am capable of handling much more than I give myself credit for.

- I will take positive action on what I do control to impact my future.

- I can speak calmly and slowly to myself to alleviate my anxiety.

- I am safe and secure from anxiety, it cannot overtake me if I don't allow it to.

- Just because a particular event, situation, or interaction turned out poorly for me in the past does not mean it will always turn out poorly for me.

- Discomfort is not the same as danger or destruction. This situation will not bring danger or destruction. It may bring some discomfort, which I can handle.

- This situation is not as big and bad as my mind is trying to trick me into seeing it as. This is a negative illusion that I am creating and I can imagine a more likely, reasonable scenario if I want to.

- There's nothing my Higher Power and I can't handle together.

CARRIE'S STORY

When Carrie contacted me for coaching, she was feeling extremely overwhelmed at home and at work. She had a toddler at home and a job as a Sales Representative where she felt stuck professionally, while struggling to remain on top of all her projects and deadlines. She felt negative a lot of the time, and believed that her critical self-talk was her worst enemy.

When Carrie took the RESCRIPT Quiz, her catastrophizing score was in the very high range. She shared that at home, she found herself reading into everything her husband said and did, worrying that he was upset with her about something. At work, she catastrophized that her clients were unhappy with her, analyzed what her boss was thinking about her work, and mentally conjured that she was going to get fired. To impress her boss, she said yes to all kinds of extra work, even when she knew it was way too much. She regularly came home from work stressed, constantly checking and responding to her emails out of fear she'd get behind. She felt like these habits negatively impacted her time at home with her husband and young son.

Carrie and I did a lot of work together on RESCRIPTing her negative self-talk. When she caught herself catastrophizing, she reminded herself of situations she catastrophized over in the past that never resulted in her feared outcomes. She also worked on contemplating what she could do to effectively manage the situation should the worst-case scenario arise.

She made a regular practice of immediately asking herself, "What do I control in this situation?" once she noticed she was worrying and then taking the first step in acting upon the concern. And for the aspects of situations she did not control, she practiced speaking calmly to herself, assuring herself that catastrophizing over what she does not control doesn't help her or the situation, it just hurts her and wastes precious time.

Carrie and I also worked on strategies to plan out her work and personal commitments each week so she could prioritize, track her progress, and feel less overwhelmed. She created daily task lists and organizational routines. Additionally, she practiced being honest about what tasks she could take on based on her existing project deadlines. Carrie also began to create clear boundaries for how to address work when she was home with her family.

Ultimately, Carrie became more self-compassionate, more assertive in setting critical boundaries, as well as calmer and more confident overall. Her relationship with her husband improved, she was able to make more time to be involved with her son's preschool events, and was more present mentally and emotionally while at home.

At work, Carrie became more assertive, began to feel more confident in sharing her ideas, and was recognized by her boss for offering strong recommendations. Carrie ultimately earned a promotion to Territory Manager. Carrie significantly decreased her stress level and learned to challenge her catastrophizing.

PRACTICE #5

R- RESTRICT REGRETS

"Don't look back, you're not going that way."

~ Mary Engelbreit

THE LIMITING SCRIPTS OF REGRET

Shoulda, woulda, coulda. That's the language of regret. Life is full of choices. Some go well, some do not. We could have done it differently, should have said something else, and maybe it would have worked out better than it did. When experiencing regret, our Inner Antagonist continuously flips the pages of our story back to our most unhappy moments. Then it whips out a yellow highlighter and highlights all the actions we took that led us to the unhappiness.

In order to experience regret, we must first believe we bear some or all of the responsibility for the outcome of an event, hence there must have been a personal choice involved (not someone else's choice). To experience regret, we must also believe that a different decision would have had a preferred outcome. Hence, regret occurs in relation to our decisions when we believe that the outcome of our selected choice is less desirable/worse than the potential outcomes of the choice(s) we did not select. It is typically followed up by beliefs that we somehow should have known better than to choose as we did, berating ourselves for choosing unwisely, desires to undo or redo what we did, and imagining all the opportunities we've lost out on as a result of our choice.

Regret is one of the most intensely and commonly experienced negative emotions.[25] As an emotion, regret is unique because it's not a basic emotion we develop right away, and it doesn't have a specific facial expression, like for example, anger, disgust, fear, happiness, sadness, or surprise. We develop the experience of regret around early elementary school age when we begin to more sophisticatedly imagine other possibilities than the way things actually are.[26] It requires abstract thinking capabilities, as well as our ability to compare and contrast. Furthermore, regret is also unique because most other negative emotions like fear, anger, disgust, anxiety, and disappointment can be experienced without choice, but regret cannot (guilt and shame, similar to regret, require choice—these will be discussed further in the Invite Imperfection chapter).

Regret also has an interesting relationship with worry and catastrophizing. While regret is typically examined in its relationship to the past, we also can project regret we might feel over a future decision, leading us to worry and catastrophize over the potential outcomes of that decision. Projecting future regret can sometimes lead us to avoid making decisions in order to evade potential risks. When dealing with the future, regret is more of a mental than emotional experience. When we are regretting the past, it can be both mental and emotional.

Our responses to feelings of regret vary. If undoing the choice is a possibility, it is typically the favored response. For example, if I didn't register to take college courses in September, and then during the first week of classes, I hear my friends talking about school and I feel like I made a bad decision, I can undo my choice by going to the registrar and signing up for classes starting the following week. Sometimes, we get to undo a choice because the window to make the change after feeling regret is still open.

In order to alleviate the distress brought on by regret, when we cannot undo our decision, we may choose to renounce responsibility for the problematic outcome, justify why we did what we did, or might take a healthier psychological approach by determining what positives resulted from our choice versus focusing too heavily on the negatives.

Why do we regret?

It's important to note that regret as a mental and emotional experience is not all bad. Experiencing regrets can help us to learn from our mistakes and change our behaviors in order to avoid repeating problems and resulting painful emotions. However, sometimes our Inner Antagonist take regret to an extreme and unproductive level, using it to chastise and continuously torture us.

We experience regret because human beings are not fond of missed opportunities, particularly if they believe those opportunities may have been within their reach.

We are more likely to experience regret when it's easy to imagine an outcome different than the one that occurred. For example, consider these two similar scenarios:

On a Tuesday, I am at work for my job as a bank teller, and someone commits an armed robbery at my bank that day, which leads me to feel severe psychological distress.

A. **Scenario A**: If I was scheduled to go into work that Tuesday, I am unlikely to experience regret for going to work that day because it doesn't seem as if a different outcome was possible or likely.

B. **Scenario B**: If I was scheduled to be off from work that Tuesday, but I decided to go in anyway to make some extra money, I am much more likely to feel regret because an alternate outcome (keeping my day off and not being present during this traumatic event) is easy to imagine.

We do not need to know for certain what alternative outcomes exist to experience regret—we will simply mentally conjure those alternatives.

What do we regret?

There are some areas of life people experience greater levels of regret than others. What we regret tends to vary based on age/time of life and includes a combination of reflecting on things we did and things we didn't do. However overall, people's most common regrets are in the areas of education, career, and relationships.[27] Below are examples of some common regrets I've come across in my work with clients:

1. **Relationships**: Breaking off a particular romantic relationship, marrying one person instead of another, not working harder to maintain a marriage, not telling someone "I love you" more or at all, arguments and cut-off in family relationships, not forgiving or apologizing, not staying in more frequent contact with family and friends, not spending more time with loved ones, not being kinder to family and friends, not making more time for loved ones before they passed away, investing time in people that were toxic.

2. **Career:** Choosing a practical career instead of a career with more passion and purpose, following our parents' career desires instead of our own dreams, working too much at the expense of other areas of our life.

3. **Finance:** Spending too much money, not saving more money, making/not making certain investment decisions.

4. **Living Environment**: Not moving to another neighborhood/city/state/country.

5. **Community Engagement**: Not volunteering more, not doing enough to help the local/global community.

6. **Physical Health:** Not eating healthier, not exercising more, not sleeping more.

7. **Mental & Emotional Health**: Not speaking up about feelings, not standing up for convictions, not being more authentic and vulnerable, allowing fear to stop specific actions, worrying too much, caring too much about what others think, not expressing more confidence, not pursuing personal happiness.

8. **Intellectual Growth**: Not completing a degree, not studying more when in school, not learning a particular skill.

9. **Recreation & Relaxation**: Not traveling more, not investing more time in hobbies and passions, not taking more time for self-care.

10. **Spirituality:** Not connecting with a higher power sooner, not maintaining consistent spiritual/religious practices.

Connectedness is a core human need, so it is no surprise that regrets relevant to relationships are at the top of most people's regrets. We strongly desire to feel like we belong and feel connected to others, thus when we believe we've made choices in our lives that have threatened or damaged our connections with others, we feel the greatest level of regret.

We also place a high regard in our society upon things relevant to our intellectual and professional achievement. Thus, we often regret actions or inactions in these areas of life as well. Furthermore, when discussing regret, people often talk about compromises they've made between career/educational pursuits and relationships. More specifically, some express regret for spending excessive time on education and career at the expense of time with their family and friends. Whereas others express regret for spending too much time with family and friends and neglecting career and educational pursuits.

Interestingly, while our actions generate greater regret in the short-term, our inactions foster more regret in the long-term.[28] When people discuss recent regrets, they are generally connections with things they have done. However, when people look back on their lives, they express significantly more regret related to the things they did not do. Hence, with age it is also more likely for regrets to be focused more on inactions versus actions.

How does regret harm us?

When we spend excessive time wallowing in our regrets, we are less likely to feel satisfied with our lives, experience greater levels of depression and anxiety, have a more difficult time coping with challenging life events, and may experience physical health/ somatic manifestations as well.

We must accept that as human beings, we make errors in judgment, and that this is okay. Allowing our Inner Antagonist to enact unending punishment upon us does not undo anything, it simply harms us.

How does Restricting Regret RESCRIPT our story?

Restricting regrets allows us the freedom to be human. We allow ourselves to understand that every person makes choices that end in unpleasant outcomes. We are able to see that we can live with the results of all our choices, even the ones we don't love, and take positive action in any way we can moving forward. We amplify our Inner Advocate, thus freeing ourselves from living in our past and empowering ourselves to be present in the now and feel hopeful for the future.

Feeling unending regret is not required to learn from our mistakes. We can recognize that our actions may have intentionally or unintentionally caused harm to us or others. This is critical. However, we can offer sincere apologies when warranted, make amends when possible, experience self-compassion, and use what we learn for continuous self-growth.

In my own life and in my work with clients, I have found that releasing regrets lifts negative limits we put on ourselves and our lives. We can move forward, only when we are looking forward.

SOME HIGHLIGHTS FROM RESEARCH STUDIES ON REGRET

- Roese, Epstude, Fessel, Morrison, Smallman, and colleagues found that those who experience higher levels of regret are more likely to experience more general distress, greater anxiety, and increased depression.[29]

- A study by Schmidt and Van revealed that focusing your thoughts on your regrets prior to going to bed significantly delays falling asleep.[30]

- Becerra Pérez, Menear, Brehaut, and Legaré discovered that long-term concentration on regrets reduces people's satisfaction with their lives, decreases their well-being, and can negatively impact their overall mental health.[31]

- A study by Gao, Zhang, Wang, Xu, Hong, and Jiang discovered that experiencing regret consumes individuals' self-control resources and leads to poorer problem-solving performance on subsequent tasks, whereas seeking silver linings about the regret triggering situation improves people's problem-solving performance.[32]

- Research by Lewis and Borders revealed that women with lower degrees of regret experience higher levels of satisfaction with their lives.[33]

LIMITING NARRATIONS OF REGRET RESCRIPTED

Let's examine how we can RESCRIPT the stories we tell ourselves when we experience regret:

1. "I really wish I had gone to college when I had the chance."

    RESCRIPTed...
    "I may not have gone to college right out of high school, but at the age of 30, I'm ready. I am enrolling in my local

community college and I'm going to get my degree! Better late than never!"

2. "I wish I never would've dated Tom since he treated me so horribly."

    RESCRIPTed...

    "Tom treated me pretty badly when we were dating. Some say I should've never stayed with him so long. But, all these years later I realize how much I learned from that experience. And, I've been able to pass that wisdom along to my friends who may also be in unhealthy relationships."

3. "I should've never said that, it completely ruined my friendship with Sarah."

    RESCRIPTed...

    "I think that what I said to Sarah may have really damaged our relationship. It was not my finest moment. All I can do now is try to make it right by apologizing and trying to start again. Even if she does not want to be friends anymore, at least I will know I did all I could to make amends."

4. "I wish I would've spent more time with my kids when they were little instead of working so much."

    RESCRIPTed...

    "I worked a lot when my kids were young, and missed some time with them. But, I can't go back and change things now. At the time, I thought making money to provide for their future was the most important thing. My priorities are different now, and so I am going to be cutting back some at work and making more time for my family."

5. "I'm such an idiot, I completely messed up by not taking part in a once in a lifetime opportunity."

    RESCRIPTed...

    "This is not my finest decision for sure and I likely missed a great opportunity. But, I am human and don't always make fabulous choices. Yet, just as I have before, I will be just fine. Wallowing in regret does me no good. I will take this as a lesson and make sure I engage similar growth opportunities in the future."

LIMITLESS LIVING LIBRARY – STRATEGIES TO RESTRICT REGRETS SECTION

In addition to these strategies, you can modify and use strategies from other chapters to restrict your regrets!

Restrict Regret Strategy #1: Helping or Harming Review

During or following your next episode of regretful thinking, ask yourself the following:

1. What is/was my purpose/intent in this episode of regretful thinking?

2. How does/did regretful thinking harm me?

3. How does/did regretful thinking help me?

4. What is/was avoided through regretful thinking?

5. What is/was addressed through regretful thinking?

6. What would I say to a friend who was thinking about regrets?

7. What more effective things could I say to myself right now?

8. What more effective strategies exist to achieve my original purpose/intent?

9. What did I learn about my regretful thinking from this review?

Restrict Regret Strategy #2:
Terminate Trying to Time Transport

Have you ever found yourself closing your eyes tightly, thinking back on that decisive moment, desperately wishing to go back in time, hoping that if you just think hard enough, maybe you'll be transported back in time to get your do over? Most of us have been there.

Whether it's something we said or did, or didn't say or do, sometimes we spend our time wondering about what would've been. We never get to travel back in time to reset a different reality; we simply mentally relive the trauma of the negative experience over and over again.

The next time you find yourself in a mental state of begging to go back, imagine yourself sitting inside the DeLorean from the movie "Back to the Future." Except, every time you press the time transport buttons, you just keep time-looping the pain, hurt, and anguish of the negative experience that occurred rather than positively changing the decision that drove it. Now, imagine that you finally realize that the only way to stop reliving the anguish is to get out of the DeLorean and Terminate Trying to Time Transport altogether. You finally recognize that the only way to diminish the hurt is to move forward, not backward. You can positively influence what's to come, without trying to change what has already happened.

Restrict Regret Strategy #3:
Cancel "The Could've Beens"

Sometimes situations arise where we wonder what could've been if we had made a different choice. Could our stories have been different? We find ourselves imagining all the better storylines that could've been possible if we had simply chosen differently. While there may be storylines we didn't get to experience as a result of our decision, wallowing in "could've been" stories discounts the value of the stories that actually are. There will always be positive relationships, opportunities, and moments we may not have experienced if we hadn't chosen as we did.

Imagine "The Could've Beens" as a pilot TV series. It's been on for weeks now, and it just keeps flipping from storyline to storyline. Some have been really good, others iffy, and some have made you sad while viewing. It's a little hard to follow and the stories and characters are not always that believable. To watch "The Could've Beens," you've been missing another series you've watched for years, "The Actually Ares." You just got a little bored with it, a bit frustrated with its storylines, maybe a tad annoyed with the characters on occasion, and started wondering what else was out there. That's what led you to start viewing "The Could've Beens." But now that you really think about it, there's a lot of things you've liked about "The Actually Ares."

Now ask yourself these questions about *your* "Actually Ares":

1. What storylines have you really liked?

2. What characters and character relationships have you enjoyed?

3. What are some key scenes that have really stood out that you loved?

So, check it out—you just heard that "The Actually Ares" has a new head writer and she's looking for viewer feedback and suggestions for future storylines.

1. What new, believable storylines would you like to see to get you feeling excited about the series again?

2. Any storylines you'd like to see less of or eliminate altogether?

3. What new, believable characters and character relationships would you like to see?

4. Any characters you'd like to see less of or write off the series altogether?

5. What are some new, believable key scenes you would love to see?

6. Any scene types you'd like to see less of or eliminate altogether?

The great thing is that in "The Actually Ares," it's YOU that is truly the writer, and you get to savor all those great storylines, character relationships, and scenes you've lived, as well as write new life into your story through the actions you take to author new storylines, character relationships, and scenes. You don't need the fake storylines of the "The Could've Beens" when you have the real ones from "The Actually Ares." Cancel "The Could've Beens" pilot series. "The Actually Ares" has some great highlights and the series isn't over yet. Keep writing!

Restrict Regret Strategy #4:
Leverage the Lesson Learned

"If I knew then what I know now, I would've..." Most of us have uttered such a phrase before. It's the indication that we feel a sense of regret over a choice we made, have learned things since, and would change that decision if we had it to make again. However, mulling over the way we'd use today's wisdom to change yesterday's choices is unproductive. However, what is productive is contemplating how we have already leveraged the lessons learned and will continue to do so.

Next time you are pondering an "I would've..." ask yourself the following questions:

1. What lessons have I learned from this situation/decision?

2. How have I already used this wisdom to positively impact my life?

3. How have I leveraged this lesson learned to help someone else in need of guidance?

4. How can I use this wisdom in similar situations?

5. How will I focus my mind on what I've gained instead of what I've lost?

Restrict Regret Strategy #5:
Self-Forgiveness Liberation Letter

When we are deep into an episode of regretful thinking, we are often very hard on ourselves. We beat ourselves up over things we believe we should've said or done differently. We might be blaming ourselves for perceived contributions to unfortunate circumstances. And, we may feel angry with ourselves for the choices we've made and any resulting negative circumstances.

The thing is, we ALL make poor choices sometimes. No person gets out of this life without some poor decisions. That doesn't mean you have to continuously torture yourself over those errors in judgment. But, how can we liberate ourselves from self-blame and regret?

We can begin by getting the regret we've been drowning ourselves in, out of us and onto paper. Get out a piece of paper, a pad, or start a Word document on your computer. Think about the focus of your regret and what specifically you are upset with yourself about.

Address your letter to your name, "Dear MyName,"

Now, begin by writing about what decision you are beating yourself up over, why, and how you've been feeling. However, refrain from using the letter as another opportunity for self-loathing or self-shaming. Then, commit to letting go of any self-punishing thoughts, emotions, and behaviors that you have engaged in since making this decision. Quiet your Inner Antagonist and amplify your Inner Advocate by sharing what self-compassionate and beneficial thoughts, emotions, and behaviors you commit to experiencing now that you have forgiven and liberated yourself.

Each time you find your mind trying to dwell again on the regretful thoughts and emotions, read this letter to yourself, quietly or aloud.

Below is a sample liberation letter.

Dear MyName,

For too long, I have been feeling angry with you for making the decision to stop speaking to your cousin, Tom, because you were told by a mutual friend that he was taking drugs again after being clean for five years. I have been upset with you because I wish you would've chosen to put aside your disappointment and judgment and reached out to Tom instead when he probably could've used your support and love. Despite being unsure in your heart of your choice, you stuck with it, and I have been angry at you for that. When Tom overdosed and passed away just a month later, I began blaming you for his death and feeling like if you just would've reached out and supported him instead, maybe he would still be alive. Losing Tom, especially after choosing not to speak with him, hurt more than anything. These regretful and blaming thoughts and feelings have been beyond torturous over this past year, and I really want to liberate us from them. You are not the awful human being I've been painting you to be and you don't deserve to be tortured like this. At that point in time, you made the choice to go with a tough love approach because you thought it made sense. When you decided not to speak to Tom, you had no idea that you would not have time to change your mind. Sometimes life gives us lots of time, sometimes it doesn't. I don't have to like the decision you made, but I do need to learn to live with it peacefully and compassionately. I am not going to emotionally and mentally abuse you over this anymore. I'm committing myself to liberating us from these toxic feelings. I'm not carrying them around anymore. I forgive you. I'm choosing to replace the toxic feelings with feelings of compassion, forgiveness, and understanding. We've learned important things

165

from this experience that we take with us. And, I'm choosing to leverage the lessons I've learned to help myself and others, and focus my thoughts on the family relationships I've strengthened as a result of this experience. I'm also choosing to treasure our memories of Tom because we had 10 times as many good memories with him than anything else.

Sincerely,
MyName

Writing and reading your letter whenever you need to helps you to truly forgive yourself and liberate yourself from a vicious cycle of self-abuse. And, it helps you to replace the self-punishment with self-compassion.

Restrict Regret Strategy #6:
Regret Narration RESCRIPTing

Consider some recent and/or long-standing regrets you have experienced in various areas of your life that have kept you stuck in a life limiting story. Using the narration RESCRIPTing examples and other illustrations from this chapter as a guide, RESCRIPT some of your regretful thoughts into statements that are more realistic, encouraging, and empowering.

What regrets will you restrict through RESCRIPTing...

1. Regarding your relationships?
   • Regretful Thought:
   • RESCRIPTed:

2. Regarding your career?
   • Regretful Thought:
   • RESCRIPTed:

3. Regarding your financial life?
   • Regretful Thought:
   • RESCRIPTed:

4. Regarding your living environment?
   - Regretful Thought:
   - RESCRIPTed:

5. Regarding your engagement within your community?
   - Regretful Thought:
   - RESCRIPTed:

6. Regarding your physical health?
   - Regretful Thought:
   - RESCRIPTed:

7. Regarding your mental and emotional health?
   - Regretful Thought:
   - RESCRIPTed:

8. Regarding your intellectual growth?
   - Regretful Thought:
   - RESCRIPTed:

9. Regarding your recreation and relaxation?
   - Regretful Thought:
   - RESCRIPTed:

10. Regarding your spirituality practices?
    - Regretful Thought:
    - RESCRIPTed:

Commit yourself to restricting your regrets!

Restrict Regret Strategy #7:
Acknowledgements & Affirmations

Here are some acknowledgements and affirmations you can recite any time you need to restrict regrets!

I acknowledge and affirm that...

- No one gets a rewind button.

- No matter how much I think about things I regret, I will never undo what's done.

- Decisions are not simply good or bad, but fall on a spectrum in between both.

- Making a mistake does not mean I must feel guilty for the rest of my life.

- Each choice I've made offers me lessons I needed to learn.

- Every decision I've made has given me wisdom to guide me with future choices.

- The knowledge I've gained from my mistakes enables me to help others through similar situations.

- Some choices I've made may have disabled some positive opportunities, relationships, and experiences, but they've also enabled different positive opportunities, relationships, and experiences.

- If there are aspects of my regrets that I am able to positively act upon, I will begin doing so, if there are not, I will use the wisdom in what I've learned.

JUSTIN'S STORY

When I first spoke with Justin, he was feeling extremely stuck in his career. He was looking for ways to begin making moves in a positive direction. However, persistent regrets were bogging him down.

Justin was a Talent Acquisition Specialist for a large technology products and services provider. It was a relatively new job at his current company, however he had held similar titles at several other technology companies throughout his career. He quickly realized that the work responsibilities in this position were below his capabilities, the job was not growing him professionally, and the workplace culture was unfriendly.

He was experiencing intense regret for taking the position because he believed he could not leave anytime soon since he had just started the job.

Justin and I did some deep career exploration together. Through this process, Justin shared that he had always wanted a Director of Talent Acquisition title, but felt he'd already ruined that trajectory by continuing to make lateral moves. He expressed regret for not trying harder to pursue a Director role.

Through the process of identifying his passions and purpose, Justin also shared that he strongly disliked the tech industry, but stayed because it's where he'd always been. His real dream had always been to work in the sports industry, but he felt it was too late to break in, and he felt regret over this as well.

Justin and I did a lot of work together on RESCRIPTing his self-talk so he could restrict the regrets he had been focusing on, and use what he'd gained and learned from his choices. We also did some strengths assessing, achievement defining, and worked to build his belief that the dreams he had were still very much within his reach.

Not long after we began working together, Justin felt ready to get back on the job market and target only Director of Talent Acquisition titles within the sports industry specifically. Justin was surprised to land an interview quickly and was offered the position he'd always wanted in the industry he'd always dreamed of working within. He also received a nice salary bump!

Restricting regrets helped Justin to get out of his own way to achieving his professional dreams.

PRACTICE #6

I- INVITE IMPERFECTION VS. INFALLIBILITY/PERFECTIONISM

"Where perfectionism exists, shame is always lurking."

~ Brené Brown

THE LIMITING SCRIPTS OF INVITING INFALLIBILITY/PERFECTIONISM

Rarely do we brag about being an "imperfection-ist." In fact, it's so uncommon that spell check is telling me that it's not even a word! However, we all know that perfectionist IS a word, and it's often one many of us use with great pride to describe ourselves. "Yes, thank you. My house is clean and organized all the time. I can't really function when it isn't. I'm such a neat freak. I suppose you could say I'm a perfectionist." So proud. Yet, so exhausting.

What is takes to maintain the standards of infallibility/perfectionism can actually make us *believe* that we cannot function when that standard isn't met. And, if we believe it strongly enough, we behave it. That means we might find ourselves in mental, emotional, and behavioral states of dysfunction and disarray when we fail to meet one of our own perfectionistic rules.

Inviting imperfection is something I've worked to embrace whole-heartedly in my own life. However, that doesn't mean the voices of perfectionism don't creep up and start yapping sometimes. You know that Inner Antagonist can be quite persistent.

For me, there was nothing like writing a book to kick my Inner Antagonist into high gear with perfectionistic demands. And, let me tell you, the demands got weirder and weirder.

"Every chapter MUST follow an identical structure."
"Every chapter MUST be the same number of pages."
"Every chapter MUST have the same number of RESCRIPTing strategies."
"Every RESCRIPT strategy MUST be alliterative." (I have an alliteration quirk, I'm sure that's been super clear though!)

What is that? What kind of bizarre rules are these anyway?

Nonetheless, in the beginning stages of writing, I was actually trying to follow these rules and demands. Fortunately, I caught that I was making up rules, acknowledged that these rules were making the writing process take way longer than it needed to, and noticed they were making me feel needlessly dissatisfied with my writing. I knew if I was going to actually complete this book, I was going to have to rewrite my rules and let this book be imperfect. Doing so was both challenging and liberating.

To liberate ourselves by inviting imperfection into our lives, we must first be willing to modify any beliefs that perfectionism is something to be proud of. Let's start by examining what it is and what it's not.

Perfectionism involves demanding unrealistically high standards for ourselves with regard to our performance or appearance, and experiencing intense distress when we do not meet these standards. Perfectionists' definition of success is often quite narrow, whereas failure is defined quite broadly—it's anything that is not the exact, narrow definition of success. This is an inaccurate definition, but when a perfectionist believes they've failed, they often perseverate on this failure, struggling to see successes or positive qualities, and sometimes even defining self-worth largely on a perceived failure. Perfectionism involves stringent self-evaluations and thus a strong desire to avoid mistakes.

One example of perfectionism might be a college student who gets an A in a course they studied vigorously for, but experiences intense disappointment, devastation, and self-criticism because their final grade for the course was a 97, not 100. Another example of perfectionism could be a person believing they have failed in their career because they were not selected for a promotion.

Perfectionism needs to be distinguished from its well-adjusted cousin—realistic high striving. Similar to perfectionists, realistic high strivers have high personal standards and a strong desire to excel and achieve. Standards provide us with a way of monitoring how we are doing in various areas of our lives. However, realistic high strivers are less rigid with their standards and move through failures with less self-criticism, greater resilience, and without allowing failures to crush their sense of self-worth. When considering the previous examples of perfectionism, a realistic high striver would experience joy and pride for their course grade of an A (97), and still be able to see themselves as professionally successful without attaining the job promotion. Hence, realistic high striving is healthy and positive, whereas perfectionism can be quite damaging.

We can be perfectionistic in some areas and realistic high strivers in others. And, we can also be realistic high strivers in an area of our lives, and then find ourselves being perfectionistic in this same area during another period. We are not all or nothing. We can vacillate. However, since perfectionism can be mentally and emotionally harmful, it's critical to develop strategies to manage and mitigate perfectionistic thoughts and behaviors when they do strike.

Why do we become perfectionistic?

Our Inner Antagonist often develops its perfectionistic standards based on observing or experiencing patterned rewards or punishment as a result of particular behaviors. Thus, like many other habits, both negative and positive, we typically learn perfectionism by seeing it role modeled by someone close to us, observing someone close to us being rewarded for successes that were achieved through perfectionistic types of behaviors or punished for particular types of failures, or by experiencing these types of rewards and punishment first-hand.

If we have a parent who engages in perfectionistic thoughts, feelings, and behaviors relevant to their weight or other aspects of physical appearance, we might model what we see, especially if we also observe rewards, such as positive attention and compliments for the results of this perfectionism. If we observe a sibling engaging in perfectionistic studying and grade striving, and also see a parent reward our sibling for positive results, we may determine that these behaviors will garner us the same rewards if we engage in them too. And, finally, if we are simultaneously involved in multiple curricular and extra-curricular activities as a child, and are consistently complimented by parents, teachers, friends, and others for how well we "juggle it all," we may surmise that being busy all the time is a necessary characteristic for being valuable and receiving respect.

It is important to note that not all children who have had such experiences will develop perfectionistic tendencies. Personality characteristics and temperament play a role as well. Some individuals may be more prone to seek recognition from others to determine self-worth. Furthermore, as is often the case, we also can take what we see and are rewarded/punished for to another level, twisting reality to make ourselves believe that rigid standards of success are the way to achieve self-worth. However, no matter what we learn or what our predispositions may be, we can always retrain ourselves to invite imperfection.

What are we perfectionistic about?

There is a plethora of things people can be perfectionistic about, but below are a few examples of areas of perfectionism. Note the very specific and narrow standards.

1. **Relationships**: Believing that a divorce indicates being a complete failure in relationships, believing that not being able to give 100% to your kids because of career responsibilities is indicative of being a failure as a parent, thinking you can never let anyone down or else you're a bad person.

2. **Career:** Believing that not getting a particular job means you are a professional failure, thinking that one or two areas of critique in your performance evaluation means you are doing a horrible job.

3. **Finance:** Believing that having any debt means you've failed at managing your money, believing that if you don't make at least $100K a year you are a financial failure.

4. **Living Environment**: Believing that if your house is ever unkempt or disordered you are failing at maintaining a home, thinking that if you don't live in a big house or mansion you have failed at success.

5. **Community Engagement**: Believing that volunteering only once a month is failing to serve your community enough, thinking that you have to work to solve every community issue you are passionate about or you aren't doing enough.

6. **Physical Health:** Thinking that not exercising every single day equates with failing at exercising, believing that eating more than 1000 calories a day is failing at healthy eating.

7. **Mental & Emotional Health**: Believing that occasionally feeling sad or angry means you are failing at being mentally and emotionally healthy, thinking that it is weak

if you spend any time at all nurturing your mental and emotional health.

8. **Intellectual Growth**: Thinking that anything less than an A (or 100) is failing academically, believing that you must be studying every day and not engaging in any non-academic activities to be a success in college.

9. **Recreation & Relaxation**: Believing that less than two vacations a year is a recreational failure, believing that allowing yourself any down time to relax means that you are lazy and unproductive.

10. **Spirituality:** Thinking that missing religious services for one week means that you've failed your faith, thinking that any unkind thought or deed means that your higher power cannot love you.

As you see in these examples, perfectionism is about rules. We all have rules that guide our lives. Perfectionistic rules are focused on achieving a very specific, rigid standard that is deemed to equate with success.

When being perfectionistic, our Inner Antagonist often wrongly assumes that we are only valuable if we are perfect, plus perfectionism is devoid of self-compassion. Perfectionists often struggle to forgive themselves for simply being human and imperfect. They believe their imperfections are reasons to experience deep shame or guilt. Shame is believing that something we've experienced or done makes us unworthy of love and connection. Guilt, on the other hand, is feeling responsibility and/or remorse for a real or perceived offense against another person. Thus, perfectionists may not want others to know their authentic selves for fear they will be shunned. These feelings may even result in challenges in genuinely connecting with others because a perfectionist may believe they must hide aspects of who they truly are. They may feel as if being seen as perfect is the next best thing to actually being perfect, so they hide imperfections. A perfectionist's harsh self-judgment feels warranted to them.

Another side of perfectionism that is damaging is wanting others, or life overall, to conform to unrealistic standards. This can also be extremely damaging to personal relationships and incite much unnecessary disappointment and angst.

How does perfectionism harm us?

Perfectionists are more likely to become depressed, anxious, or even suicidal when they do not perform according to their rules and standards. Perfectionism can provoke feelings of hopelessness, and consequently a maladaptive method of managing life's challenges and problems by avoiding them altogether. Some perfectionistic consequences are less severe than others, however perfectionism is rarely bereft of harm.

How does Inviting Imperfection RESCRIPT our story?

Inviting imperfection into our lives is a liberating experience. We allow the voice of our Inner Advocate to be amplified so we can be authentic with others, no longer having to hide our flaws from the world. We can tell others about our mistakes, screw-ups, flaws, traumas, and challenges if we wish, knowing that we are worthy of love in our entirety. We relieve ourselves of the fear, pressures, and anxiety that needing to be perfect evokes. We can be calm and self-compassionate. We can be forgiving of others' flaws and the flaws of life overall, knowing that these flaws are simply threads in life's colorful tapestry. Inviting imperfections means we get to break the rules!

SOME HIGHLIGHTS FROM RESEARCH STUDIES ON PERFECTIONISM

- Research by Jerabek and Muoio of PsychTests found that over half of those surveyed reported only feeling satisfied with a task when they've completed it perfectly, continuously worrying about making mistakes, perpetually stressing about what others think of them, and hating the thought of being labeled as average in anything.[34]

- A study by Flett, Madorsky, Hewitt, and Heisel revealed that high levels of perfectionism are correlated with rumination, intrusive thoughts, and psychological distress, including depression and anxiety.[35]

- Handley, Egan, Kane, and Rees revealed that perfectionistic thinking, including excessive concern over mistakes and having unrealistically high personal standards, increases pathological worrying and anxiety symptomatology.[36]

- Ferrari, Yap, Scott, Einstein, and Ciarrochi determined that practicing self-compassion weakens the negative impact that perfectionism has on depression symptoms.[37]

- Brené Brown has researched and written extensively on shame, vulnerability, and perfectionism, and maintains that perfectionism impedes success and often breeds depression and anxiety. Moreover, she's found that sharing our stories authentically requires self-compassion and the courage to be imperfect.[38]

LIMITING NARRATIONS OF PERFECTIONISM RESCRIPTED

Let's examine how we can RESCRIPT the stories we tell ourselves when we require infallibility and invite perfectionistic behaviors:

1. "I can't believe I just made that mistake on the exam, I'm so stupid."

   RESCRIPTed...
   "I made a pretty big mistake on that exam. But, I have been doing really well up until this point and need to forgive myself. I'm not a robot, I'm a human being. I make mistakes. I'm certainly not a failure by any means."

2. "I looked like an idiot when I didn't know the answer to that question in the meeting, I suck at this job."

RESCRIPTed…
"I got caught off guard with that question in the meeting today, but it's no big deal, I'm going to research the answer and get back to the team. No one is all knowing. But, we can all learn more and share that information."

3. "If I could just lose 20 pounds, then maybe I'd finally look good."

RESCRIPTed…
"I may not be a size 6, but I feel pretty darn good when I look in the mirror! I am very comfortable in my own skin and don't need to be supermodel thin to be beautiful."

4. "Other people seem to be able to successfully juggle work, family, and everything else, but I totally suck at it."

RESCRIPTed…
"I have a lot on my plate juggling work, family, and everything else. And, I drop more than a few balls along the way. But, no one can do it all, even when it seems like it from the outside. No one ever gets to see what happens behind all of our closed doors. We are all in this juggle struggle together!"

5. "Cindy is a much better mom than me, I always seem to mess up with my kids."

RESCRIPTed…
"When I'm scrolling through Facebook posts, it seems like Cindy is the perfect mom, managing a full-time job, PTO, soccer, gymnastics, and gourmet cooking. But, I know that no parent does it perfectly, no matter what posts may seem to reflect. I struggle to hold it all together. I bet Cindy does too. And, its fine, we are all flawed humans."

LIMITLESS LIVING LIBRARY – STRATEGIES TO INVITE IMPERFECTION SECTION

In addition to the strategies in this section, there are numerous strategies from other chapters that can be leveraged as well, with some mild modification.

Invite Imperfection Strategy #1:
Helping or Harming Review

During or following your next episode of perfectionistic thinking, ask yourself the following:

1. What is/was my purpose/intent in this episode of perfectionistic thinking?

2. How does/did this perfectionistic thinking harm me?

3. How does/did this perfectionistic thinking help me?

4. What is/was avoided through perfectionistic thinking?

5. What is/was addressed through this perfectionistic thinking?

6. What would I say to a friend who was being perfectionistic?

7. What more effective things could I say to myself right now?

8. What more effective strategies exist to achieve my original purpose/intent?

9. What did I learn about my perfectionistic thinking from this review?

Invite Imperfection Strategy #2:
Scrutinize Your "Should"-er

Let's face it, your Should-er is a nag and it's super judge-y. It guilt trips you. You'll know when its talking to you because it sounds kind of like, "I really should exercise," "I really should

179

join that committee," "I really should do them that favor," "I should be able to handle this," "I should be in a relationship by now," "I should've done a better job," "I shouldn't do this if I can't do it perfectly," and "This shouldn't bother me so much." No matter what your Should-er is saying, it generally doesn't leave you feeling great during or afterwards. Sometimes what your Should-er is saying might be something you actually *want* to do. But, other times it's *not*. Rather than blindly obeying its recommendations, Scrutinize Your Should-er to make sure it's not tied to any unrealistic, perfectionistic beliefs!

When you hear your Should-er nagging, ask yourself the following questions:

1. Is there an underlying perfectionistic belief driving this should? If so, which one?

2. Is this should in line or in conflict with my values? How?

3. Is this should in line or in conflict with my ultimate desires? How?

4. Is this should expecting something unrealistic of me? If so, what?

5. Is obeying this should potentially going to overwhelm my time and/or energy? If so, how?

6. Is obeying this should potentially going to cause any domino effect of challenges for me? If so, how?

7. Is obeying this should potentially going to leave me with negative feelings? If so, how?

8. After scrutinizing my Should-er, is its recommendation something I will follow? Why or why not?

Sometimes, we just jump right into obeying our Should-er and face a monsoon of issues because of it. Other times, we find that it just gave us a nudge to do something we wanted to do. But, before doing what it suggests, a little scrutinizing might just help us make a more informed decision and avoid any unnecessary, perfectionism-driven issues.

Invite Imperfection Strategy #3:
Rewrite Your Rules

Is your rule book keeping you trapped in a story you want to escape from? We all have rule books, even if we don't realize it. And the crazy part is that we are the ones that created them for ourselves! But for most of us, these rules are so longstanding and engrained in our minds, that they become automatic—we don't even notice we are living by them. Or if we do, we often forget the most important thing—we wrote our rulebook, so if the rules are limiting us, we can rewrite them!

We have two sets of rules—those we create for ourselves (internal) and those we create for life/others (external). For example, a rule we create for ourselves might sound something like this, "I should never let anyone know about my mistakes in life and work." A rule we create for life/others might sound something like this, "Life and people should not get in the way of my scheduled work/life plans because I take great care to create my schedule." Before we can rewrite our rules, it's helpful to understand: (1) the fears behind them, (2) their positive functions, (3) their negative functions, (4) how we've handled breaking them in the past, and (5) what we'd like to change about them. Want to start rewriting some of your limiting rules?

First, contemplate at least three limiting rules you've created for yourself and respond to the questions below. You can use the example to guide you.

Rules for Yourself
Example:

Rule #1: I should never let anyone know about my mistakes in life and work.

- I fear that if I break this rule, people will see me as a flawed fraud, will not have any respect for me, will not like me, and I will be alone.

- This rule impacts my life positively because it drives me to make well thought out decisions to some degree.

- This rule impacts my life negatively because it makes me ingenuine, feel insecure about people really knowing me, and closes me off from honest relationships.

- There have been times when I have broken this rule and shared a mistake I made with others. When I was a kid, there were times I got made fun of by classmates for a mistake in school. But, as I've gotten older, it hasn't been as negatively dramatic. Sometimes I thought a person thought less of me, but later realized they didn't. And, those who did think less of me, I ended up realizing weren't people I wanted in my life. I managed my rule breaking by retreating/walling off sometimes, and other times by telling myself it was good to be genuine, though I sometimes felt worried about what was to come.

- I'd like to change this rule by making it less rigid because it traps me in a lonely, insecure, inauthentic box where I'm afraid to be myself and let people know me fully.

- **Rule #1 Rewritten**: I will be confidently genuine about who I am, flaws and all, because all people make mistakes and it doesn't make me less worthy.

Your turn!

1. Rule for Myself #1:

- What do you fear will happen if you break this rule?

- How does this rule impact your life positively?

- How does this rule impact your life negatively?

- Have you ever broken this rule? If yes, what was the outcome? What strategies did you use to handle/manage your rule breaking?

- What would you like to change about this rule to be more realistic and compassionate with yourself?

- **Rule for Myself #1 Rewritten**:

Repeat for your other core perfectionistic rules for yourself!

Second, contemplate at least five limiting rules you've created for life/others and respond to the questions below. You can use the example to guide you.

Rules for Others & Life
Example:

Rule for Others/Life #1: Life and people should not get in the way of my scheduled work/life plans because I take great care to create my schedule.

- I fear that if life breaks this rule, it will completely mess up my whole day, possibly even my week, totally stress me out, and I won't be able to get everything I need to do done, I won't reach my ultimate goals, and then I will let people down, and they will be angry with me and think I'm irresponsible.

- This rule impacts my life positively because it makes me a very scheduled, responsible person who can get a lot done in my work, my life, and for others.

- This rule impacts my life negatively because it makes me inflexible, easily stressed by glitches, and resentful of life for being unfair and others for being inconsiderate.

- Life has broken this rule many times. Typically, it was inconveniencing, stressful, and frustrating, but I still managed to get things done, sometimes later than I wanted. Rarely did anyone get really mad at me like I feared, occasionally someone would get a little frustrated if I was late on a deadline/needed to move an appointment, but nothing life shattering. Often people surprised me by offering even more extra time than I asked for! While it was overwhelming for a period of time, it didn't last forever and I survived. To handle/manage life breaking this rule, I looked at my schedule, let people know something unexpected came up, that I needed to move an appointment/get something in a little later, apologized for the inconvenience, and made sure I came through on the new deadline/appointment.

- I'd like to make this rule less black and white, and less catastrophe-based. I want it to be kinder to others by realizing people may need me sometimes when I have something else planned and that does not make them inconsiderate, life is unfair and sometimes inconvenient, but I can deal/have dealt with it all just fine.

- **Rule for Others/Life #1 Rewritten**: Life/others will sometimes interrupt my plan/schedule and I don't need to be resentful of them for it because I can manage it without catastrophe.

Your turn!

1. Rule for Others/Life #1:

- What do you fear will happen if life/others break this rule?

- How does this rule impact your life positively?

- How does this rule impact your life negatively?

- Have life/others ever broken this rule? If yes, what was the outcome? What strategies did you use to handle/manage life/other's rule breaking?

- What would you like to change about this rule to be more realistic and compassionate with life/others?

- **Rule for Others/Life #1 Rewritten:**

Repeat for your other core perfectionistic rules for others and life overall.

The next time you catch yourself trying to enforce your old rules, remind yourself, "I made these rules and I can change them because they aren't working for me anymore. I'm going to live by my compassionately rewritten rules."

Invite Imperfection Strategy #4: Rebel Against Your Rules

Remember being a teenager? Your parents would set rules for your behavior, and whether you were bothered by those rules or not, you felt some burning desire to rebel against them? "You're not allowed to see your friends until you finish your homework!" "You can't go to that party!" "You're not allowed to go out with that boy!" "You can't stay out past midnight!"

Well today, it's your Inner Antagonist who's setting the rules—well, at least the rules that are ultra-critical, stringent, unrealistic, and largely unattainable. Except, now that you're an adult, you're past all that teenage rebellious stuff, now you're trying to be a responsible rule abider. But, what if you suspended that responsibility for a day...or two...or three...or more? What if you mustered up some of that rebelliousness from years ago, and Rebelled Against Your Rules?

When perfection is what you're striving for, the mere thought of rebelling against any of your rules might seem wrong, awful, and maybe even dangerous. We get scared about what might happen if we don't abide. The best way to find out is to try, scary as it might be.

1. **Step One**: Pick one of your perfectionistic, unrealistic, extreme, angst-provoking, life limiting rules to rebel against.

2. **Step Two**: Select a day this week to not abide! This means that when your Inner Antagonist starts barking orders, you tell it, "No!" and do not submit to its demand.

3. **Step Three**: Write down what happens or doesn't happen after your rebellion.

4. **Step Four**: Write down how you felt before, during, and after your rule rebellion, and how you coped with any negative feelings.

5. **Step Five**: Repeat with the same or another rule!

A little rebellion is good for the soul. I promise it won't turn you into a completely careless, reckless human being. We just need to balance the scales a bit. We need to remind ourselves that you've got to live a little, you've got to take a risk sometimes, you've got to trust that you won't lose control of yourself just because you do something a little differently, you're valuable and worthy beyond rules of perfection.

Invite Imperfection Strategy #5:
Share Your Shames

For someone aiming for perfection, one of the most uncomfortable things can be sharing the things you feel ashamed of with others. Doing so can induce feelings of embarrassment and vulnerability. However, practicing doing the very thing that brings us such discomfort is actually the start of liberating ourselves from perfectionism.

The object of this exercise is not to aimlessly share everything we've felt shameful about with anyone and everyone. We must, indeed, be discerning with our sharing. There will always be certain things we prefer to share with very select people, and there's nothing wrong with this. The intent of this exercise is to help us become progressively more comfortable with being authentic and vulnerable with others. This, in turn, helps us to become more comfortable with ourselves, imperfections and all.

1. **Step One:** Pick something you have felt shameful about to share with someone. When in the practicing phase, it's often easier to select something that feels less personal and less threatening to share. For example, it would likely be easier to imagine sharing, "My house is often dirty, I just hide my messes or make sure I clean really good before people come over" versus "I was arrested for shoplifting." Neither of these things we may feel shame about make us unlovable, but one is much less personal than the other.

2. **Step Two:** Select a person to share with. It can be someone close to you or someone you don't know well, whichever feels less uncomfortable. I say less uncomfortable instead of more comfortable because in the beginning, all sharing of perceived imperfections can feel pretty uncomfortable, so select the less challenging option for you.

3. **Step Three:** Write down what happens or doesn't happen after Sharing Your Shames.

4. **Step Four:** Write down how you felt before, during, and after your sharing, and how you coped with any negative feelings.

5. **Step Five:** Repeat the process with the same or a different thing you have felt shame about, with the same or a different person.

With time and repetition, Sharing Our Shames with others helps us to invite imperfections, diminishes our fear of them, and demonstrates to us that others' responses are not as terrible as we imagine, and that we are strong enough to manage perceptions of imperfection…because we are ALL imperfect and all have had feelings of shame.

Invite Imperfection Strategy #6: Get Out & Give Up Your Guilts

Guilt is one of the most painful experiences of perfectionism. We can experience guilt when we think, feel, or behave in ways we perceive as being unkind or harmful to others. Some of these perceptions are based on societal standards, while others are based on our own specific rules. People often describe guilt as weighing them down. It's a heavy emotion to carry around.

Of course, guilt is not all bad. Feeling guilt can demonstrate that we feel remorse for an act we committed that intentionally or unintentionally harmed another living being. It can demonstrate empathy. And when we use these feelings to change future actions, guilt can be positive. However, many of us struggle to let go of our guilt and instead carry it around unceasingly and allow it to eat away at us.

One way to take the weight off of us is to get out our guilts, and commit to giving them up. Contemplate some of the guilts you've been carrying around that have been weighing you down. Furthermore, contemplate the thoughts, feelings, or behaviors that commonly bring up feelings of guilt for you.

Now, practice getting them out and then commit to giving them up:

1. I have been feeling guilt because....

   - I commit to giving up this guilt because....
   - Instead of weighing myself down with guilt, I will....

Example: "I have been feeling guilt because I missed so many of my daughter's school-related and extra-curricular events during her elementary school years. I have spent a lot of time beating myself up over this, feeling like I've been a terrible mother. I commit myself to giving up this guilt because I acknowledge that the rules I've created for myself to live by as a parent have been absolutely unrealistic and as a result, my perceptions of myself as a parent have been distorted. While I would have loved to attend every one of my daughter's events, when I didn't it was because I was working in a career and position I busted my butt to achieve. Instead of weighing myself down with this guilt, I will remind myself of the times I left work early to catch my daughter's soccer games, spent my nights and non-working weekends having fun with my husband and daughter, and used my vacation time to go on trips with my family. I've spent real quality time with my daughter having deep conversations, listening to her dreams, and offering her guidance. Plus, I've role modeled a strong work ethic, love, and shown her that a woman can achieve success and happiness professionally and personally. I will also role model a mom who is confident in her choices, and not berating herself all the time. I will replace my guilty thoughts and feelings with focusing my mind and heart on my love for my daughter, and the ways I show her that love."

2. I often feel guilt when....

- I commit to giving up this guilt because....
- Instead of weighing myself down with guilt, I will....

Example: "I often feel guilty when I can't give as much time as I'd like to helping someone who needs help, or when I am unable to help due to other commitments. I commit to giving up this guilt because I realize I set a completely unrealistic standard for myself when it comes to this. I recognize that I am only one person and cannot give 100% help to everyone 100% of the time. Feeling guilty over this is kind of like punishing myself for not really doing anything wrong, just for being a human being. Instead of weighing myself down with this guilt, I will simply offer what help I can, when I can within reasonable bounds of what I have going on in my life. If I must say no, I will say no, without guilt, knowing that a person cannot say yes to everything and still have time to sleep. I will remind myself that no one expects this type of standard from me except me and since I set the standard, I can change it to one that is kinder to me!"

Once you've gotten out and given up your guilts, read your statements any time you need a reminder of how your guilt doesn't serve you. No one does everything flawlessly. We all make choices that result in benefits and drawbacks. That's just life.

Acknowledging these realities is healthy, kicking the crap out of yourself over them is not.

Invite Imperfection Strategy #7: Catch & Cut the Social Comparisons

Social comparison is a soul killer. You talk to others or go on social media and hear/see what you *think* are people's perfect lives, and you start nitpicking all the imperfections in your own life by comparison. By the end of this social comparison episode, you are feeling awful about all the ways you think you're failing in life. Not cool. Cut it out. Your Inner Antagonist's volume needs to be turned down.

The next time you catch yourself in social comparison, mulling over how imperfect you and your life are in comparison to someone else's, ask yourself the following questions:

1. On a scale from 1 to 10, how certain am I that this person/their life is perfect?

2. What information do I *not* have about this person's life that might debunk my theory that they/their life is perfect?

3. What am I afraid will happen if this person might be more perfect than me?

4. Can I survive if this person is stronger at something than I am? How?

5. How is comparing myself to this person helping me?

6. How is comparing myself to this person harming me?

7. What thoughts and actions will I implement to cut the comparison habits?

8. What will I tell myself the next time I catch myself comparing myself to someone else?

Your story is your story. Their story is their story. Yours isn't their business and theirs isn't your business. Comparing yourself to others can get us caught up in harmful perfectionistic flaw-finding. Live and love the journey you're on, the imperfections are part of the ride—*everyone's* ride has them. We just aren't privy to knowing everyone else's.

Invite Imperfection Strategy #8:
Favorite Facets of My Flaws

As much as we each have strengths, we also have imperfections—the things we struggle with. We can either worry that we are unlovable because of them and attempt to hide these imperfections from others, or we can embrace them as part of the tapestry of our unique beauty. However, there are often facets of these imperfections that offer us something uniquely cool. When we intentionally examine and identify our Favorite Facets of Our Flaws, we learn to love ourselves wholly, authentically, and without need for some unrealistic standard of perfection.

1. What are some things you have considered to be personal flaws?

2. What are some of your favorite facets of those flaws?

3. How do you plan to own and rock those favorite flaws of yours?

Here's some of mine!

- Some have called me long-winded. I know it takes me a while to say what I want to say. If a message can be delivered in a sentence, I'll deliver it in 20. I used to feel embarrassed about this. I felt like people were thinking, "Spit it out already!" Now, I love this flaw because I view it as a key reason I have made a living teaching, speaking, coaching, and writing. Some may call it long-winded—I call it comprehensive. I think really hard about what I want to say and I make sure I leave no page unturned. I give complete scenarios!

- I have talked to lots of people over the years that recall their college years as some of the best of their lives because of how engaged and involved they were on campus. I was a super mediocre college student. I had more Cs and C+s than I can count. I didn't do any leadership on campus, didn't talk to advisors, didn't get involved socially, and made all kinds of academic and personal mistakes. For so long, I felt like these years were some kind of hideous stain on my life, especially when I transformed into "perfectionism girl" in grad school. Fortunately, these stained, bruised, marred years of my life are among my favorite flaws. My favorite facets of my college performance flaws are how it has helped me to be a better teacher and advisor to my students. I genuinely understand my students' struggles, mistakes, and anxieties. And, I can guide them from a place of deep empathy, understanding, and personal learning. I can also assure them that these challenges are just a chapter in a riveting story that will have its ups and downs, but never a chapter where falling down means staying down forever.

Invite Imperfection Strategy #9:
Perfectionistic Narration RESCRIPTing

Consider some recent and/or long-standing perfectionistic thoughts you've had in various areas of your life that have kept you stuck in a life limiting story. Using the narration RESCRIPTing examples and other illustrations from this chapter as a guide, RESCRIPT some of your perfectionsitic thoughts into statements that are more realistic, encouraging, and empowering.

What imperfections will you invite through RESCRIPTing...

1. Regarding your relationships?
   - Perfectionistic Thought:

- RESCRIPTed:

2. Regarding your career?
   - Perfectionistic Thought:
   - RESCRIPTed:

3. Regarding your financial life?
   - Perfectionistic Thought:
   - RESCRIPTed:

4. Regarding your living environment?
   - Perfectionistic Thought:
   - RESCRIPTed:

5. Regarding your engagement within your community?
   - Perfectionistic Thought:
   - RESCRIPTed:

6. Regarding your physical health?
   - Perfectionistic Thought:
   - RESCRIPTed:

7. Regarding your mental and emotional health?
   - Perfectionistic Thought:
   - RESCRIPTed:

8. Regarding your intellectual growth?
   - Perfectionistic Thought:
   - RESCRIPTed:

9. Regarding your recreation and relaxation?
   - Perfectionistic Thought:
   - RESCRIPTed:

10. Regarding your spirituality practices?
    - Perfectionistic Thought:
    - RESCRIPTed:

Commit yourself to inviting imperfection!

Invite Imperfection Strategy #10: Acknowledgements & Affirmations

Here are some acknowledgements and affirmations you can recite any time you need to invite imperfection!

I acknowledge and affirm that...

- There is no actual standard for perfect because everyone defines it differently.

- My perfectionism filter sometimes hears others' comments with harsh meaning about me that was not actually part of their message.

- I will embrace ALL of who I am.

- I make mistakes sometimes that cause challenges for me and occasionally others, and I'm using what I learn instead of emotionally beating myself up.

- Sometimes I drop one of the many balls I am juggling in the air, and I know I am still just as competent.

- I created the rules for perfection that I've been living by, so I can revamp them into self-compassionate, realistic rules to strive high while embracing my imperfections.

- I can share all of who I am with others, imperfections included, knowing that every part of me deserves love.

- I do not have to carry guilt for all the ways I've been imperfect, I can give up my guilts knowing that beating myself up for my mistakes doesn't make anything better.

- I do not need to do all things perfectly to be valuable, everyone has their own journey and I will own and love the imperfect journey I am on.

MELODY'S STORY

When Melody and I first spoke, it was immediately evident that she had very high standards for herself in every area of her life—especially her relationships and career. And while high standards can be healthy and positive, the rules Melody had been setting for herself were highly unrealistic, and impossible to achieve. As a result, Melody was often beating herself up feeling like a failure at home and at work.

When Melody completed the Rewrite Your Rules exercise, one of the rigid perfectionistic rules she discovered was that she believed she should never let anyone down. She defined this so stringently that she usually said yes to everyone's requests of her, and thus frequently felt overwhelmed with everything she had on her plate, particularly at work. She felt she needed to do work in the morning before she went to the office, when she got home after 5pm, and often on the weekends in order to keep up with everything she'd committed herself to so she didn't let anyone down at work. Furthermore, whenever her daughter or husband said anything less than complimentary, Melody perceived it as if she'd failed them by somehow not doing enough, which helped to facilitate arguments and rifts if her relationships with them.

Melody and I did a lot of work together on rewriting her rules and speaking calmly and compassionately to herself. She practiced setting boundaries on what she would and would not do in and outside of work, despite the discomfort of letting someone down. She listened more closely to and scrutinized her should-er in order to decipher if it was suggesting a genuine want or a perfectionistic demand. She worked to acknowledge her limits while recognizing these limits did not equate with incompetence.

Through our RESCRIPTing work, Melody made some transformational changes in her life. She started saying no confidently when a should or perfectionistic rule to please set in. She began making her time and emotional/mental well-being a greater priority. She RESCRIPTed her rules when she caught herself demanding that she obey them. Furthermore, she worked on hearing her loved ones and colleague's words without her critical, auditory filter, recognizing that it was her own perfectionistic rules that made their words sound like criticisms.

Melody ultimately set greater boundaries between her personal and professional life, allowing her time away from work, and enabling a more reasonable work schedule in the office. Even more important to Melody, her relationships with her husband and daughter progressively became more and more harmonious. She and her husband also became closer once she invited imperfections. Melody also shared that she developed a very close and authentic relationship with her daughter, the kind she'd always dreamed of.

PRACTICE #7

P- PURSUE PASSION & PURPOSE VS. PUTTING UP WITH PASSIVITY

"To have meaning, our lives require both passion and purpose. A life without passion is like a furnace without fuel, and without purpose, like a ship without a rudder."

~ Mardy Grothe

THE LIMITING SCRIPTS OF PUTTING UP WITH PASSIVITY

"I just feel like I'm stuck in a rut." I hear this a lot when clients first reach out to me. This rut often refers to the ways life has come to feel plain and predictable. We get stuck in ruts like these because somewhere along the way, we resign ourselves to believing this might just be all there is to life. Maybe it's supposed to just be routine all the time, maybe it's not supposed to feel exciting anyway. This is passivity—submitting to the belief that life (or any given area of our lives) is destined to become habitual, stale, and a daily grind we simply have to put up with and push through. When we put up with passivity, we might begin to believe that a life fueled by passion and purpose isn't a real thing people can even have. This belief is one of many ways our Inner Antagonist keeps us stuck and stagnant.

Passion lies in *what* we love to do and be engaged in—these are activities that bring us joy and experiences we love so much we can lose track of time when doing them. Purpose, on the other hand, lies in the *why* behind the things we do—the missions, values, or beliefs that inspire us to do what we do and ignite a sense of meaning and calling to serve a cause that's bigger than us. And despite how we may sometimes feel, we *can* experience both passion and purpose in our lives. However, putting up with passivity is an obstacle we must overcome in this pursuit.

Why do we put up with passivity?

We see it modeled. Sometimes we saw our parents or others close to us putting up with passivity when we were growing up. We may also have seen it modeled on TV and in movies. We may have watched and heard talk of routine, how practical work is more important than being passionate about work, how mission and service doesn't pay the bills, or how we should enjoy being young because there's no time for play and fun once you're an adult. And we started to believe there was some trade-off that happened once we grew up. In actuality, there doesn't have to be a trade-off at all. We can have practicality, passion, and purpose all at once if we believe we can.

We buy into the language and message we hear. "You know, the same old, same old." "Just doing the daily grind." "Same shit, different day." "Same thing, day in and day out." "Same old story." These are just a few of the very common phrases people say when asked, "How've you been?" First, we hear it. Next, we start saying it. Then, we start believing it. If we say something enough, we assume we must be saying it because it's true. We make it our truth. We must start saying something different to create a new, more passionate, more purposeful truth.

We get caught up in just getting things done. Projects at the office, errands at home—there will always be things that just need to get done. There's deadlines and consequences if we don't meet them, so we make the endless projects and errands a priority. When we contemplate anything else beyond what has to get done, it makes our brains tired. 'Want to do' activities get pushed aside, passion and purpose-driven projects become viewed as luxury not necessity. And, in the short-term, perhaps we can survive. But in the long-term, without passion and purpose fueling us, we lose steam and fizzle out. We lose power, lose direction, and simply stand still.

What are we passive about?

We can become passive in one or various areas of our lives. Below are some examples of Inner Antagonistic thoughts relevant to putting up with passivity.

1. **Relationships:** Believing that our time to have a romantic relationship has passed and there's no point to getting back out there, thinking that marriages/long-term romantic relationships are supposed to get dull after time, thinking kids today are just into technology so there's no point trying to do other kinds of fun things as a family, believing that once you're settled into life and work your time for having a fun night out with friends is over, thinking it's impossible to find friends you can trust and who share your values, there's no point in talking with strangers while I'm out doing things because why should I connect with people I don't even know and may never see again.

2. **Career:** Believing that your job just needs to pay the bills, thinking that nobody likes their job so why should you care if you hate yours, believing that if you didn't find a career that feels meaningful by now then you never will, thinking that purpose-driven careers can't pay the bills, thinking that you're trapped in your job because you've got responsibilities.

3. **Finance:** Believing that the financial goals you once dreamed of are just impossible so why bother trying anymore, thinking that putting any money towards a passion or purpose-driven project is impractical when you have bills to pay.

4. **Living Environment**: Believing that the house projects you want to get started on are just too much work so you should forget about them, thinking that making that move to a new city/state/country is just not in the cards for you.

5. **Community Engagement**: Believing that if you have not yet figured out what causes matter most to you then you never will, thinking that if you haven't gotten involved in bettering your community yet then it's too late to start now, thinking that speaking up and taking action in the community for what you believe in is useless because nobody is going to listen to you anyway, believing you can't make any real change in the world because you're just one person.

6. **Physical Health:** Thinking that if you haven't already gotten into a healthy eating or exercise routine by now then you never will, believing it just takes too much energy to make health changes and you don't have time for all that.

7. **Mental & Emotional Health**: Believing that you're just an anxious or depressive kind of person and there's really nothing you can do to change that, thinking that most people really aren't all that happy anyway so you should just get used to feeling dissatisfied with life.

8. **Intellectual Growth**: Thinking that it's too late or just not possible to work on a new degree or certification, believing our time to learn a new subject/topic has passed.

9. **Recreation & Relaxation**: Thinking that if you haven't figured out what hobbies you are passionate about by now you aren't going to, believing that the activities you used to love doing are a thing of the past because you have real life responsibilities now, thinking that nobody has time to relax and recharge anymore so why bother trying to find time.

10. **Spirituality:** Believing that you'll never figure out your greater purpose if you haven't yet, thinking that a higher power may have a plan and purpose for some people but maybe not you.

How does putting up with passivity harm us?

When we get stuck in a rut by putting up with passivity, we begin to lose a sense of hope for the future and overall zest for life. We feel like maybe there's nothing more than what already is. We lose energy and motivation to believe in and work towards a life that feels more passionate and purposeful. We wonder if a life with more engagement, meaning, inspiration, and joy is even a possibility. This kind of passivity can lead to feeling despondent due to believing we are trapped in a stagnant story.

How does pursuing passion and purpose RESCRIPT our story?

A life of passion and purpose is a life with an empowered Inner Advocate. When we believe in and live our lives with passion, we experience greater happiness, life satisfaction, gratitude, hope, achievement motivation, and even self-confidence. We are also more likely to be kind to others and experience less envy. Having a sense of life purpose gives us foundation and direction, as well as increases our happiness and life satisfaction. And, when we have passion and purpose in our career specifically, we experience greater work commitment, job satisfaction, balance between work and other areas of life, and less job burnout. And, there's no time in our lives when living with passion and purpose isn't beneficial. Older adults/seniors who engage in life with passion and purpose also experience increased happiness, life satisfaction, zest, and excitement, as well as decreased feelings of sorrow and disappointment.

One of the things I'm most grateful for is allowing my passions and purpose to drive my direction in all areas of my life, especially within my career. There were times when doing so made perfect sense, others when I discovered new aspects of my passions and purpose by taking chances on unknown opportunities, and times when following my passion and purpose appeared to be the less practical thing to do, but I took a calculated risk anyway.

When contemplating career passions and potential college majors at the young age of 17, all I knew was that I loved to write (English major?) and I loved to help people (Psychology major?). These were my two most consistent passions. After much introspection and some guidance from my parents, I chose to declare a major in Psychology, and left behind a potential career in writing...or so I thought.

While majoring in Psychology at Rutgers University - Douglass College, I discovered a passion for abnormal psychology. I considered pursuing a career as a psychiatric hospital psychologist. To get a feel for the work, I completed a week-long externship at a psychiatric hospital. It was one of the most amazing experiences of my life. However, I came to believe it may not be the right fit for me as some of the psychologists there expressed discontent due to the challenges of impacting lasting, positive change for many of their patients. I had also spent two years in college working as a Therapeutic Assistant with teens in foster care who were experiencing emotional difficulties. I loved this role, my connection with the teenagers, and enjoyed the experience of making a positive impact. It was this work experience that began to more clearly define what I believe to be my guiding life purpose—to help others see all the good in themselves, others, and life overall. This position also led me to apply to graduate programs in Counseling Psychology with a redefined intent of becoming a family psychologist.

During my first year of graduate school at the Rutgers Graduate School of Education, I asked my advisor/mentor if the program was connected with any field work opportunities working with families or teens. She told me that she would investigate this for me, but in the meantime, her colleague at Career Services was looking for an intern and I should set up a meeting with her. I had no idea what career counselors did, but I set up that meeting. It led to a two-year long career counseling internship and essentially was the pivotal experience that guided much of my subsequent career trajectory.

My supervisor's initial vision for me was that I would work predominantly with the first-year students, helping them to choose a major. I did enjoy that work, particular the career and personality assessment process. However, I stumbled upon something I enjoyed much more—helping students write their résumés, cover letters, and graduate school personal statements. All of a sudden, my passion for writing was fusing with my passion for helping people, and it felt like magic to me. I also truly loved helping students search online for jobs and graduate programs, which ignited a passion for all things research. I asked my supervisor if I could do more of the writing and research work with students and she gave me the green light.

While interning at Career Services, I also acquired a few Research Assistant positions with faculty members, as well as a position as an Academic Coach at the Learning Center. As an Academic Coach, I helped students develop their study skills, and inadvertently learned how to study properly myself. I also helped them assess their learning styles, and once again found I really enjoyed assessing students' uniqueness and helping them use it for their ultimate success. My next position as a Residence Hall Director for my final three years of graduate school solidified a new career trajectory in the helping professions. I no longer wished to work with families, I wanted to work with college students.

And after completing my doctoral degree, that's just what I did. I got a position counseling and advising first-generation, low-income college students, and I absolutely loved working with my students. I was expressing all of my passions and I felt I was fulfilling my greater purpose. I had an idea to start providing résumé, cover letter, and graduate personal statement writing services. I pitched it to my supervisors, and got the green light again. I also had another wonderful mentor who introduced me to teaching, which had once been my greatest fear, and I discovered that I loved it. I was getting to live my passions and fulfil my purpose in numerous ways. But, I felt that I wanted to make an impact on a more macro level, so I pursued a management position.

Three years out of graduate school, I became the director for two programs serving first-generation, low-income college students. I was getting to make major programmatic changes and launching career development and academic initiatives that benefited students as a larger group and it was wonderful. During this time, I also started a side business writing résumés because I loved it so much. I had been writing résumés as a hobby for fun, for family, friends, and friends of friends for many years, so I started the side business essentially to earn while I played. I was also teaching one class per semester at my local community college during that time.

Then, a year later, my son was born and I gave up the résumé writing and teaching to spend my time outside of full-time work with my son and husband. We were blessed to have my parents and in-laws alternating providing care for our son while my husband and I were at the office. However, my desire to have more time with my son, in conjunction with missing résumé writing and teaching, made me feel much less passionate and purposeful in my full-time program director role. As much as I adored my students, my heart was telling me I needed a career shift in order to be true to my evolving passions and purpose.

After six months of planning, I decided to resign from my salaried position to pursue full-time entrepreneurship. It was a risk and I was rightfully scared. But, I literally felt like I was being called by something bigger than me to make the change. So I did. I started writing resumes during the day while home with my son, and teaching a few classes per semester at my two alma-maters at night after my husband arrived home from work.

Once my son started preschool, I began doing individual career and life coaching too, which allowed me to do more assessment again. Connections I made led me to serving as a co-author in several self-help and career books, and co-authoring articles in psychology academic journals. And, one of these books led me to facilitate community wellness groups focused on optimism. The writing career I thought I gave up on before it ever began, at the age of 17, had found its way back to me. My work today is split between writing and helping, the two passions that have been with me all along. And, through these passions, I get to fulfil my greater purpose of helping others identify and honor all the good within and around them.

I strongly believe that we thrive most when we express our passions and purpose in our life and work. We can do this through career changes/transitions, concurrent roles, comprehensive roles, or through activities outside of work, such as volunteer work, hobbies, and relational activities with family and friends. Our passions and greater purpose are likely to evolve over time and we must evolve our roles with them for sustainable happiness at work and in life overall.

SOME HIGHLIGHTS FROM RESEARCH STUDIES ON PASSION & PURPOSE

- Research by Froh, Kashdan, Yurkewicz, Fan, Allen, and Glowacki indicates that youth with high levels of passion to help others and engagement in activities experience greater happiness, life satisfaction, gratitude, hope, and self-esteem, as well as less depression, envy, antisocial behaviors, and delinquency.[39]

- A study by Bundick found that those who engage in discussions about their values, life goals, and purpose experience higher levels of goal directedness and life satisfaction.[40]

- Vallerand, Paquet, Philippe, and Charest discovered that those who experience greater harmonious passion (an internal desire that leads people to want to engage in an activity they enjoy) experience increased work satisfaction, decreased work conflict with other areas of their life, and less work burnout.[41]

- A study by Duffy, Bott, Allan, Torrey, and Dik demonstrated that those who feel they have a calling and are living their calling experience greater career commitment, work meaning, and job satisfaction.[42]

- Berg, Grant, and Johnson found that individuals with unfulfilled professional callings found other ways to pursue meaning by taking on new work tasks that related to their calling, changing their perception of the meaning of their job by aligning it with a larger pro-social purpose, and engaging in meaningful volunteer activities outside of work, which enhanced happiness and sense of purpose.[43]

LIMITING NARRATIONS OF PUTTING UP WITH PASSIVITY RESCRIPTED

Let's examine how we can RESCRIPT the stories we tell ourselves when we put up with passivity:

1. "I hate Mondays, it's back to the grind again."

   RESCRIPTed...
   "Lately, I've been dreading Mondays. I need to spice things up at work and pitch this project idea I have that I'm really excited about!"

2. "I do this job for the money, so what if its soul-sucking work."

   RESCRIPTed...
   "This job may pay fantastically, but the work is zapping my energy. It's time for a change! I'd rather make a little less and love the work I do every day! I'm ready to pursue a dream I once thought I left behind. It's never too late."

3. "I feel like every day is just the same routine, over and over."

RESCRIPTed...

"I may live by routines in some fashion, but I always ignite excitement into my days by taking on new challenges, furthering my learning through online courses, and visiting places I've never traveled to."

4. "I guess at my age, I have to get used to the fact that my days of excitement are over."

RESCRIPTed...

"I may be a midlife woman, but I still pursue projects I am passionate about, like my art, writing, and music. As long as I am living, there will be a fire within me!"

5. "Some people are lucky enough to do work that feels meaningful, but I'll never be."

RESCRIPTed...

"While I sometimes feel removed from the greater mission of my company, I often remind myself that the work I do behind the scenes has a greater purpose of making people's lives simpler. That gives me a sense of meaning. I also make sure I do volunteer work in my community, which serves a greater purpose through helping those in need."

LIMITLESS LIVING LIBRARY - STRATEGIES TO PURSUE PASSION & PURPOSE SECTION

In addition to these strategies, you can modify and use strategies from other chapters to pursue your passion and purpose!

Pursue Passion & Purpose Strategy #1: Helping or Harming Review

During or following your next episode of thinking you should put up with passivity, ask yourself the following:

1. What is my purpose/intent in putting up with passivity?

2. How does putting up with passivity harm me?

3. How does putting up with passivity help me?

4. What is avoided through putting up with passivity?

5. What is addressed through putting up with passivity?

6. What would I say to a friend who was putting up with passivity?

7. What more effective things could I say to myself right now?

8. What more effective strategies exist to achieve my original purpose/intent?

9. What did I learn about my putting up with passivity from this review?

Pursue Passion & Purpose Strategy #2: Prohibit the Passive Phrases

Pay close attention to the limiting, passive phrases you tell yourself and others that keep you living without the passion and purpose that could make life limitless. These phrases might sound something like:

- "I'm just the type of person/I'm just not the type of person that…"

- "I'm just naturally/not naturally…"

- "I just have tendencies to…"

- "That's just/just not how I am…"

- "It's just not possible for me to…"

- "That's just the way my life always goes"

- "That's just the way _____ always turns out for me"

- "That's just the way life is"

- "Oh well, I guess this is as good as things are gonna get for me"

- "Oh well, what can you do anyway?"

Remember, we typically believe the things we say, even if we don't have any proof that they're true! When you catch yourself saying limiting, passive phrases like these, ask yourself the following questions:

1. Who says that's how I have to be/life has to be/this has to be?

2. Why do I want to let myself believe something that is keeping me stuck?

3. What passionate/purposeful phrases can I tell myself instead to get me unstuck?

Prohibit the Passive Phrases you are telling yourself. Give yourself the opportunity to live with passion and purpose!

Pursue Passion & Purpose Strategy #3: Identify Your Inspirations

There are times in life when we find ourselves genuinely inspired by the traits and deeds of others. Perhaps it's someone we know or someone we've read, learned, or heard about. When we are trying to discover our own passions and purpose, it can help to contemplate who inspires us and why.

1. Who are three people who inspire you the most?

2. What is it about these individuals' characteristics and contributions to the world that inspire you?

3. How did these individuals accomplish the things they did? What resources did they leverage? How did they overcome obstacles?

4. What passions and purposes are embodied through these individuals' characteristics and contributions?

5. What aspects of these passions and purposes feel most connected to what matters most to you?

By reviewing your responses, determine how you will use your inspirations to guide your life and work with greater passion and purpose!

Pursue Passion & Purpose Strategy #4: Leave Your Legacy

When considering our purpose in the world, it helps to think about what legacy we hope to leave after we are gone. Each of us has an undetermined number of years on this planet. However, the way we use those years helps establish what aspects of our time here lives on well beyond our physical presence. Let's contemplate the legacy you hope to leave.

1. What moments have you felt you were doing what you were put on this planet to do?

2. What times in your life did you do something that made you feel connected to something greater than you?

3. What values help guide how you live your life?

4. What mottos do you live by?

5. What adversities have you overcome in life and how can you use your experience to help others?

6. How do you most commonly enjoy helping others?

7. If you could write a book to help the world, what would it be about?

8. If you could invent something to change the world, what would it be?

9. If you could teach others anything, what knowledge would you impart?

10. What positive impact do you want to be remembered for?

11. What do you want others to say about you and your life when you are gone?

Review your responses to the questions above. Now ask yourself:

1. What small steps can you begin to take immediately to ensure you leave your legacy?

2. What bigger steps can you plan out to ensure that you leave your legacy?

Your life matters. Your actions leave imprints of your heart, soul, and purpose on others and this world long after you are gone. Own your legacy.

Pursue Passion & Purpose Strategy #5: Champion Your Cause(s)

Passion and purpose are often stirred within us based upon particular issues and causes in the world. To help uncover what brings us a sense of meaning and engagement in something bigger than us, we can hone in on the causes that get our blood flowing. Let's examine the causes that matter to you.

1. What issues discussed on the news get you fired up and why?

2. What TV commercials or other advertisements related to particular causes or non-profit associations invoke strong emotions for you? What types of emotions?

3. What world problems would you love to fix and why?

4. What injustices in the world spark a desire in you to fight and why?

5. What local or global community service projects have you done or wish you could do and why?

Now that you've examined the causes you feel passionate about, let's contemplate how you can begin to Champion Your Cause(s). While giving funds is a wonderful way to contribute to causes we care about, it often brings us a much greater sense of meaning and purpose when we become more directly engaged in volunteering our time to cause(s). However, we often don't know exactly how to go about doing that. Fortunately, there are some great resources available to help us. One of my favorites is www.volunteermatch. org. On VolunteerMatch, you can sort volunteer opportunities by location (physical location or virtual/online), keywords, and cause areas. You can learn about the frequency of volunteering, tasks involved, and who to contact to inquire further and get started. Let's explore!

Based upon your responses to the questions above, go on VolunteerMatch and begin to explore options available to volunteer in order to Champion Your Cause. Select your top 10 favorite volunteer options to explore. Email and CALL the sites to get more information. Once you've done all your research, commit to the volunteer opportunity that feels most in line with your cause(s) and your needs!

Pursue Passion & Purpose Strategy #6:
Mold Your Work Around Your Mission(s)

Whether you are working in a career you want to remain in or defining new career pursuits, you can always Mold Your Work Around Your Mission. A mission is the greater good behind your work. Sometimes when we start a career, we understand our work mission, but lose that feeling of being mission-driven over time. Other times, we haven't even considered the greater mission of our specific job/role. Examining or reexamining our work mission is vital for infusing a feeling of meaning and purpose in our careers. Let's examine your work's mission!

1. Who are the direct and indirect customers your work serves/will serve?

2. How does/will your work enhance the work or life of your direct and indirect customers?

3. What work projects and work problem solving has felt the most meaningful and rewarding for you?

4. What different careers have you contemplated because the mission seemed meaningful and rewarding?

5. What are your greatest work strengths and how do you want to use them to serve your work mission?

Using your responses above, now answer the following:

1. What do you feel is/are your most important work mission(s)?

2. How can you mold your current work activities and intentions more around your mission(s)?

3. If you decide you want to leave your current role, what other career pursuits or jobs resonate with your mission(s)?

4. What actions can you start taking now to move towards work that is molded around your mission(s)?

Utilize tools from the Engage Growth Goals chapter to draw out an action plan with short and long-term activities you can implement to Mold Your Work Around Your Mission!

Pursue Passion & Purpose Strategy #7: Value Your Voice

Passion and purpose don't just get expressed through our paid work and volunteer initiatives, they get expressed in the conversations we have with family, friends, and strangers, and in the other ways we use our voice to speak up for what we believe in. However, to use our voice, we must first Value Our Voice. Too many times we remain silent about the injustices we hear about and see on/in the media or right in front of us. Our silence can be based in fear, and sometimes those fears are based in believing our words are not important and won't have an impact. Our voices have value—when we use them, we can influence (but not control) thoughts, feelings, and actions. We can even inspire others to use their voices as well. And in doing so, we can feel pride in the knowledge that we've given value and new life to our passions and purpose.

Practice valuing your voice in your private and public conversations. Others may not always agree, they may even argue, but we don't need validation or permission. We can live without it. When we are speaking on behalf of the greater good, to disrupt injustices, to empower compassion, we are living with passion and purpose.

Pursue Passion & Purpose Strategy #8: Zero in on Your Zone

When you engage in work and activities that light your fire, it feels great! We all have moments when we feel in the zone, totally immersed in an activity we really love. These moments can occur in any of the key areas of our lives. The more time we spend on our passions, the more alive and motivated we feel. Let's explore your passions and Zero in on Your Zone!

1. When was the last time you could barely sleep because you were so excited about something you were working on?

2. What activities do you enjoy so much and get so immersed in that you lose track of time when doing them?

3. When you've had free time to surf the internet, what topics do you get absorbed in researching and exploring?

4. What section of the bookstore can you get totally engrossed in while browsing through?

5. What classes have you taken where you were so into what you were learning that the time just flew by?

6. What topics of conversation have you engaged in with someone that felt so interesting that you stopped noticing everything else going on around you?

In reviewing your responses, what activities and topics get you feeling in the zone, totally engaged in what you are doing? Now that you have Zeroed in on Your Zone, make consistent time in your life and schedule to pursue these passions!

Pursue Passion & Purpose Strategy #9:
Lifelong Adventure Agenda

Imagine that for the rest of your life, from today forward, you are on a lifelong adventure. You can go anywhere and do anything you want. No time, money, capability restrictions, or situational impediments at all. Let's brainstorm what your adventure will be like!

1. What cities, states, countries, and sites are on your itinerary?

2. What important items are you packing to take with you and why?

3. How will you get to your destinations?

4. Who will be coming along on your adventure and why?

5. Who will you meet along your journey?

6. What activities will you be engaging in?

7. What will you be learning and how will you be learning it?

8. What and how will you be contributing to the people and places you visit?

9. How often and in what ways will you rest and recharge on your journey?

10. What else will you be doing on your adventure?

11. When will you be doing what?

Now that you've brainstormed and dreamed, contemplate how you might transform some of these dreams into realities.

1. What research would you need to do?

2. What steps would you need to take?

3. What internal and external resources will you leverage?

4. How will you plot out your adventures weekly/monthly/ yearly to accomplish them?

Use your responses to design your Lifelong Adventure Agenda with adventures and potential dates. You can use tools from the Engage Growth Goals chapter to help you. Begin taking the small steps needed to embark on your passion and purpose adventures!

**Pursue Passion & Purpose Strategy #10:
Make Your Passions a Priority**

When we have lots on our plate, often the first things we toss in the trash are our passions and purpose projects. We tell ourselves things like, "I just don't have time for that right now," "It's just not a priority," "It's not a good time right now," or "My passions have no deadlines like everything else, so no one will be upset if I don't do this right now." The thing is—your responsibilities aren't going to magically disappear to make enough room for your passions and YOU'LL be upset if you don't make your passions a priority!

Make your own benchmarks and deadlines for your passion project actions, and put your passions on your calendar. Use the planning tools from the Engage Growth Goals chapter to help you take action on your passions. You work hard and deserve to have your passions come to fruition in your life. Amplify your Inner Advocate and Make Your Passions a Priority!

**Pursue Passion & Purpose Strategy #11:
Professional Passions & Values Appraisal**

Whether we are in high school, college, or a working professional contemplating a new career, we need simple and accessible tools to uncover what career options exist that we might feel passionate about and that are aligned with our values. Fortunately, there are some excellent tools online that are free to use! Wondering what your career passions and values might be?

Step 1: Complete the My Next Career Move Interest Profiler at: www.mynextmove.org/explore/ip. There are 60 questions (10 for each of the six interest categories). They are scored on a 5-point

Likert Scale from a possible score of 0 (lowest) to 4 (highest). The lowest score for an entire interest category is 0 and the highest possible score is 40. In theory, a score of 0 represents extreme disinterest, scores of 1 – 10 represent disinterest, scores of 11 – 20 represent neutrality, scores of 21 – 30 represent interest, and scores of 31 – 40 represent extreme interest. However, even if your highest scores are on the lower end, it still can indicate your strongest interests among the six categories.

Step 2: Read about your top three interest areas on the O*Net Online website: www.onetonline.org/find/descriptor/browse/Interests

Step 3: Use the drop-down menus at www.onetonline.org/explore/interests/Social to select your top three interest categories learned from the My Next Career Move Interest Profiler. First, search by your top three interests in order of highest, second highest, and third highest. For example, Social + Artistic + Enterprising. Then, search Social + Artistic. Then, Social + Enterprising. Then, Artistic + Enterprising. Then, Social only. For each search, click on the hyperlinks to occupations in the list O*Net generates that sound interesting based on title. Read through the descriptions in full detail. Click on other career lists generated at the bottom of these job description pages if they look interesting.

Step 4: Complete the CA Career Zone Work Importance Profiler at: www.cacareerzone.org/wip. There are 42 questions that assess six work values categories. They are first assessed via questions that ask you to rank particular work values statements by importance to you and then via yes/no questions about specific work values.

Step 5: Read about your top three work values on the O*Net Online website: www.onetonline.org/find/descriptor/browse/Work_Values

Step 6: Use the drop-down menus at www.onetonline.org/explore/workvalues/Achievement to select your top three work values learned from the Work Importance Profiler. First, search by your top three values in order of highest, second highest, and third highest. For example, Achievement + Independence + Relationships. Then, search Achievement + Independence. Then, Achievement + Relationships. Then, Independence + Relationships. Then, Achievement only. For each search, click on the hyperlinks to occupations in the list O*Net generates that sound interesting based on title. Read through the descriptions in full detail. Click on other career lists generated at the bottom of these job description pages if they look interesting. Are there occupations that meet both your career interests and values?

Step 7: If you would like additional information about the occupations you read about on O*Net, you can go to the Bureau of Labor Statistics Occupational Outlook Handbook (www.bls.gov/ooh/a-z-index.htm#V) and/or Occupational Employment Statistics (www.bls.gov/oes/current/oessrcst.htm) sites for further research.

Step 8: Based on the information you have gathered, rank your top 5 to 10 occupations of potential interest.

Step 9: Go on LinkedIn (www.linkedin.com) and research people who work in potential occupations of interest. Connect with people working in these roles/industries and write them a brief message requesting a short informational interview to gain more real-world job information.

Pursue Passion & Purpose Strategy #12:
Putting Up with Passivity Narration RESCRIPTing

Consider some recent and/or long-standing experiences you've had with putting up with passivity in various areas of your life that have kept you stuck in a life limiting story. Using the narration RESCRIPTing examples and other illustrations from this chapter as a guide, RESCRIPT some of your putting up with passivity thoughts into statements that are more realistic, encouraging, and empowering.

What passions and purpose will you pursue through RESCRIPTing...

1. Regarding your relationships?
   - Putting Up with Passivity Thought:
   - RESCRIPTed:

2. Regarding your career?
   - Putting Up with Passivity Thought:
   - RESCRIPTed:

3. Regarding your financial life?
   - Putting Up with Passivity Thought:
   - RESCRIPTed:

4. Regarding your living environment?
   - Putting Up with Passivity Thought:
   - RESCRIPTed:

5. Regarding your engagement within your community?
   - Putting Up with Passivity Thought:
   - RESCRIPTed:

6. Regarding your physical health?
   - Putting Up with Passivity Thought:
   - RESCRIPTed:

7. Regarding your mental and emotional health?
   - Putting Up with Passivity Thought:
   - RESCRIPTed:

8. Regarding your intellectual growth?
   - Putting Up with Passivity Thought:
   - RESCRIPTed:

9. Regarding your recreation and relaxation?
   - Putting Up with Passivity Thought:
   - RESCRIPTed:

10. Regarding your spirituality practices?
    - Putting Up with Passivity Thought:
    - RESCRIPTed:

Commit yourself to pursuing your passions and purpose!

Pursue Passion & Purpose Strategy #13: Acknowledgements & Affirmations

Here are some acknowledgements and affirmations you can recite any time you need a boost in your motivation to pursue your passion and purpose!

I acknowledge and affirm that...

- Just because I haven't discovered my passions or greater purpose yet, doesn't mean I'm not going to.

- I don't have to live my life passively or put up with feeling stuck—if I want more adventure and meaning in my story, I'll create it.

- I have the right to pursue my passions and purpose.

- I can and will have more moments that light my soul on fire.

- I will do work or service that brings me a sense of meaning.

- Every person has a greater purpose and I deserve to pursue mine.

- Engaging in purpose-driven activities makes my heart overflow.

- Engaging in activities I feel passionate about makes me feel excited about life.

Lilly's Story

When I first spoke with Lilly, she was feeling burnt out with her work hours and bored with her job responsibilities. She had been working in the financial services industry since graduating high school. Lilly earned her Associates, Bachelors, and Masters degrees in Business with a focus in Finance while working, and had progressively risen up the career ladder to a Director of Financial Services role. Despite having followed her career goals, she suddenly found herself feeling unfulfilled and overwhelmed.

Lilly and I did a comprehensive exploration of her strengths, passions, and purpose. Through this process, we discovered that Lilly most enjoyed entrepreneurial types of pursuits, developing financial systems and strategies, and training professionals and clients in these systems. In her current role, she felt stifled, and did not feel she was getting to engage her passions fully. Furthermore, she hated the inflexibility of her hours and the impact it had on her family and personal life. Lilly uncovered that she felt her greater purpose was to help others develop financial strategies that would enable them to pursue the activities and dreams they desired for themselves and their families all the way through their retirement years.

We explored and discussed a variety of new options, many which Lilly had never considered. Lilly ultimately felt called to launch her own financial planning and advising practice, as well as pursue part-time college teaching opportunities in business and finance. We plotted out the research, coursework, certifications, and steps Lilly would need to take to start her business and embark on a teaching career, simultaneously.

Lilly was steadfast in taking the steps towards living her life with renewed passion and purpose. She launched her business and began teaching courses at a local college. Within a few months, Lilly left her salaried Director of Financial Services position to pursue her entrepreneurial initiatives full-time.

Over the last several years, Lilly's business has grown to include training both individuals and businesses through one-on-one financial planning and advising, corporate trainings, and conference presentations. Lilly has also increased the repertoire of college courses she teaches. The changes Lilly made have enabled her to feel passion in her work, live her greater purpose, and create the flexibility she desired for her family and personal life.

PRACTICE #8

T- THINK THANKFULLY VS. THANKLESSLY/DEPRIVED

"Gratitude unlocks the fullness of life.
It turns what we have into enough, and more."

~ Melody Beattie

THE LIMITING SCRIPTS OF THINKING THANKLESSLY/DEPRIVED

Too much is never enough. Whose quote is that? I honestly don't know, maybe because I've heard it said so many times. Basically—we want more. More love, more stuff, more thrills, more accolades—MORE!

Thinking thanklessly/deprived is when we find ourselves believing that in some way, shape, or form, we are missing something that would be the thing to finally make us happy and fulfilled. Perhaps we believe that others have what's required to have a fulfilling life, but we are still waiting, not quite there yet. Maybe more money, a bigger house, a remodeled kitchen, a luxury car, a bigger diamond ring, a high-powered job, a more lavish vacation, getting married, having a family—yes, that would do it.

It's something different for every person, but most of us have felt it at some point—that feeling that if we just had that one more thing, then we could finally be happy. But we don't have it yet, so we are living in some kind of deprivation. Our Inner Antagonist fixates on what is missing, and slowly but surely, we can no longer see what we already have.

Why do we think deprived?

We saw it modeled. Maybe when we were growing up, we heard our parents or other influential adults talking about that one more thing they needed to finally make it in life. Maybe it was moving to a bigger house or a more affluent town, perhaps it was that promotion or pay raise, or maybe it was the designer clothing, brand-name handbag, luxury vehicle, or the 14-carat gold necklace. Somewhere along the line we learned—money buys happiness, more is better, and what we have isn't enough.

The media brainwashes the heck out of us. Just turn on the TV and within a few short moments you should see it. It's the commercial that tells you that this product will finally make you feel better about yourself and your life, the reality TV show that says people that get on TV live in big-ass houses, the entertainment channel that is obsessively interested in what designer labels celebrities are wearing on the red carpet tonight, the rom-com that features that sad, lonely woman who finally finds her knight in shining armor who gives her the sugar-daddy, protection, manly man-ness, and baby that makes her a happy, worthwhile woman. We don't even realize it while it's happening, but it's seeping right into our brains. And, suddenly, we are the "I need more, more, more" drones the media and advertisers created us to be.

Mental rubbernecking might be at it again. Aside from what happens externally—what we are raised seeing and hearing, what the media tells us, in some situations, our brains might just view perceived deprivations as a threat to our well-being and zero in on them. We might be operating on a negativity bias, focusing our metaphorical lenses on what we don't have while struggling to clearly see all we do have.

What do we think deprived about?

Each of us has a unique focus of what makes us feel deprived in our lives. However, these are some relatively common focuses of deprived Inner Antagonistic thoughts.

1. **Relationships**: Believing our partner doesn't pamper us enough, thinking that being unmarried or childless means we are missing something critical for happiness.

2. **Career:** Thinking that not being a manager means we have missed our potential, thinking that our career track isn't respectable enough to be valued in our social circles.

3. **Finance:** Believing that we don't make a high enough salary to feel good about ourselves, thinking we haven't saved enough money to be respectable in our community.

4. **Living Environment**: Thinking our house isn't big enough to feel successful, believing our décor isn't modern enough to feel good about our home.

5. **Community Engagement**: Believing our status in the community isn't well-known enough, thinking our social impact isn't vast enough to be considered worthwhile.

6. **Physical Health:** Thinking we need to buy the best organic food products to be seen as physically healthy among peers, believing we must be able to afford gym membership or a personal trainer to achieve the best physical health.

7. **Mental & Emotional Health**: Believing that we are still too Type-A to consider ourselves mentally and emotionally healthy, thinking we must experience some kind of grand psychological transformation to feel mentally and emotionally evolved enough.

8. **Intellectual Growth**: Thinking that the things we are knowledgeable about aren't as interesting or valuable as other people's, believing our education isn't prestigious enough to be valuable.

9. **Recreation & Relaxation**: Believing that other people have time for fun and relaxation but we don't, thinking that our hobbies are too boring to compare with the exciting hobbies others have.

10. **Spirituality:** Believing we must be able to participate in a major spiritual pilgrimage to attain spiritual enlightenment, thinking our higher power hasn't given us enough to be happy.

How does thinking deprived harm us?

Thinking deprived leaves us believing we have voids that need to be filled. When we genuinely believe we have voids or holes, we seek ways to fill them. We often seek ineffective and sometimes self-destructive ways of doing so. Whether we excessively spend money we do not have, seek love through indiscriminate sex, or pursue career respect in our social circles through high-powered titles working 80 hours a week with no time off, we ultimately lose something. We widen our voids and move ourselves further away from the wholeness and satisfaction we seek. We find it progressively harder and harder to see all the blessings we already possess.

How does thinking thankfully RESCRIPT our story?

Before I begin to talk about the healing power of gratitude, I want to note that there are times in life when we experience genuine deprivations that can be extremely hard to cope with— loss of a home, a job, a loved one; marginal financial resources; or less access to resources that support our wellbeing. These are particularly difficult deprivations and it's understandable that when experiencing them, our minds might struggle not to focus on them. Yet, it may be even more critical during these times that we call upon the internal or external resources that we do have. No matter what we experience in life, gratitude practices can help us cultivate the internal calm and clarity we need to move us forward.

Whether we are experiencing tough times or just feeling stuck and frustrated, implementing regular gratitude practices in our lives can help to foster transformations. Our Inner Advocate awakens. Our ability to empower ourselves and seek solutions to challenges strengthens. Our happiness increases, we feel more satisfied with our lives overall, our optimism for the future amplifies, our resilience grows, stress and depression decrease, and we feel a greater connection to others. I have seen it happen with my clients and students. I have experienced it firsthand.

It is meaningfully fitting that my RESCRIPT Framework ends on thinking thankfully. All who know me well are very aware that I speak about gratitude a lot. In one-on-one coaching, workshops, wellness groups, the classroom, my home, and elsewhere, gratitude is a frequent topic of discussion. The reason for this is that I will always credit intentional gratitude practices with completely changing me and my life.

Sometimes I cannot believe that I ever lived my life without gratitude at the very center of it. In fact, that time of my life seems so far removed from where I am today, that it almost feels like the life I remember is not my own. But, it is. And as silly as it may sound, I am grateful that I know what it is to live without a strong center of gratitude, because it ensures that I will never go back to that place again.

For at least 10 years, I existed in a state of waiting for and wanting more. If I wasn't in a relationship, I pitied myself for being alone and wished I wasn't. If I wasn't doing well in a college class, I envied those who were because I felt I deserved to know whatever secret they had to be successful. When I was in graduate school and people my age were working, making money, and buying houses, I felt like my time would never come and I'd just keep living in limbo forever. I lived my life in my past and in my future, and my present slipped right by me without even a glance. I mourned past losses, regretted previous mistakes, and pondered all kinds of "what ifs." I looked to the future for the time when I'd get to finally be happy, while simultaneously catastrophizing all of the ways things would never really work out for me. I beat myself up for not being perfect and believed I was as far from it as I could be. I had moments of being self-destructive and had pretty low self-esteem overall.

To fill all of my perceived voids and deprivations, I shopped. In fact, I earned the first D of my life during my first year of college because instead of going to Geology class, I went shopping. I thought, "Hey, how tough can understanding rocks really be?" Clearly, I came to realize, rocks are hard (bad pun intended).

More and more, I saw happiness in life to be achieved through buying material things. The true irony was that all the stuff I accumulated didn't really bring me happiness at all. A new purse could make me feel pretty excited for a day or two, but generally, I either felt guilty for buying it afterwards or the novelty of it simply wore off. In many ways, it really deepened the void more than anything else. I needed more things, more frequently in order to feel happy, and the happiness lasted for shorter and shorter periods of time. Most of the time, I just felt sad, angry, or anxious.

The emotional toll of waiting for and wanting more was already enough. But, it impacted my body too. It began with severe back pain. My lower back felt like the top half of my body was grinding on the bottom portion. It was excruciating at times. I also struggled to sleep at night. It wasn't back problems that kept me awake, it was my mind. I would lay there and think and think and think. I would stress over the future and the past as I tried to fall asleep. It took me an average of two hours, sometimes more, to shut my mind off. I had nightmares often. I'd dream I had a job or a class that I'd forgotten about, and now there was a project due or a test to take and I wasn't prepared.

In the morning, I'd wake up and my jaw would be so stiff, I'd have to wiggle it around a few times so it would open right. I understood TMJ and knew I must be grinding my teeth at night, though I couldn't recall doing it. Then, my jaw started to unhinge itself during the day. I'd be talking with someone and my jaw would pop out of place and I'd have to move it back into place. Afterwards, it would sound like sand was inside of my jaw since it was so ground down.

Then came the panic attacks. They began infrequently, but then started happening more and more regularly, and lasted for longer periods of time. I finally realized something needed to change.

It was around this time that I sought out therapy for the first time. My amazing therapist taught me emotional coping tools that I have taken with me to this day. However, it was a trip to the bookstore that offered me the specific tool that became, and has remained, the core of how I live and work, the practice that changed everything. For some reason in the bookstore that day, I was immediately drawn to Louise Hay's *Gratitude: A Way of Life* sitting on the shelf.[44]

I bought it. Though I had no idea at the time, it would finally turn out to be a purchase that filled the voids. Or, more accurately, a purchase that made me see there were never voids in the first place.

The book shared stories of people who had changed their lives by practicing gratitude. In all honestly, at first, this seemed pretty hokey to me. I really didn't get how being more thankful could make all that much of a difference. However, I decided it was worth a try. I was at a low point and needed all the coping strategies I could find.

I began a practice of trying to recall the things I was grateful for at the end of each day. It was far from an easy undertaking initially. Sometimes it was hard to come up with much of anything. I was looking for big things, monumental moments, but experiences like that don't come as often. And I was still clouded by the things I felt went wrong that day, or even yesterday. I realized quickly that I had to shift my focus. And it took real cognitive, emotional, and behavioral work. I had to be intentional in quieting my Inner Antagonist, so I could finally hear my Inner Advocate and see myself, others, and the world through her eyes.

Thus, I shifted my focus to look for things as they were happening instead of waiting to recall moments at night. It was then that I started to see all the good that was happening. It was the little things I started to see, like the person who held the door for me at the grocery store, the person that let me make a left turn on a busy street, the conversation I had with a stranger/friend/family member, my cat sitting on my lap, the birds tweeting on a Spring morning, the professionals paving potholes in the streets in the middle of winter so drivers wouldn't wreck their cars, a staff member who went beyond the call of duty, a colleague who understood and related to my perspective, a supervisor who supported my development, a student of mine who thanked me for helping them, or an opportunity that would help me grow personally or professionally. As time went on, the things I was thankful for even expanded to seeing how a bad experience usually gave me insight that helped me understand and counsel others, and how a seemingly missed opportunity magically led me to one more suited for me.

Thinking thankfully also had the most amazing contagious impact on other aspects of my life. All of a sudden, my faith grew. When I became grateful for the greater purpose in life's challenges, I stopped questioning my higher power. I started realizing that my higher power knew things I didn't, I could hand over control to my higher power, and then I could breathe more easily. This made pains and even tragedies easier to deal with. A higher power has a plan for us and we do not have to know what it is to live life contently.

Gratitude diminished my anxiety and worrying. When I became grateful for the little things, I worried less about achieving all the big things. And because gratitude grew my faith, I recognized that if the big things I wanted were right for me and meant to be, they would be. I could plan and strategize for the future, but I didn't control it. And it was okay. The back pain, jaw unhinging, and panic attacks eventually went away and now I fall right to sleep, most nights within five to ten minutes (that's what my FitBit says). And, I only have my "stress dream," as I call it, a maximum of once every few years now—usually about a math class I apparently forgot to take and now it's the final and I never went to class and don't even have the book!

Being grateful allowed me to embrace myself and my life, and let go of materialism and envy. With gratitude, I became thankful for my perceived wrong turns, poor choices, losses, flaws, and quirks. They taught me about myself and others, they made me who I am, some of them held beautiful moments that simply didn't last forever, and they all meant I was alive and trying. Embracing the ugly made me see my uglies as beautiful, and this led me to finally be comfortable in my own skin. This made me show my authentic, quirky me at all times, it made me bare my soul without fear of what others would think of me. It allowed me to not want what others have, because their haves are not my journey. And I love traveling my own unique journey now. Plus, I no longer perceive myself as having voids, so shopping doesn't quite do it for me the same way anymore. When I do want to work out my feelings, now I just write or talk about them. I don't need to hide them.

Gratitude enabled me to embrace others. If I am grateful for and love myself, flaws and all, I can do the same with those around me. I can see that even when a person does something I disagree with, they still hold their own unique beauty. Their journey is their own and none of us can know exactly what another needs. We cannot know the entirety of another's experience. We cannot know their heart and soul completely. We want to be allowed to live our lives with acceptance, and we must embrace others and treat them with compassion. If we disagree so strongly with another, we can choose to stop engaging with them. But, we do not need to seek revenge or intentionally hurt anyone.

In sum, there hasn't been an area of my life that gratitude hasn't impacted. I feel as if it has transformed me on a cellular level, and certainly rewired my brain to see all the good in myself, my life, others, and in this world as a whole.

I've been practicing daily gratitude (really, multiple times a day-ly) for about 18 years now. Saying thank you to my higher power and all who provide me a service or kindness is a pretty automatic response today. When something has this kind of impact on your life, you feel compelled to share that gift with everyone you can. And, this is what I've tried to do. I integrate gratitude practice tools into my work with clients and students. And, I have shared this gift with my favorite person on earth—my now nine-year-old son, Joshua. I started doing my once solitary bedtime thankfuls with Josh when he was five years old.

When we first began, Josh had trouble coming up with more than one thing. When he did, they were often material items like, "I'm thankful you bought me a toy today. I'm thankful I have lots of toys. I'm thankful I got a cool goodie bag at the party today." However, within a month, he was rattling off sometimes 15 or more things he was thankful for that day—typically people and experiences versus material things. Four years later, being thankful is so natural for Josh, he deems just about everything as worthy of gratitude. "I'm thankful that I got to go to school today. I'm thankful I have a nice bed. I'm thankful I have a great family. I'm thankful I played with my cousins today. I'm thankful we have a good God. I'm thankful God made us a beautiful world. I'm thankful for thankfuls." Gratitude is indeed the greatest gift of all.

As parents, my husband and I also wanted Josh to understand the importance of showing gratitude for all we have by giving to those who may not have some of those things. While it was challenging to find volunteer opportunities for kids as young as five, some research on VolunteerMatch.org and in my community newspaper led to two volunteer opportunities we've been doing together for the last four years. We do food sorting and shelving together once or twice a month at our local food pantry. It's still one of Josh's favorite things to do (playing piano takes the #1 spot though). If I wake him up in the morning and tell him we are going to the food pantry that night, he will yell, "Yay!" and jump right up. Before our first time volunteering, we showed Josh the documentary, American Winter (www.americanwinterfilm. com). It is a documentary film that chronicles the impact of the recession on several formerly middle-class families, most of whom lost their jobs and/or homes, and utilized the services of their local food pantries. While it was a heavy film for a five-year-old, it helped Josh to understand why we volunteer at the pantry. When my parents asked him about it, Josh said, "We watched this movie about families and kids who didn't have jobs, houses, and food, and they had to go to the food pantry. So, we go there so we can give people food if they don't have any." My hope is that volunteering will be an expression of gratitude that Josh keeps up throughout his lifetime.

Josh also told me back then that he wanted to thank God by keeping God's beautiful world beautiful by cleaning it up. So, each year, we do our township's annual community clean-up. I've seen the impact thinking thankfully has had on my son's compassion for himself, others, all living creatures, and the planet.

I am a true believer that gratitude is transformational magic. If gratitude was an individual or business entity, I'd apply to be its PR Agent.

SOME HIGHLIGHTS FROM RESEARCH STUDIES ON THINKING THANKFULLY

- Expressing thanks and appreciation to team members, colleagues, and supervisors at work can be incredibly impactful. A study by Jerabek & Muoio of PsychTests discovered that those who feel unappreciated at work are far more likely than those who feel appreciated to believe their work stress is more than they can handle, to say they no longer care about how well they do their job, and to feel alienated from their colleagues and their job overall.[45]

- Robert Emmons, the world's leading gratitude researcher, has found that those who engage in gratitude experience greater happiness, optimism, and alertness, and tend to be more forgiving, generous, and compassionate. Perhaps most intriguing, practicing gratitude is correlated with having a stronger immune system, lower blood pressure, and better sleep.[46]

- Froh, Bono, Fan, Emmons, Henderson, and colleagues found that children who engaged in classroom-based gratitude activities, including keeping a gratitude journal, became more aware of how their thoughts impact their choices in social interactions, began to express gratitude more frequently, and were perceived by teachers to be happier when compared with children who did not receive gratitude instruction.[47]

- Seligman, Steen, Park, & Peterson found that those who wrote and delivered a letter of gratitude or kept a gratitude journal experienced both immediate and longer term increases in happiness and decreases in depression.[48]

- Gordon, Arnette, & Smith conducted a study of couples and discovered that feeling and expressing gratitude is connected with higher levels of marital satisfaction and happiness.[49]

LIMITING NARRATIONS OF DEPRIVED RESCRIPTED

Let's examine how we can RESCRIPT the stories we tell ourselves when we think deprived:

1. "I wish my house was as big and beautiful as Jennifer's house."

RESCRIPTed...

"Jennifer's new house really is beautiful and huge! My house is definitely not a mansion and has some 1980's décor, but every day I look at each room and feel so blessed to live here. It's got my family's personality in every space. It's home and I truly love it. It's my solace."

2. "Some people get so lucky to have a close family, but I sure didn't."

RESCRIPTed...

"My family isn't particularly close like some people's families are, and we've had our share of drama. But, my one cousin and I have had each other's back since we were kids and I know I can always count on her. She is one of my greatest blessings."

3. "I never get lucky with great career opportunities like other people do."

RESCRIPTed...

"I haven't always made a ton of money at the jobs I've had. But, one thing I've been blessed with is awesome colleagues, many of whom I'm still close with to this day."

4. "Some people's lives are so easy, but mine has been pretty rough."

RESCRIPTed...

"I've been through some pretty tough things in my life, but they have taught me resilience. I feel stronger because of the challenges I've faced. I'm actually grateful for many of them."

5. "I don't have enough of what I need to be happy."

RESCRIPTed...

"I may not have the most money, the fanciest car, or the biggest house, but I have all I need to be happy. I have an amazing family, causes I believe in and actively support, and goals I love pursuing."

LIMITLESS LIVING LIBRARY – STRATEGIES TO THINK THANKFULLY SECTION

In addition to these strategies, you can modify and use strategies from other chapters to think thankfully!

Think Thankfully Strategy #1:
Helping or Harming Review

During or following your next episode of thinking deprived, ask yourself the following:

1. What is my purpose/intent in thinking deprived?

2. How does thinking deprived harm me?

3. How does thinking deprived help me?

4. What is avoided through thinking deprived?

5. What is addressed through thinking deprived?

6. What would I say to a friend who was thinking deprived?

7. What more effective things could I say to myself right now?

8. What more effective strategies exist to achieve my original purpose/intent?

9. What did I learn about my deprived thinking from this review?

Think Thankfully Strategy #2:
Thank Your Treasures & Triumphs

Each of us has experiences, people, external resources, and personal strengths that are treasures in our lives, as well as experiences of triumph through achievement. These are blessings to feel thankful for. Let's explore your treasures and triumphs!

Take time to consider the people in your life that you are grateful for—friends, family, neighbors, pastor, mail carrier, doctor, hair stylist, restaurant server, or even the stranger you just talked with on line at the supermarket. These individuals contribute to bringing you joy and comfort. When we remind ourselves of all the people in our lives that make it better, we feel calmer and more at peace. We must savor our moments with those we love and encounter in our travels.

1. Who are the people you are grateful to have in your life currently and why?

When you look back on your life thus far, there have been journeys and moments that have brought you joy, satisfaction, or a feeling of achievement. Perhaps it was a concert you attended as a teenager, a college course you loved, graduation from college, a great project at work, a promotion, a painting you worked on for weeks, a vacation to Europe, or volunteering at the soup kitchen. Close your eyes and bring yourself back to those experiences, breathe them in, then go out and experience some more of what life has to offer.

2. What positive life experiences are you thankful for and why?

Each of us has external resources to draw comfort from, whether it's a home, food on the table, money to pay the bills, good health, a reliable vehicle, or a great job opportunity. Especially when we are feeling that we do not have enough, its critical to remind ourselves of everything that we already have.

3. What external resources are you thankful for and why?

Each of us has unique strengths, gifts given to us by a higher power. The greatest way to show our gratitude for these gifts is to make sure we express them and give them to others. By doing so, we multiply their positive impact.

4. What personal strengths are you thankful for and why?

Think Thankfully Strategy #3:
Thank Your Trials & Tribulations

Each of us experience trials and tribulations in our lives—traumatic or challenging life experiences, losses of important relationships, shortages of external resources that might make life easier, and personal imperfections that sometimes make things tougher for us. The trials and tribulations we encounter can easily become a source of feeling deprived in our lives—like we have had it tougher than someone else or are missing things we need to be happy. However, as odd as it may sound, we can actually choose to Thank Our Trials & Tribulations. Let's contemplate this thankful versus deprived perspective.

The loss of relationships through death or severed ties can leave us feeling lonely, rejected, and even fearful to fully connect in present or future relationships. However, even a relationship that ends provides us with gifts. There are positive memories you can still savor from these relationships. People that are no longer in our lives still helped us to learn and grow in some way. No relationship is wasted. We can decide to keep the good from them, let go of hurt and fear, and recognize that our future connections, whether short or long, will give us new gifts and joys.

1. What relationships that are no longer part of your life are you thankful for and why?

The challenging experiences we face often provide us with some of the greatest wisdom and transformation in our lives. Rather than allowing previous challenges to poison our minds, we can consider what gifts they have given us. Whether it's an argument with our partner, loss of a job, loss of a home, car accident, or serious illness, we learn something about ourselves and gain strength that propels us toward something different or sometimes even better.

2. What challenging life experiences are you thankful for and why?

It may seem counterintuitive, but we can even be grateful for shortages in our lives. Perhaps living on a smaller salary has taught us what things we really need, helped us to be more economical with our money, and led us to appreciate a vacation or dinner out more fully than we did when we had a larger income. Perhaps the personal sacrifices we've made to support family or friends has taught us to appreciate the virtue of self-sacrifice. We all live with one shortage or another at various points in our lives. They teach us to appreciate the little things, for it's those little things that truly mean the most.

3. What shortage of an external resource are you thankful for and why?

As much as we each have strengths, we also have imperfections—the things we struggle with. We can either worry that we are unlovable because of them and attempt to hide these imperfections from others, or we can embrace them as part of the tapestry of our unique beauty. Gratitude for our imperfections removes any shame we may have about them. When we become grateful for our flaws, we learn to love ourselves wholly, authentically, and without need for some unrealistic standard of perfection. It allows us to be honest about ourselves, and in doing so, we help offer others permission to do the same.

4. What personal flaws are you grateful for and why?

Think Thankfully Strategy #4:
Celebrate Non-Catastrophes

This is an especially great gratitude practice for those who struggle with catastrophizing, because it takes care of enhancing two kinds of positive thinking at once! There are days when we feared a catastrophe or problem was going to happen, and then…it doesn't. This is a great thing to be thankful for—Celebrate Non-Catastrophes!

1. What catastrophes that never actually happened are you thankful for?

Think Thankfully Strategy #5:
Recognize Others in Writing

In our lives there are often people we feel particularly thankful for that we realize we have not properly thanked. It could be someone who has had a long-term positive impact in our lives like a parent, other family member, close friend, or long-time mentor, or perhaps a teacher, coach, or mentor from years ago. We also experience more specific moments of gratitude for friends, colleagues, and neighbors. Additionally, we may feel thankful for those who provide a service to us in our daily lives, such as a public official (i.e., police, fire fighter, postal worker, public works staff member) or a professional (i.e., your dentist, doctor, child's teacher). Often, these individuals who care for our community, our health, our education, and other needs do not get properly thanked for the great work they do. How often do we give a real, proper thank you to these individuals? One great way to express thanks is to Recognize Others in Writing. Here are some ways to do so!

1. **If you want to offer a more comprehensive and impactful thank you, write a letter.** Specifically note the things you are thankful for and why. If the person you are thanking is a particularly influential and important person in your life, you can take it a step further and instead of sending it in postal mail, you could deliver it in person. Ask the person if the two of you can meet, but don't tell them about the letter beforehand. When you meet, read the letter to the person. Pay attention to how reading the letter makes you feel in the moment. Spend time with the recipient afterwards talking about the effects of the letter and what she/he has done for you. Additionally, if you feel grateful for someone who has already passed on, it can also be therapeutic to write out a letter of gratitude to that person.

2. **If you want a quicker thank you, send a text or email.** Consider the people in your professional and personal life for whom you are grateful. Make a practice of sending at least one brief thank you email or text each week to someone

you are thankful for, specifically citing a reason or two why you appreciate their presence in your life or workplace.

3. **If you want to do something somewhere in between comprehensive and brief, give a thank you card.** This can be an especially cool thing to initiate at work. You can ask employees to keep an eye out for moments when a co-worker helps them out or contributes in a way that positively impacts them or the organization as a whole. Create a practice that involves employees giving a thank you card to colleagues they feel grateful for. Particularly pay attention to thanking those who rarely get thanked.

4. **For a quick and kind gesture of thanks, post a post it note**. You can do this at home on a mirror, the fridge, or somewhere else that's prominent to say a quick thank you to a family member. You can do this at work as well. You can even create a special place for workplace gratitude. Using a large bulletin board, post sticky notes to specific co-workers that you are thankful for and state why. This allows the gratitude to be publicly displayed where everyone can see it.

Think Thankfully Strategy #6: Kindle Kindness

Kindling Kindness in every area of our lives is a great way to say thank you to our higher power. When we show kindness to all living creatures and our planet, we express our gratitude to our higher power for everything that was created for us. Each day, make a practice of smiling at others, saying hello, and helping someone out in any way you can. Be gentle with animals and insects (yes, insects—if they aren't bothering us, we don't really need to crush them, do we?!). Treat animals with love, care, and respect. Be good to the earth, keep it clean, pick up trash if you see it laying around, don't litter. These are just some small ways we can make a daily practice of thanking our higher power for everything that's been given to us.

Think Thankfully Strategy #7:
Eradicate Envy

In previous chapters, we've talked about how social comparison is a soul killer. It's the breeder of envy. When we look around, we will always find someone who has something we don't have—a bigger house, fancier car, higher paying job, more close relationships. However, once we allow ourselves to look at all the blessings we do have and recognize that someone else's journey has its own unique treasures and tribulations, we can Eradicate Envy. When we eradicate envy, we free ourselves from its poison. We can celebrate others' treasures, while simultaneously having gratitude for our own gifts.

Think Thankfully Strategy #8:
Compliments Instead of Complaints

When you find yourself desiring to complain or gossip about a person, do the opposite, the unthinkable—find a way to compliment the person instead! You can compliment the person directly by saying the compliment to them, or indirectly by saying it about them to someone else. This forces us to contemplate something good that we can appreciate in a person who doesn't generally illicit positive feelings within us. It's quite an effective strategy for growing gratitude and diminishing negative thoughts and feelings.

Think Thankfully Strategy #9:
Talk Thankfully

To think thankfully, we must Talk Thankfully. If we spend a lot of time talking with others about the experiences, people, and things we perceive we are deprived of in our lives, we will think we are indeed deprived. As we've talked about, we believe what we tell other people about our lives. However, if we focus on talking more about our blessings than our burdens, we begin to see our lives through a lens of abundance. Speak less of your deprivations and more of the good things in your life in your conversations with others. Then, watch the abundance you see in your life grow!

Think Thankfully Strategy #10:
Acquire More Adventures Than Assets

There's nothing wrong with things—a nice pair of shoes, bigger TV, new couch, or new car are pretty nice! However, it's when we focus too much of our pursuit of happiness on material assets that we end up feeling more deprived, despite how much we acquire. However, when we focus more energy on acquiring adventures/ experiences, we increase our joy and our gratitude. This is because experiences have a longer lasting impact. We can recall the places, people, thrill, achievement, knowledge, skills, or other positive aspects and feelings associated with the experience long after it's over. Whereas the novelty and excitement of material things tends to wear off more quickly, leaving us seeking a new thing to make us feel fulfilled again. So, in your pursuit of fulfillment, you don't have to banish buying things altogether. Just focus greater time, resources, and energy on acquiring experiences—this will lead to a feeling of greater abundance!

Think Thankfully Strategy #11:
Savor Each Second

Gratitude requires presence. It requires savoring. If our minds are focused on the past or the future, we miss what's happening right now, hence we miss moments we can feel grateful for. And, if our minds are not fully present and focused on where we are, who we are with, and what we are doing, we cannot savor our experiences. To savor means to soak it in, really feel it, truly enjoy.

We need to train ourselves to Savor Each Second we experience. To engross ourselves in deep conversations. To listen more and talk less. To passionately embrace and feel the warmth of those we love. To profoundly see the radiant colors of the sky, grass, and trees. To intensely smell the fragrance of the flowers. To keenly taste the flavor of each bite of a meal. To acutely listen to the melody of the music and the meaning in the lyrics. We don't savor nearly enough. Instead, we multitask, we technologize, we ruminate, we stress—and the now drifts right by. Let's make a practice of being present to Savor Each Second, so that we may truly experience life and grow our awareness of all we have to be grateful for.

Think Thankfully Strategy #12:
All-Around Life Appreciation Appraisal

Conduct a comprehensive appraisal of all you appreciate in your life to date. In each area of your life, what experiences, achievements, people, and things are you grateful for? What brings you happiness? Take a moment to truly savor these blessings and keep nurturing them!

** Worksheet available in Appendix H and in my free "RESCRIPT Your Story Workbook" available at www.ColleenGeorges.com **

Think Thankfully Strategy #13:
Three Thankfuls at Twilight

Each night before you go to sleep, for one month, write down three experiences, people, and/or things you are grateful for that day. The items can be relatively small in importance (e.g., "my co-worker made the coffee today") or relatively large (e.g., "I earned a big promotion"). The goal of the exercise is to remember a good experience, person, or thing in your life—then enjoy the good emotions that come with it! Review your experiences at the end of each week and at the end of the month, savoring your positive memories. If you enjoy the activity, consider making Three Thankfuls at Twilight a continuous practice. Furthermore, after a while it may be enough to simply say the things you are thankful for each night out loud to yourself. You can also make it a couple or family ritual to discuss your thankfuls together!

** Worksheet available in Appendix I and in my free "RESCRIPT Your Story Workbook" available at www.ColleenGeorges.com **

Think Thankfully Strategy #14:
Deprived Thinking Narration RESCRIPTing

Consider some recent and/or long-standing deprived think-ing in which you've engaged, in various areas of your life, that has kept you stuck in a life limiting story. Using the narration RESCRIPTing examples and other illustrations from this chapter as a guide, RESCRIPT some of your deprived thinking narra-tives into statements that are more realistic, encouraging, and empowering.

What will you begin to think thankfully about through RESCRIPTing...

1. Regarding your relationships?
   • Deprived Thought:
   • RESCRIPTed:

2. Regarding your career?
   • Deprived Thought:
   • RESCRIPTed:

3. Regarding your financial life?
   • Deprived Thought:
   • RESCRIPTed:

4. Regarding your living environment?
   • Deprived Thought:
   • RESCRIPTed:

5. Regarding your engagement within your community?
   • Deprived Thought:
   • RESCRIPTed:

6. Regarding your physical health?
   • Deprived Thought:
   • RESCRIPTed:

7. Regarding your mental and emotional health?
   - Deprived Thought:
   - RESCRIPTed:

8. Regarding your intellectual growth?
   - Deprived Thought:
   - RESCRIPTed:

9. Regarding your recreation and relaxation?
   - Deprived Thought:
   - RESCRIPTed:

10. Regarding your spirituality practices?
    - Deprived Thought:
    - RESCRIPTed:

Commit yourself to thinking thankfully!

Think Thankfully Strategy #15: Acknowledgements & Affirmations

Here are some acknowledgements and affirmations you can recite any time you need a boost in your thinking thankfully motivation!

I acknowledge and affirm that…

- I can and will wake up with a grateful heart each day, ready for a day filled with beautiful moments and encounters.

- I already have many things to be thankful for.

- I don't need to have all the things I want to feel grateful, I must instead want what I've got.

- Complaining about my problems regularly makes me feel less grateful.

- Contemplating all the problems I don't have makes me feel more grateful.

- Talking about the internal and external resources I have makes me feel thankful.

- I can experience loss and frustrations, and still feel gratitude for the good I still have in my life.

- I am allowed to feel deprived sometimes, but I do not have to remain in that deprived emotional state.

- There are reasons to feel grateful occurring all the time, but sometimes I need to shift my focus to notice them.

- I do not need to be thanked for every kind deed I do for me to feel good about the deed; doing good is its own reward.

- I can choose to focus on what I am grateful for, even when I have had a tough period in my life.

- Taking time each day to really look at and appreciate the beauty of nature—the sky, trees, flowers, and animals—makes me feel so grateful and enables me to live in the present moment.

- I can and will scan my world for the best in others, the beauty in nature, and the joy in my small and big accomplishments.

- I can and will say thank you to family, friends, and neighbors who extend me a kindness, even the most basic kind.

- I can and will acknowledge and thank all who provide me a service—the cashier, restaurant server, mail carrier, gas station attendant, bus driver—all who work to serve others.

- I can and will thank the stranger who opened the door for me, who let me make the left turn while driving, who took time to be kind when they did not have to do so.

- When I face a problem, I can and will experience my frustrations while simultaneously acknowledging the wisdom life's challenges have offered me.

- When my mind drifts to the things, experiences, or connections I want but do not currently have, I can and will remind myself of the blessings I already have in my life, both big and small.

- As I lay my head on my pillow at night, I can and will review all the experiences, people, and things I am most grateful for today and overall, and thank my higher power for my blessings.

- I can and will close my eyes at night with peace in my soul, knowing that all I need to be happy is already within and around me.

MY STUDENTS' STORIES

As I talked about in the Seeking Strengths chapter, I taught a Positive Psychology-based course that incorporated several Positive Psychology exercises that students were asked to use in their professional and personal lives.

With regard to thinking thankfully, I asked my students to complete two distinct exercises:

1) Gratitude Journal:

   - For four weeks before going to sleep each night, write down three things you are grateful for from your day (big or small) and why you are grateful.
   - Reflect upon the experience.

2) Gratitude Letter:

   - Write a detailed letter of appreciation to a person in your life who you are grateful for, but who you feel you have not yet adequately thanked.
   - Set up a time to meet with the individual without sharing the intent, and read the letter to them *or* stay with them as they read the letter you wrote.
   - Reflect upon the experience.

In reflecting upon keeping a Gratitude Journal for one month, students shared some amazing experiences. Coming up with things to be grateful for was difficult initially, however with daily practice it became hard *not* to do. My students cited noticing a new ability to appreciate little things they'd never thought about before and finding themselves thinking of their blessings readily throughout their day. Practicing gratitude helped my students transform their perceptions of what they had thought was a bad day into viewing it as a good day. They found themselves suddenly looking for good in all things, even in unfortunate events, and diminishing episodes of negative rumination. They noted positive changes in the way they handled life's challenges. Reviewing what they were grateful for at night made them feel accomplished, as well as optimistic and excited about the next day, instead of stressed. Those who had struggled to fall or stay asleep began sleeping more quickly and soundly.

Both keeping a Gratitude Journal and writing/delivering a Gratitude Letter to a person they were grateful for had lasting positive impacts on my students' relationships. Appreciating other's kindnesses made them want to do more kind things for others and tell people how much they appreciated them. Loved ones even noted positive changes in my students' attitudes and demeanors after implementing gratitude practices into their lives. Most students noted the gratitude exercises to be the most positively impactful activities in the course, and several students have shared with me in the years since that they have continued to use gratitude practices in their personal and professional lives. Furthermore, students reported experiencing increases in their overall life satisfaction, self-forgiveness, hope, life meaning, and gratitude.

PART 3

THE NEW LIMITLESS LIFE STORY

"Your life is your story. Write well. Edit often."

~ Susan Statham

MAKING RESCRIPTING
A LIFESTYLE

"Life is an adventure, it's not a package tour."

~ Eckhart Tolle

Stories Only Get Written When You Keep Writing Them

You made it! You've learned to RESCRIPT your story and allow your Inner Advocate to be heard! This is a big deal because you know it's not easy to do and it takes a ton of work. With time and practice, RESCRIPTing becomes simpler and more natural, we begin removing the limits from our life story, and empower our story's Protagonist to embark on any adventure desired. However, to truly make RESCRIPTing a lifestyle, we can't simply rely on the RESCRIPTing we've already done and assume it will take our stories far enough. There are still so many more exciting chapters to come. But, stories only get written when you keep writing them.

It's not uncommon in life to learn something new, implement it for a while, get sidetracked by something, and then go back to old limiting habits (which often include getting mad at ourselves for getting sidetracked!). Here's the deal—sidetracked is fine, it happens! It doesn't mean anything major unless you tell yourself it does.

Let me tell you a quick story. I talked about how I've been doing nightly gratitude for about 18 years now. Well, about a year ago, I slowly fell off my routine. I got sidetracked staying up late working a lot on various work and personal projects and gradually stopped doing bedtime thankfuls with my son. A couple days of not doing evening gratitude turned into weeks, and weeks turned into a couple of months. And something happened; I started feeling deprived. I had this sudden desire to buy all new furniture for my house, and redo my bathrooms and kitchen, and then I just wanted to move to a different house altogether, maybe another town. I became mentally fixated on these thoughts. But the thoughts of these new and shiny things didn't make me excited, they were making me feel stressed and down. I started feeling dissatisfied, cranky, and easily irritated. But, one day, like a really obvious epiphany, I thought, "Damn, I haven't been practicing my gratitude for awhile now." And my very next thought was, "Could that be what's been going on with me lately?" So, I was very intentional in starting back on doing my evening thankfuls with my son. And the wildest thing happened. The deprived thinking just stopped. The crankiness and irritability stopped. My mood lifted and I felt satisfied with life again. Craziness. Years and years and years of regular gratitude practice didn't mean I could just stop. The cup only runneth over when we refill it.

A RESCRIPTing lifestyle is a daily thing. We must keep paying attention to what our Inner Antagonist is telling us about who we are and what we are capable of. We must keep RESCRIPTing our thoughts and amplifying the voice of our Inner Advocate. We must keep actively and intentionally using the RESCRIPT strategies to Release Rumination, Engage Growth Goals, Seek Strengths, Challenge Catastrophizing, Restrict Regret, Invite Imperfection, Pursue Passion & Purpose, and Think Thankfully. And, if we get sidetracked, no big deal, we just start up again.

What does a RESCRIPTed lifestyle look like?

A RESCRIPTed lifestyle looks different depending on you and what you want for your story. However, here are few good indicators of a RESCRIPTed lifestyle.

1. **Relationships**:
   - We take time to talk to people we don't know in our daily travels because we value all human beings.
   - We recognize the value in diversity, and cultivate relationships with people from different backgrounds, demographics, and perspectives.
   - When we are with loved ones, we are really with them, fully present, paying attention to their words and actions, and offering them our whole heart.
   - We are intentional in bringing others up versus dragging them now.
   - We are compassionate and forgiving with others.

2. **Career:**
   - We pursue our passions and purpose in our work and offer our strengths to make a positive impact in our workplace and on those our work serves.
   - We trust that we have what it takes to take on and master new opportunities.

3. **Finance:**
   - We save enough money to care for us and our family in the future.
   - We spend enough money to really live and experience life's adventures.

4. **Living Environment**:
   - We make our home a sanctuary that reflects our unique style.
   - We love the home we are in, whatever location, size, and décor because it keeps us warm and dry.

5. **Community Engagement**:
   - We speak to our neighbors and help them when we can.
   - We serve the greater good of our local, larger, or global community because we genuinely care about the wellbeing of others we do not know.

6. **Physical Health:**
   - We put quality fuel in our bodies, while still allowing ourselves to savor a cheeseburger.
   - We do what it takes to keep our bodies strong and healthy, while honoring and respecting our unique shape and size.
   - We give our body the sleep it needs and deserves to keep us going every day.

7. **Mental & Emotional Health**:
   - We allow ourselves to really feel our feelings, the positive and the negative, but we savor the positive longer and let go more quickly of the negative.
   - We allow ourselves to laugh a lot, including at ourselves.
   - We love ourselves and have no shame in saying it.
   - We say nice things to ourselves in a kind tone.
   - We are self-compassionate.

8. **Intellectual Growth**:
   - We never stop learning, including learning from others who may have different backgrounds or perspectives.
   - We keep our brains growing by soaking up new knowledge and experience.

9. **Recreation & Relaxation**:
   - We define productivity to include fun and recharging.
   - We explore and maintain our many passions, hobbies, and interests.
   - We honor ourselves with various forms of relaxation.

10. **Spirituality:**
- We allow faith to be a guide and a reliever of worry.
- We trust that we don't need to understand everything that happens in our lives, others' lives, and in life overall.
- We trust that our higher power has a plan for us and we don't need to know what it is, we just need to listen to our heart.

LIMITLESS LIVING LIBRARY – STRATEGIES TO MAKE RESCRIPTING A LIFESTYLE SECTION

You've got a lot of strategies to RESCRIPT your Inner Antagonist's narrations from the previous chapters, but here are just a few more to make RESCRIPTing a lifestyle.

RESCRIPT Lifestyle Strategy #1:
Weekly Thought Tracking & RESCRIPTing

For one week, track the things your Inner Antagonist is saying to you--in essence your limiting and self-critical thoughts. Make note what types/categories of limiting thoughts they are (rumination, evading, scrutinizing shortcomings, catastrophizing, regret, infallibility/perfectionism, putting up with passivity, thinking thankless/deprived), and what situation triggered them.

First, use the chart below to note the frequency of different types of limiting, self-critical thoughts you've had over the week. You don't need to write out the thoughts or topics, just the number of occurrences.

Frequency of Limiting, Inner Antagonist Thoughts							
	Mon.	Tues.	Weds.	Thurs.	Fri.	Sat.	Sun.
Rumination							
Evading Growth Goals							
Scrutinizing Shortcomings							
Catastrophizing							

Regret							
Infallibility/Perfectionism							
Putting Up with Passivity							
Thinking Thanklessly/ Deprived							

Second, jot down at least five of your most negatively impactful limiting thoughts—the ones that bothered you most, and prevented you from doing more important, positive things. Note what situation(s) triggered the thoughts. Finally, RESCRIPT your thoughts to remove the limits and self-criticism.

Inner Antagonist Thought:

- Type of Thought (RESCRIPT Category):

- Trigger Situation:

- *Thought Limitlessly RESCRIPTed:*

RESCRIPT Lifestyle Strategy #2: Be It Before You Believe It

Sometimes we spend our time waiting to think differently so we can act differently. However, change doesn't always come in that order. There are plenty of times in life when you must Be It Before You Believe It. In order to change your thoughts about yourself, your life, others, or the world, you often must begin by acting in the ways you wish to believe. If you are feeling cynical about humanity, intentionally be kind to others even when you believe they might not appreciate it, or volunteer your time for a cause if you believe the world is in peril. If you believe you cannot be a stronger public speaker, volunteer yourself to run a workshop at your job or in the community to force yourself to be what you've told yourself you can't. If you believe you can't be a person who's on top of keeping an organized and uncluttered home, rent a dumpster for your driveway for a week, and see how quickly you'll start decluttering! These activities also create some urgency to accomplish your goals.

If you believe you cannot love your face and yourself without putting on your makeup, leave the house without it and hold your head high and confident. I actually did this for a year nearly two decades ago to prove this to myself and overcome insecurities. It turned out I could feel beautiful and love myself without the makeup (but I still love wearing it!). Whatever way of thinking isn't serving you that you want to change, consider beginning by changing your behavior. You might just find that your perspective completely shifts for the positive in the process!

RESCRIPT Lifestyle Strategy #3: Shorten Critical Carol's Scene

Scene 2: Critical Carol walks in the door. Yep, she's back. Your Critical Carol negative thoughts *will* come walking through the door. You can pretty much count on it. However, YOU get to decide how long Carol and her critical perspective can stay! Don't want to be rude to Carol even though she never has anything nice to say? That's okay, you can let her stay, but put a cap on her visit so she doesn't ruin your day. When Carol waltzes in with her nasty attitude, decide how long you want to put up with it today. Five minutes, maybe 10 tops? Let her spew all her negativity, analyze the heck out of everything you are doing in your life, share her gloom and doom, but after a short, specific period of time, tell her it's been real and you've got an important appointment to wash your hair or something like that. Her criticizing outlook doesn't deserve more than a few minutes of your time. Shut her down!

RESCRIPT Lifestyle Strategy #4: Don't Breathe in the Poison

Sometimes our anxieties start with others' talk rather than our own. And in engaging with particular people who are in chaos, we become chaotic as well. We've heard about toxic people. A toxic person will try to draw you into their poisonous negativity. Perhaps they will complain about the same issues they've complained about before, but refuse to do the work to change, and expect you to pity and try to fix it for them. Or, perhaps they will say or do something offensive and hurtful to you, expecting you will defend yourself, offend them back, and engage in a poisonous, unproductive argument. Sometimes a person can be a constant toxicity in our lives, and sometimes a person can be toxic to us only at certain times. Whichever the case, we must become familiar with the warning signs that the toxicity is about to fill the air.

When we notice the person engaging in toxic behaviors, we must not engage in the expected pattern with them. If we engage, we are in essence breathing in their poison, succumbing to it ourselves. When we choose to disengage, it is like putting on a protective mask. Disengaging does not always mean leaving the room (though sometimes it might). It means not falling into a negative back-and-forth trap of the person offending and you defending, or the person wallowing in their poison and then you trying to save the other person from their own poison. Instead, resist the urge to defend, offend back, or swoop in to save. You can instead keep a neutral facial expression and body posture, while responding calmly with neutral phrases such as, "It's unfortunate that you feel that way." "It sounds like you're really frustrated." "I hear what you're saying." "That sounds really difficult." By remaining neutral and non-engaged, we do not breathe in the poison and thus do not experience mental chaos, heightened emotions, or physical symptoms of frustration or anxiety.

RESCRIPT Lifestyle Strategy #5:
Heightening Hope & Ebbing Expectations

Let me begin by saying that I'm not intending to give expectations a totally bad rap here. There are some aspects of expectations that are positive—if we expect good things, we are more likely to be motivated to put the work in to achieve those good things. However, there are certain aspects of expectations that must be kept in check (or ebbed), or they can get us into emotional and mental trouble sometimes. Understanding the differences and similarities between hope and expectations is key.

Hope and expectations have similarities, and although some dictionary definitions and thesauruses use the words interchangeably, they are not quite the same thing. They both involve a belief and feeling about the future. But, it's the differences between them that impact our reactions to what actually occurs in the future.

When contemplating positive outcomes, to hope is to believe in general that good things *can* happen. It can also mean to believe that a very specific good thing *will* happen. When you hope for something, you *believe* in and *want* the good. But, you don't *need* it. Hope is positive, faithful, flexible, and resilient. It keeps giving even in the midst of challenges. It lets you know that you will be okay no matter what. It knows that when time and circumstance and the stars align, the good thing(s) *will* be. Hope sees a present and future of abundance and does not focus on perceived deficits.

When considering positive outcomes, to expect is to believe that a specific good thing *will* happen. But, then expectations take it to another level by making us believe that the specific good thing *should* happen and *must* happen for us. At their worst, expectations can begin to have us believing good things in general *should* and *must* be happening for us regularly. And, what happens when we don't get the thing we wanted? Or, when overall we face problems? We cling rigidly to our expectations and get terribly disappointed or even resentful of reality. The unmet expectations lead us to see our lives as in a deficit, missing the things we believed we needed, because expectations don't just want, they *need*. So, when things go differently than what we expected, we *believe we can't handle the reality* of the situation. This can lead us to give up, stop trying, believing our chances have already come and gone. Hence, expectations, when not ebbed or checked, can be inflexible, unceasing, and unwilling to accept and adapt to reality.

So, how do we spot the differences in our thought phrases? Here are some examples to help decipher the differences and RESCRIPT rigidly expecting thoughts into flexibly hopeful thoughts.

Expectation sounds like:

"This job opportunity will work out great for me. Because, if it doesn't, I seriously can't handle it. I *know* this job *has* to be the one for me – I *need* this!"

Hope sounds like:

"I think this job opportunity *can* work out great for me. But if it doesn't, I'll be just fine too, because I always maintain hope that good career possibilities can happen for me and will when the time and job are right."

Expectation sounds like:

"This conversation is going to be the one that finally gets through to him and makes him understand and change. I know this is it. It has to be. It will be such a waste of time if he doesn't listen to me. I need him to hear me and change already!"

Hope sounds like:

"I'm hopeful this conversation will get through to him and help him understand and make changes. I believe it can. But, even if he's not ready to hear me today, I'll feel good knowing I took the time to talk with him. I'd love to see our talk help him make positive changes, but I'll be fine if it doesn't have that impact. Positive changes will come when he's ready."

Listen to your thoughts about upcoming situations and make sure you remove rigidity and neediness from your desires. Replace it with adaptability and affirmation that you can, and will be, okay with a different outcome. Hope heals and keeps us positive, resilient, and empowered in our life's pursuits.

RESCRIPT Lifestyle Strategy #6:
Check Your Can'ts & Own Your Won'ts

"I can't change." "I can't do that." "You don't understand! I just can't!" We use the word can't quite liberally in various areas of our lives. Sometimes we use it so often, we truly believe it—we believe we can't, we believe we are limited, we believe we are trapped.

Sometimes, our can'ts are indeed real. Yet, most of the time, our can'ts aren't really can'ts at all—they're won'ts. Can't isn't a choice, but won't is a choice. Can't has no control, but won't does have control.

So, the next time you hear yourself using the word can't, check your can't and examine it. In the context of this particular situation, ask yourself:

1. Is my can't legit? Am I truly unable?

2. What evidence do I have that supports my can't claim?

3. Or, is the truth that I am choosing not to?

Once you Check Your Can'ts, Own Your Won'ts. Take responsibility for them! In the context of this particular situation, ask yourself:

1. Why won't I?

2. How do I feel about my reasons for why I won't?

3. Are they good enough reasons for me?

4. What do I gain by choosing not to do this?

5. What do I lose by choosing not to do this?

6. Based on this information, do I want to keep my won't or toss it in the trash?

7. If I toss my won't aside, what steps will I take right now to do the thing I was telling myself I can't do?

If you decide to keep your won't, own it! If you decide it's not good enough for you, change your mind! You control what you will and will not do. Empower yourself by using language that owns your choices!

RESCRIPT Lifestyle Strategy #7:
Minor Disruption or Major Disaster

Life throws curveballs our way—roadwork detours that make us late to our destinations, fender benders that cost time and money, products we purchased delivered with damages, an air conditioner that breaks on a hot day, a computer that crashes, or people who treat us unfairly.

When those curveballs come, we might react pretty badly. We may curse, yell, or stomp our feet. But, maybe we even take it a step further by ruminating incessantly over it and catastrophizing over all the issues and problems we will have now as a result. Too often, we mentally and emotionally transform situations that are more of a minor disruption into a major disaster. When we make that choice, we simultaneously choose to let these situations steal our joy, ruin our day, ruin our week, or ruin our month.

The next time a curveball comes at you and you feel ready to let it steal your joy, ask yourself:

1. On a scale from 1 to 10, with 1 representing a minor disruption and 10 representing a major disaster, where does this situation fall?

2. Looking at this situation a year or two from today, how will I most likely view it—as a disruption or a disaster in my life's story?

3. If I shared this situation with an unbiased observer, how would they most likely view it—as a life disruption or a life disaster?

4. Based on my assessments, is this situation big enough and important enough to steal my joy and take over my thoughts?

5. How can I change the way I view this situation so I can let it go from my thoughts?

6. What can I say to myself to allow this situation to be more of a disruption rather than a disaster?

7. What can I do to make sure I maintain my joy despite this disruption?

You control how you let frustrating situations impact you, your thoughts, your feelings, your behaviors, your time, and your energy. If it's closer to a disruption, don't give it power to be a disaster—choose to keep your joy anyway!

RESCRIPT Lifestyle Strategy #8:
Simply Say Stop!

No matter what negative narrating our Inner Antagonist is trying to script, we CAN stop it in its tracks. In fact, it often begins with Simply Saying Stop! If you catch yourself, ruminating, evading growth goals, scrutinizing shortcomings, catastrophizing, regretting, inviting perfectionism, putting up with passivity, or thinking deprived, simply and kindly say to yourself, "Stop Your Name! We aren't doing that. We have better things to do. Stop." When we say stop, it disrupts the flow of the negative thought process. Each time your Inner Antagonist tries to drag you back in, Simply say Stop!

RESCRIPT Lifestyle Strategy #9:
Thought Travel

Ever been somewhere so beautiful, so peaceful, so enjoyable, you didn't want to leave? A place you loved so much, you are missing it and want to be back there again? Perhaps right now time, funds, and/or other circumstances are stopping you from traveling there physically, and you find yourself thinking negatively and feeling frustrated. What you *can* do is Thought Travel.

Especially in times when we are feeling stressed, overwhelmed, or unhappy, Thought Travel can be just the thing you need to remove yourself from the negative and transport yourself to the positive.

Step One: Pick the destination you want to Thought Travel to.

Step Two: Set your senses:

1. **Sight**: Look at some photos you took while you were there. Study the visual details. Commit them to your memory.

2. **Sound**: What sounds remind you of your positive place? The ocean waves, coqui frogs, crickets, birds, owls? Play the sounds from a video you took while you were there or find some similar sounds online that you can play.

3. **Smell**: What smells do you remember? The woods, suntan lotion, flowers? Get some essential oils that are similar to those smells and sprinkle some on your clothes or fabrics around you, or dab some under your nose or on your wrists.

4. **Taste**: What tastes do you recall? A margarita, boardwalk French fries, a cultural cuisine? See what similar foods/drinks you can find at the supermarket or a local restaurant and bring it home with you to indulge your taste buds.

5. **Touch**: What textures remind you of your positive place? Perhaps the sensation of sand in between your fingers, sun of your shoulders, or cool air on your face? See if you can engage your touch sensations by going outside in the warm or cool air, taking a little sand from a souvenir jar in your hand, or other sensations you can access that remind you of your positive place.

You don't need to engage all five senses, just as many as possible.

Step Three: Pick a location to embark on your Thought Travel journey. You could lay on the couch or bed or go outdoors. Simply select a place that is comfortable and peaceful.

Step Four: Close your eyes while in your selected location and utilize your senses resources to begin your journey. Imagine yourself there. See the sites…hear the sounds…smell the smells… taste the tastes…feel the sensations. Keep your eyes closed and feel yourself there again. Walk around your destination in your mind. Mentally re-experience your positive memories. Stay in your Thought Travel destination as long as you like, until you feel ready to return. And once you return, keep the peace and joy with you. And, Thought Travel there (or somewhere different) anytime you like.

RESCRIPT Lifestyle Strategy #10:
Lighten Up Life with Laughter

Sometimes, we just take life too seriously. We get so weighed down in thinking, planning, routines, and getting things done, that life can feel super serious and super heavy. One of the simplest ways to Lighten Up Life is with Laughter. Stress piling up and you feel like you're going to burst in frustration? Burst into laughter instead. Someone just said something that irritated you? Laugh it off (you can do this in your mind, by the way, if doing so in their presence is a bit much!). Have some downtime finally and don't know how to use it? Watch a RomCom, go to a comedy club, act silly with your kids—and laugh you're a$$ off! Yup. Laughter is truly the best medicine.

RESCRIPT Lifestyle Strategy #11:
Smile Yourself Happier

When we feel good, smiling can be easy. When we are sad, stressed, or angry, smiling is pretty tough. We are most certainly allowed to feel negative emotions and definitely do not need to be smiling all the time. In fact, smiling might be the last thing we want to do when we are in a bad mood. However, it may very well be one of the keys to pulling ourselves out of negative emotions. When we smile, even when the related happy feelings are not there yet, our brains begin to release the same chemicals they release when we are actually happy. You know what happens then? We begin to feel happier. It can help pull us out of negative thoughts and into positive feelings. Smiling regularly improves our outlook on life. Smiling also has a positive impact on others around us—it improves our relationships and interactions with others. It can help others feel good too, because it can have a contagious effect. Whether you are feeling good or not so good, whether you are alone or with others, practice smiling on purpose. Smiling is genuinely good for the soul.

RESCRIPT Lifestyle Strategy #12:
Immerse Yourself in Music

When asked about what we enjoy doing, one of the most universal responses is listening to music. Music taps into something deeper within us. It elicits strong emotions. It connects us to memories. It has the power to inspire and motivate us. It inspires us to connect with something more uninhibited within us. Contemplate for a moment:

1. What songs always make you sing out loud?

2. What songs make it impossible for you not to move around or dance?

3. What songs always make you feel inspired to be better?

4. What songs motivate you to achieve your potential?

5. What songs just make you feel happy?

6. What songs when you close your eyes can you feel yourself immersed in the music?

Off the top of my head, Irene Cara's "Fame" makes me sing out loud (but, so does pretty much every song as I love to sing!), Chaka Khan's "Ain't Nobody" always gets me moving, Michael Jackson's "Man in the Mirror" inspires me to be a better human, the Laverne & Shirley theme song "Making Our Dreams Come True" motivates me to achieve, Pharrell Williams's "Happy" always makes me feel happy, and I can close my eyes and be immersed

in the music for the theme song for HBO's "Succession" especially when my son plays it on piano (I call it "swimming" in
the music). Yes, I'm a child of the 1980's who also has a lifelong
television obsession.

Use the music you thought of to inspire the feelings and actions
you want to experience, any time you need that extra push, or
even when you don't need an extra push, because why not?!

RESCRIPT Lifestyle Strategy #13:
Nurture Yourself with Nature

One of the easiest places to forget about or distract your thoughts
away from your struggles is outdoors. When we are outside, we
experience our connection to nature and life more fully and
meaningfully. Whether it's taking a walk around your neighborhood, using your work lunch break to walk around outside, sitting in your backyard or the park, walking through the woods,
or going to a botanical garden, being outdoors lifts our mood
and relieves stress.

The next time you feel work or personal stress bringing you down,
get outdoors and take in nature. Look at the colors of the sky,
grass, flowers, and trees. Listen to the sounds of the birds, other
animals, and insects. Smell the fragrance of the flowers. Look at
the shapes and movement of the clouds. Watch the animals and
insects as they play. Feel the sun, rain, or snow on your skin. Take
it all in. Savor it. And, Nurture Yourself with Nature.

RESCRIPT Lifestyle Strategy #14:
Make Sure You Move

This one is simple, yet not simple. When we aren't feeling great,
movement and various forms of exercise often seem particularly
unappealing. However, the endorphins our brains release when
we move and exercise facilitate greater happiness. You can pick
your favored form of movement, whether it's a walk around the
neighborhood, a run, some time on your treadmill, or dancing

to music in your living room. But, if you need a boost in positive thinking and feeling—make sure you move!

RESCRIPT Lifestyle Strategy #15:
Week of Wonder

Give yourself a Week of Wonder! This is a week where you set out to intentionally focus on a particular positive thinking/feeling/behavior each day of the week. An example would be Strengths Sunday, Meaning Monday, Tenacious Tuesday, Wish Wednesday, Thank You Thursday, Flow Friday, and Smile Saturday. You can make the days in your Week of Wonder about anything positive YOU want to focus on (and they don't have to be alliterative, lol!). Once you decide what your Week of Wonder will focus on, decide on what types of relevant things you'd like to do that day!

RESCRIPT Lifestyle Strategy #16:
Love Letter to You

Have you ever written a love letter to someone? Good possibility you have. Ever write one to yourself? Good possibility you haven't. Why not? To keep your story positively RESCRIPTed, let your Inner Advocate grab the pen and tell you what it loves about you! Contemplate the questions below to help get you started. Then use them to address a Love Letter to You, signed by you, and then read it aloud, especially during rough times.

1. What do you love about you?

2. What makes you awesome?

3. What do you love about your life?

4. What makes your life awesome?

RESCRIPT Lifestyle Strategy #17:
The RESCRIPT Manifesto

You can post and read this RESCRIPT Manifesto any time you need a little extra RESCRIPTing motivation!

R - I commit myself to **releasing ruminations** over negative experiences from my recent and distant past, with the understanding that continuously mulling over challenges, traumas, or tragedies that have occurred does not help me control them, it only gives them power to continue to harm and control me.

E - I commit myself to **engaging in personal and professional goals** that propel me to grow and change for the better, with the realization that evading my goals out of fear of discomfort or failure only keeps me stagnant and unfulfilled.

S - I commit myself to **seeking my strengths** instead of focusing on perceived shortcomings, with the knowledge that I have many amazing gifts to share with the world.

C - I commit myself to **challenging any catastrophizing** I find myself doing about the future, understanding that I cannot predict what lies ahead and if I'm going to imagine the future, I will instead envision a successful one.

R - I commit myself to **restricting regrets** over choices I have made, with the understanding that I cannot control or change the past, and every choice I have made has provided me with wisdom for future decisions.

I - I commit myself to **inviting my imperfections** instead of trying to hide them from the world, knowing that EVERY part of who I am makes me the uniquely awesome person I am proud to be.

P - I commit myself to **pursuing my passions and purpose** vigorously rather than allowing myself to get stuck in a mundane, passive life, understanding that when I do things I love and that give me a sense of meaning, I feel energetic and excited about life.

T - I commit myself to **thinking thankfully** about all of my internal and external resources, understanding that thinking about and expressing gratitude regularly provides me with a life of abundance.

RESCRIPT Lifestyle Strategy #18: Your Limitless Life Manifesto

Now, it's time for you to write your own Limitless Life Manifesto! Here are some question prompts to get you started:

1. What are the most important values and mottos that lead your life?

2. What thoughts do you most need to think about to create the positive changes you seek in your life?

3. What actions do you most need to take to create the positive changes you seek?

4. How do you want to make a positive impact in the world?

5. How do you want to make a positive impact on yourself and your life?

6. What phrases do you most need and want to tell yourself to keep you motivated to live your limitless life story?

Start writing and when you are finished, type it up and put it somewhere that you look at each day as a constant reminder of your limitlessness!

RESCRIPT Lifestyle Strategy #19: Your New Limitless Life Story

Now that you've learned to RESCRIPT, look back at your Old Limiting Story Review from the beginning of this book. Using what you've learned, begin to create Your New Limitless Life Story.

What New Limitless Life Stories Will You Now Tell Yourself...

- Regarding your relationships?

- Regarding your career?

- Regarding your financial life?

- Regarding your living environment?

- Regarding your engagement within your community?

- Regarding your physical health?

- Regarding your mental and emotional health?

- Regarding your intellectual growth?

- Regarding your recreation and relaxation?

- Regarding your spirituality practices?

As you make the changes you desire, you can intermittently retake the RESCRIPT Your Life Story Quiz and Life Story Satisfaction Scale to see how you are actively changing your thoughts, actions, and feelings.

And make sure you celebrate all the ways you have quieted your Inner Antagonist, amplified your Inner Advocate, and authored your limitless life!

Keep holding onto that pen, literally and metaphorically. As you evolve, keep your story evolving with you. And, keep on RESCRIPTing!

APPENDIX A

DEFINE YOUR DESIRED DESTINATIONS' DESIGN WORKSHEET

Relationships	
Desired DESTINATION Daydreams	**DESTINATION DESIGNS/Goals**
Desired Destination Daydream #1:	• Destination Design/Goal #1: • Destination Design/Goal #2:
Career	
Desired DESTINATION Daydreams	**DESTINATION DESIGNS/Goals**
Desired Destination Daydream #1:	• Destination Design/Goal #1: • Destination Design/Goal #2:
Financial	
Desired DESTINATION Daydreams	**DESTINATION DESIGNS/Goals**
Desired Destination Daydream #1:	• Destination Design/Goal #1: • Destination Design/Goal #2:
Living Environment	
Desired DESTINATION Daydreams	**DESTINATION DESIGNS/Goals**
Desired Destination Daydream #1:	• Destination Design/Goal #1: • Destination Design/Goal #2:
Community Engagement	
Desired DESTINATION Daydreams	**DESTINATION DESIGNS/Goals**
Desired Destination Daydream #1:	• Destination Design/Goal #1: • Destination Design/Goal #2:

Physical Health	
Desired DESTINATION Daydreams	**DESTINATION DESIGNS/Goals**
Desired Destination Daydream #1:	• Destination Design/Goal #1: • Destination Design/Goal #2:
Mental & Emotional Health	
Desired DESTINATION Daydreams	**DESTINATION DESIGNS/Goals**
Desired Destination Daydream #1:	• Destination Design/Goal #1: • Destination Design/Goal #2:
Intellectual Growth	
Desired DESTINATION Daydreams	**DESTINATION DESIGNS/Goals**
Desired Destination Daydream #1:	• Destination Design/Goal #1: • Destination Design/Goal #2:
Recreation & Relaxation	
Desired DESTINATION Daydreams	**DESTINATION DESIGNS/Goals**
Desired Destination Daydream #1:	• Destination Design/Goal #1: • Destination Design/Goal #2:
Spirituality	
Desired DESTINATION Daydreams	**DESTINATION DESIGNS/Goals**
Desired Destination Daydream #1:	• Destination Design/Goal #1: • Destination Design/Goal #2:

APPENDIX B
REALIZATION ROADMAP WORKSHEET

Relationships	
DESTINATION DESIGNS/Goals	**Realization Roadmap**
Destination Design/Goal #1: • Brainstorm Steps to Achieve Goal:	• If/When… Then I will…

Career	
DESTINATION DESIGNS/Goals	**Realization Roadmap**
Destination Design/Goal #1: • Brainstorm Steps to Achieve Goal:	• If/When… Then I will…

Financial	
DESTINATION DESIGNS/Goals	**Realization Roadmap**
Destination Design/Goal #1: • Brainstorm Steps to Achieve Goal:	• If/When… Then I will…

Living Environment	
DESTINATION DESIGNS/Goals	**Realization Roadmap**
Destination Design/Goal #1: • Brainstorm Steps to Achieve Goal:	• If/When… Then I will…

Community Engagement	
DESTINATION DESIGNS/Goals	**Realization Roadmap**
Destination Design/Goal #1: • Brainstorm Steps to Achieve Goal:	• If/When… Then I will…

Physical Health	
DESTINATION DESIGNS/Goals	**Realization Roadmap**
Destination Design/Goal #1: • Brainstorm Steps to Achieve Goal:	• If/When… Then I will…

Mental & Emotional Health	
DESTINATION DESIGNS/Goals	**Realization Roadmap**
Destination Design/Goal #1: • Brainstorm Steps to Achieve Goal:	• If/When… Then I will…

Intellectual Growth	
DESTINATION DESIGNS/Goals	**Realization Roadmap**
Destination Design/Goal #1: • Brainstorm Steps to Achieve Goal:	• If/When… Then I will…

Recreation & Relaxation	
DESTINATION DESIGNS/Goals	**Realization Roadmap**
Destination Design/Goal #1: • Brainstorm Steps to Achieve Goal:	• If/When… Then I will…

Spirituality	
DESTINATION DESIGNS/Goals	**Realization Roadmap**
Destination Design/Goal #1: • Brainstorm Steps to Achieve Goal:	• If/When… Then I will…

APPENDIX C

WEEK COMMITMENT CALENDAR WORKSHEET

	Monday	Tuesday	Wednesday	Thursday	Friday	Saturday	Sunday
5 AM							
6 AM							
7 AM							
8 AM							
9 AM							
10 AM							
11 AM							
12 PM							
1 PM							
2 PM							
3 PM							
4 PM							
5 PM							
6 PM							
7 PM							
8 PM							
9 PM							
10 PM							
11 PM							
12 AM							

APPENDIX D

3 PS WEEKLY ACTION AGENDA WORKSHEET

3 Ps Weekly Action Agenda Week of Month/Day/Year					
Professional:		Personal:		Passions:	
Action	Complete By What Day	Action	Complete By What Day	Action	Complete By What Day
1.		1.		1.	
2.		2.		2.	
3.		3.		3.	
4.		4.		4.	
5.		5.		5.	
6.		6.		6.	
7.		7.		7.	
8.		8.		8.	
9.		9.		9.	
10.		10.		10.	
Longer Term Projects or Actions:					
1.		1.		1.	
2.		2.		2.	
3.		3.		3.	

APPENDIX E

TIME THIEF TRACKER WORKSHEET

	Monday	Tuesday	Wednesday	Thursday	Friday	Saturday	Sunday
5 AM							
6 AM							
7 AM							
8 AM							
9 AM							
10 AM							
11 AM							
12 M							
1 PM							
2 PM							
3 PM							
4 PM							
5 PM							
6 PM							
7 PM							
8 PM							
9 PM							
10 PM							
11 PM							
12 AM							

Top Time Thieves Weekly Tally	
Time Thief #1 & Minutes/Hours Stolen:	Time Thief #4 & Minutes/Hours Stolen:
Time Thief #2 & Minutes/Hours Stolen:	Time Thief #5 & Minutes/Hours Stolen:
Time Thief #3 & Minutes/Hours Stolen:	Time Thief #6 & Minutes/Hours Stolen:

New Time Allocation for Your Time Thieves	
Time Thief #1 – When & For How Long:	Time Thief #4 – When & For How Long:
Time Thief #2 – When & For How Long:	Time Thief #5 – When & For How Long:
Time Thief #3 – When & For How Long:	Time Thief #6 – When & For How Long:

How much time do you now get back to dedicate to your goals?

APPENDIX F

UNEXPECTED UNDERTAKINGS TRACKER WORKSHEET

	Monday	Tuesday	Wednesday	Thursday	Friday	Saturday	Sunday
5 AM							
6 AM							
7 AM							
8 AM							
9 AM							
10 AM							
11 AM							
12 PM							
1 PM							
2 PM							
3 PM							
4 PM							
5 PM							
6 PM							
7 PM							
8 PM							
9 PM							
10 PM							
11 PM							
12 AM							

Unexpected Undertakings Weekly Tally	
Unexpected Undertaking #1 & Minutes/ Hours Taken:	Unexpected Undertaking #6 & Minutes/Hours Taken:
Unexpected Undertaking #2 & Minutes/ Hours Taken:	Unexpected Undertaking #7 & Minutes/Hours Taken:
Unexpected Undertaking #3 & Minutes/ Hours Taken:	Unexpected Undertaking #8 & Minutes/Hours Taken:
Unexpected Undertaking #4 & Minutes/ Hours Taken:	Unexpected Undertaking #9 & Minutes/Hours Taken:
Unexpected Undertaking #5 & Minutes/ Hours Taken:	Unexpected Undertaking #10 & Minutes/Hours Taken:

How much time each day will you build in for unexpected undertakings that may need addressing?

APPENDIX G

TRIUMPH TRACKER WORKSHEET

January	February	March
Week 1:	Week 1:	Week 1:
Week 2:	Week 2:	Week 2:
Week 3:	Week 3:	Week 3:
Week 4:	Week 4:	Week 4:
April	May	June
Week 1:	Week 1:	Week 1:
Week 2:	Week 2:	Week 2:
Week 3:	Week 3:	Week 3:
Week 4:	Week 4:	Week 4:
July	August	September
Week 1:	Week 1:	Week 1:
Week 2:	Week 2:	Week 2:
Week 3:	Week 3:	Week 3:
Week 4:	Week 4:	Week 4:
October	November	December
Week 1:	Week 1:	Week 1:
Week 2:	Week 2:	Week 2:
Week 3:	Week 3:	Week 3:
Week 4:	Week 4:	Week 4:

APPENDIX H
ALL-AROUND LIFE APPRECIATION APPRAISAL WORKSHEET

1) Relationships	
2) Career	
3) Finances	
4) Living Environment	
5) Community Engagement	
6) Physical Health	
7) Mental & Emotional Health	
8) Intellectual Growth	
9) Recreation & Relaxation	
10) Spirituality	

APPENDIX I

THREE THANKFULS AT
TWILIGHT WORKSHEET

	Monday	Tuesday	Wednesday	Thursday	Friday	Saturday	Sunday
Week #1	1. 2. 3.	1. 2. 3.	1. 2. 3.	1. 2. 3.	1. 2. 3.	1. 2. 3.	1. 2. 3.
Week #2	1. 2. 3.	1. 2. 3.	1. 2. 3.	1. 2. 3.	1. 2. 3.	1. 2. 3.	1. 2. 3.
Week #3	1. 2. 3.	1. 2. 3.	1. 2. 3.	1. 2. 3.	1. 2. 3.	1. 2. 3.	1. 2. 3.
Week #4	1. 2. 3.	1. 2. 3.	1. 2. 3.	1. 2. 3.	1. 2. 3.	1. 2. 3.	1. 2. 3.

ENDNOTES

Reliving Plots We Don't Even Like

1   Hanson, R. (2013). *Hardwiring happiness: The new brain science of contentment, calm, and confidence.* New York, NY: Harmony.

2   Freud, S. (1990). *The Ego and the Id.* New York, NY: W.W. Norton & Company.

3   Seligman, M. E. P. (1998). Building human strength: Psychology's forgotten mission. *APA Monitor, 29*(1).

Practice #1: R- Release Rumination

4   Nolen-Hoeksema, S., Wisco, B. E., & Lyubomirsky, S. (2008). Rethinking rumination. *Perspectives on Psychological Science, 3*(5), 400-424. https://doi.org/10.1111/j.1745-6924.2008.00088.x

5   Ward, A. H., Lyubomirsky, S., Sousa, L., & Nolen-Hoeksema, S. (2003). Can't quite commit: Rumination and uncertainty. *Personality & Social Psychology Bulletin, 29*(1), 96-107. https://doi.org/10.1177/0146167202238375

6   Jerabek, I. & Muoio, D. (2018). *The Thoughtlessness of Overthinking: The Disadvantages of Extreme Rumination.* http://dx.doi.org/10.13140/RG.2.2.24986.49608

7   Rude, S. S., Mazzetti, F. A., Pal, H., & Stauble, M. R. (2011). Social rejection: How best to think about it? *Cognitive Therapy and Research, 35*(3), 209-216. http://dx.doi.org/10.1007/s10608-010-9296-0

8 Hilt, L. M., & Pollak, S. D. (2012). Getting out of rumination: Comparison of three brief interventions in a sample of youth. *Journal of Abnormal Child Psychology, 40*(7), 1157-65. http://dx.doi.org/10.1007/s10802-012-9638-3

9 Kabat-Zinn, J. (2005). *Wherever you go, there you are: Mindfulness meditation in everyday life.* New York, NY: Hachette Books.

PRACTICE #2: E- ENGAGE GROWTH GOALS VS. EVADING THEM

10 Shahar, G., Kanitzki, E., Shulman, S., & Blatt, S. J. (2006). Personality, motivation and the construction of goals during the transition to adulthood. *Personality & Individual Differences, 40*(1), 53-63. http://dx.doi.org/10.1016/j.paid.2005.06.016

11 Powers, T.A., Koestner, R. & Zuroff, D.C. (2007). Self–criticism, goal motivation, and goal progress. *Journal of Social & Clinical Psychology, 26*(7), 826-840. https://doi.org/10.1521/jscp.2007.26.7.826

12 Wang, C., Shim, S. S., & Wolters, C. A. (2017). Achievement goals, motivational self-talk, and academic engagement among Chinese students. *Asia Pacific Education Review, 18*(3), 295-307. https://doi.org/10.1007/s12564-017-9495-4

13 Locke, E. A. (1996). Motivation through conscious goal setting, *Applied & Preventive Psychology, 5*(2), 117-124. https://doi.org/10.1016/S0962-1849(96)80005-9

14 Jerabek, I. & Muoio, D. (2017). *New Year, New Approach: What It Takes to Achieve Resolutions.* Retrieved from https://www.researchgate.net/publication/321918643_New_Year_New_Approach_What_It_Takes_To_Achieve_Resolutions

PRACTICE #3: S- SEEK STRENGTHS VS. SCRUTINIZING SHORTCOMINGS

15 Gander, F., Proyer, R. T., Ruch, W., & Wyss, T. (2013). Strength-based positive interventions: Further evidence for

their potential in enhancing well-being. *Journal of Happiness Studies, 14*(4), 1241–1259. https://doi.org/10.1007/s10902-012-9380-0

[16] Wood, A. M., Linley, P. A., Matlby, J., Kashdan, T. B., & Hurling, R. (2011). Using personal and psychological strengths leads to increases in well-being over time: A longitudinal study and the development of the strengths use questionnaire. *Personality & Individual Differences, 50*(1), 15-19. http://dx.doi.org/10.1016/j.paid.2010.08.004

[17] Lavy, S., & Littman-Ovadia, H. (2017). My better self: Using strengths at work and work productivity, organizational citizenship behavior, and satisfaction. *Journal of Career Development, 44*(2), 95–109. http://dx.doi.org/10.1177/0894845316634056

[18] Linley, P. A., Nielsen, K. M., Gillett, R., & Biswas-Diener, R. (2010). Using signature strengths in pursuit of goals: Effects on goal progress, need satisfaction, and well-being, and implications for coaching psychologists. *International Coaching Psychology Review, 5*(1), 6-15. Retrieved from https://www.researchgate.net/publication/281424792_Using_signature_strengths_in_pursuit_of_goals_Effects_on_goal_progress_need_satisfaction_and_well-being_and_implications_for_coaching_psychologists

[19] Quinlan, D. M., Swain, N., Cameron, C., & Vella-Brodrick, D.A. (2014). How 'other people matter' in a classroom-based strengths intervention: Exploring interpersonal strategies and classroom outcomes. *Journal of Positive Psychology, 10*(1), 77-89. https://doi.org/10.1080/17439760.2014.920407

PRACTICE #4: C- CHALLENGE CATASTROPHIZING

[20] Pisarik, C. T., Rowell, P. C., & Thompson, L. K. (2017). A phenomenological study of career anxiety among college students. *The Career Development Quarterly, 65*(4), 339-352. https://doi.org/10.1002/cdq.12112

21 Arnow, B.A., Blasey, C.M., Constantino, M.J., Robinson, R., Hunkeler, E., Lee, J., Fireman, B., Khaylis, A., Feiner, L., & Hayward, C. (2011). Catastrophizing, depression and pain-related disability. *General Hospital Psychiatry, 33*(2), 150-156. https://doi.org/10.1016/j.genhosppsych.2010.12.008

22 Jerabek, I. & Muoio, D. (2018). *Should You Be an Optimist, Pessimist, or Realist? Study Looks at Advantages & Disadvantages of Different Outlooks.* http://dx.doi.org/10.13140/RG.2.2.27518.48966

23 Sugiura, T., & Sugiura, Y. (2016). Relationships between refraining from catastrophic thinking, repetitive negative thinking, and psychological distress. *Psychological Reports, 119*(2), 374-394. https://doi.org/10.1177/0033294116663511

24 Sullivan, M., Adams, H., Ellis, T., Clark, R., Sully, C., & Thibault, P. (2017). Treatment-related reductions in catastrophizing predict return to work in individuals with post-traumatic stress disorder. *Journal of Applied Biobehavioral Research, 22*(1). https://doi.org/10.1111/jabr.12087

PRACTICE #5: R- RESTRICT REGRETS

25 Shimanoff, S. B. (1984). Commonly named emotions in everyday conversations. *Perceptual & Motor Skills, 58*(2), 514. http://dx.doi.org/10.2466/pms.1984.58.2.514

26 Burns, P., Riggs, K.J., & Beck, S.R. (2012). Executive control and the experience of regret. *Journal of Experimental Child Psychology, 111*(3), 501-515. http://dx.doi.org/10.1016/j.jecp.2011.10.003

27 Roese, N. J., & Summerville, A. (2005). What we regret most... and why. *Personality & Social Psychology Bulletin, 31*(9), 1273–1285. https://doi.org/10.1177/0146167205274693

28 Gilovich, T., & Medvec, V. H. (1995). The experience of regret: What, when, and why. *Psychological Review, 102*(2), 379-395. http://doi.org/10.1037/0033-295X.102.2.379

29   Roese, N. J., Epstude, K., Fessel, F., Morrison, M., Smallman, R., Summerville, A., . . . Segerstrom, S. (2009). Repetitive regret, depression, and anxiety: Findings from a nationally representative survey. *Journal of Social & Clinical Psychology, 28*(6), 671–688. https://doi.org/10.1521/jscp.2009.28.6.671

30   Schmidt, R. E., & Van, D. L. (2013). Feeling too regretful to fall asleep: Experimental activation of regret delays sleep onset. *Cognitive Therapy and Research, 37*(4), 872-880. https://doi.org/10.1007/s10608-013-9532-5

31   Becerra Pérez, M. M., Menear, M., Brehaut, J. C., & Legaré, F. (2016). Extent and predictors of decision regret about health care decisions: A systematic review. *Medical Decision Making, 36*(6), 777-790. https://doi.org/10.1177/0272989X16636113

32   Lewis, V. G., & Borders, L. D. (1995). Life satisfaction of single middle-aged professional women. *Journal of Counseling & Development, 74*(1), 94-100. https://doi.org/10.1002/j.1556-6676.1995.tb01829.x

33   Gao, H., Zhang, Y., Wang, F., Xu, Y., Hong, Y., & Jiang, J. (2014). Regret causes ego-depletion and finding benefits in the regrettable events alleviates ego-depletion. *The Journal of General Psychology, 141*(3), 169–206. https://doi.org/10.1080/00221309.2014.884053

PRACTICE #6: I- INVITE IMPERFECTION VS. INFALLIBILITY/PERFECTIONISM

34   Jerabek, I. & Muoio, D. (2018). *I Am Broken: New Study Reveals Young People More Likely to be Perfectionists.* http://dx.doi.org/10.13140/RG.2.2.10806.96321

35   Flett, G. L., Madorsky, D., Hewitt, P. L., & Heisel, M. J. (2002). Perfectionism cognitions, rumination, and psychological distress. *Journal of Rational-Emotive & Cognitive-Behavior Therapy, 20*(1), 33-47. http://dx.doi.org/10.1023/A:1015128904007

36   Handley, A. K., Egan, S. J., Kane, R. T., & Rees, C. S. (2014).

The relationships between perfectionism, pathological worry and generalised anxiety disorder. *BMC Psychiatry, 14*(98). https://doi.org/10.1186/1471-244X-14-98

37 Ferrari, M., Yap, K., Scott, N., Einstein, D. A., & Ciarrochi, J. (2018). Self-compassion moderates the perfectionism and depression link in both adolescence and adulthood. *PLoS One, 13*(2). https://doi.org/10.1371/journal.pone.0192022

38 Brown, B. (2010). The Gifts of Imperfection: Let go of who you think you're supposed to be and embrace who you are. Center City, MN: Hazelden Publishing.

PRACTICE #7: P- PURSUE PASSION & PURPOSE VS. PUTTING UP WITH PASSIVITY

39 Froh, J. J., Kashdan, T. B., Yurkewicz, C., Fan, J., Allen, J., & Glowacki, J. (2010). The benefits of passion and absorption in activities: Engaged living in adolescents and its role in psychological well-being. *The Journal of Positive Psychology, 5*(4), 311-332. https://doi.org/10.1080/17439760.2010.498624

40 Bundick, M. J. (2011). The benefits of reflecting on and discussing purpose in life in emerging adulthood. *New Directions for Youth Development, 2011*(132), 89–103. https://doi.org/10.1002/yd.430

41 Vallerand, R. J., Paquet, Y., Philippe, F. L., & Charest, J. (2010). On the role of passion in burnout: A process model. *Journal of Personality, 78*(1), 289-312. https://doi.org/10.1111/j.1467-6494.2009.00616.x

42 Duffy, R.D., Bott, E.M., Allan, B.A., Torrey, C.L., & Dik, B.J. (2012). Perceiving a calling, living a calling, and job satisfaction: Testing a moderated, multiple mediator model. *Journal of Counseling Psychology, 59*(1), 50-59. https://doi.org/10.1037/a0026129

43 Berg, J. M., Grant, A. M., & Johnson, V. (2010). When callings are calling: Crafting work and leisure in pursuit of unanswered

occupational callings. *Organization Science, 21*(5), 973-994. https://doi.org/10.1287/orsc.1090.0497

PRACTICE #8: T- THINK THANKFULLY VS. THANKLESSLY/DEPRIVED

[44] Hay, L. (1996). *Gratitude: A Way of Life.* Carslbad, CA: Hay House.

[45] Jerabek, I. & Muoio, D. (2018). *From Neglect to Burnout: New Study Emphasizes Importance of Employee Appreciation.* http://dx.doi.org/10.13140/RG.2.2.20653.33761

[46] Emmons, R. (2010, November 16). Why gratitude is good. *Greater Good Magazine: Science-Based Insights for Meaningful Life.* Retrieved from: http://greatergood.berkeley.edu/article/item/why_gratitude_is_good

[47] Froh, J. J., Bono, G., Fan, J., Emmons, R. A., Henderson, K., Harris, C., . . . Wood, A. M. (2014). Nice thinking! An educational intervention that teaches children to think gratefully. *School Psychology Review, 43*(2), 132-152. Retrieved from https://www.researchgate.net/publication/273061748_Nice_Thinking_An_Educational_Intervention_That_Teaches_Children_to_Think_Gratefully

[48] Seligman, M. E. P., Steen, T. A., Park, N. P., & Peterson, C. (2005). Positive psychology progress: Empirical validation of interventions. *American Psychologist, 60*(5), 410-421. http://dx.doi.org/10.1037/0003-066X.60.5.410

[49] Gordon, C. L., Arnette, R. A. M., & Smith, R. E. (2011). Have you thanked your spouse today?: Felt and expressed gratitude among married couples. *Personality & Individual Differences, 50*(3), 339-343. http://dx.doi.org/10.1016/j.paid.2010.10.012

ACKNOWLEDGEMENTS

I'm incredibly blessed to have countless individuals I am grateful for throughout my life and book journey. The toughest part is where do I begin? I'm going to do my best to do my gratitude justice.

To God: You have given me a cup runneth over. My heart is full, my life is full. Fulfilling your purpose for my life is my drive every single day. It's the best way I know to say thank you for the endless blessings you bestow upon me.

To my grandparents, Katherine, Steven, Ellen, and James: I know you've been with me every step of the way through this book writing process. You gave me endless wisdom, love, and guidance in life and have been my angel guides from above. I know you are smiling up there.

To my parents and book editors, Lori and Peter: Thank you for your unceasing belief in me. You've offered me role modeling, unconditional love, and all the support I needed to help me fulfill my dreams. You engaged in countless hours of reading a gazillion versions of my book manuscript to make sure there wasn't a double "the" or a "that" where there was supposed to be a "than," that my grammar was on point, and that my words made sense to people other than me! You are the most dedicated, thorough editors around. I'm so blessed God chose you to be my parents.

To my husband, José: When I said I wanted to leave my salaried job to be a full-time entrepreneur, you didn't question me, stress, or shut me down. You listened and said, "Let's do it." You believed in me and my business more than I did. You have been my biggest business and book PR person to every person you know. You are the definition of partner in every way. I always say that the St. Patrick's Day I met you was my lucky day.

To my son, Joshua: For months you've asked, "When will I be able to hold your book, mommy?" You've told me, "I can't wait to tell my friends that my mom wrote a book!" You are my heart, soul, and purpose. You have made me the proudest mom in every way. I promise you that the next book is going to be the children's book about being thankful that you and I write together.

To my cat daughters, Kitty and Sweetie: Throughout this writing process, you've been laying on my lap…or on top of the arm I'm trying to type with. And, I love every second of your company (though I often needed my arm back again).

To my family and friends: I've been blessed with such good family and friends in this life. You've been with me through tears, laughter, and dreams. We've had the best talks and most awesome memories. You rock.

To my students, clients, and community wellness group members: Getting to be part of your journey is one of my most treasured gifts in life. While my role is to instruct and advise you, you've taught me just as much. Your bravery and growth inspire me every single day.

To my mentors: There have been so many amazing people who have given me opportunities and guidance in my life and work. You helped lead me on my path. You helped me to get here.

To my Foreword author and human extraordinaire, Judy Torres: I'm so grateful and blessed to know you. You are one of the smartest, bravest, multi-talented, hardest working, inspirational, kindest hearted people I've ever known. Seeing you achieving your dreams fills my heart. There's nothing you can't do when you decide you're going to do it. Your Foreword brought me to happy tears. #FutureLifeCoach

To Bill O'Hanlon, author, instructor, and inspirer: You offered me the motivation to get serious about writing my book. But most importantly, when I was feeling stuck and unsure, you made me realize that everything I needed to write my book was already in my head, heart, and soul.

To Kary Oberbrunner, AAE, and the Igniting Souls Tribe: I found you exactly when I needed to. It was God's plan. You were the missing pieces of the puzzle. You gave me the guidance, resources, structure, and community I needed to make this book real. You are dream makers.

To Debbie and Chris O'Byrne at JetLaunch: You are surely the most dedicated designers in existence. You connect with authors' missions and visions and make them shine right through in your book covers and interior designs.

To Linda Joy, my brand visibility coach: You gave me the guidance and strategies I needed to launch this book. You said the things I needed to hear exactly when I needed to hear them. You helped me get my message heard.

To my book endorsers and launch team members: Your kindness in supporting my book journey has humbled me. What a gift to know people who give so freely of themselves to help others.

ABOUT THE AUTHOR

Positive Psychology coach, speaker, educator, and author, Dr. Colleen Georges, flips scripts by helping people RESCRIPT limiting life stories into empowered, limitless adventures. A recovering catastrophizer, Colleen's own experiences dealing with and overcoming anxiety, panic attacks, and low self-esteem have shaped her work helping others rewrite negatives into positives. In her TEDx Talk, "Re-Scripting the Stories We Tell Ourselves," Colleen illustrates how we can change our internal dialogue to transform the lives we live. Through her teaching, coaching, speaking, and writing, Colleen shares a core message—we can choose to leave behind shame-fueled, worry-driven, auto-piloted narratives, and instead script self-compassionate, hopeful, purpose-directed journeys.

Colleen is the founder of RESCRIPT Your Story, LLC where she provides life and career coaching, leads community wellness groups, and delivers organizational trainings and speaking engagements. Colleen is also a Rutgers University Lecturer in counseling, women's leadership, and social justice, a member of the Rutgers Speaker's Bureau, and teaches Psychology of Women at Middlesex County College.

She received her Bachelor's Degree in Psychology, Master's Degree in Counseling Psychology, and Doctorate in Counseling Psychology from Rutgers University. Colleen is a NJ Licensed Professional Counselor, Certified Comprehensive Positive Psychology Coach, Certified Professional Career Coach, Certified

Professional Life Coach, Certified Anxiety Specialist, and holds over a dozen certifications in coaching and counseling.

Colleen is a Huffington Post contributor and co-author of several best-selling self-growth books including *10 Habits of Truly Optimistic People*, *Contagious Optimism*, *Inspiration for a Woman's Soul: Opening to Gratitude & Grace*, *Midlife Transformation: Redefining Life, Love, Health and Success*, and *101 Great Ways to Enhance Your Career*. Her expertise has been featured in various media including Live Happy, Inspire Me Today, Mashable, Rewire Me, The Job Network, Care.com, New Jersey Family Magazine, and The Trenton Times.

Colleen, her husband, José, son, Joshua, and two cats, Kitty and Sweetie, live in New Jersey.

To connect with Colleen, visit: www.ColleenGeorges.com.

Dive Deeper into the RESCRIPTing Process

Take your story to the next level with Dr. Colleen's RESCRIPT Coaching Programs.

✦ Design the life story you've been dreaming of filled with passion and purpose.

✦ Feel fulfilled at home, in your community, in your career, and in your relationships.

✦ Give yourself the self-care and self-compassion you deserve without guilt.

✦ See all the good within and around you and live with gratitude and abundance.

✦ Own your power, leverage your strengths, and live authentically with confidence.

✦ And, say goodbye to negative self-talk patterns that are keeping you stuck!

Find out More at

www.ColleenGeorges.com